# Trailing the Bolsheviki:
# Twelve Thousand Miles with
# the Allies in Siberia

# AMERICANS IN REVOLUTIONARY RUSSIA

Vol. 1
Albert Rhys Williams, *Through the Russian Revolution*, edited by
William Benton Whisenhunt (2016)

Vol. 2
Princess Julia Cantacuzène, Countess Spéransky, née Grant, *Russian People: Revolutionary Recollections*, edited by Norman E. Saul (2016)

Vol. 3
Ernest Poole, *The Village: Russian Impressions*, edited by Norman E. Saul (2017)

Vol. 4
John Reed, *Ten Days That Shook the World*, edited by
William Benton Whisenhunt (2017)

Vol. 5
Louise Bryant, *Six Red Months in Russia*, edited by Lee A. Farrow (2017)

Vol. 6
Edward Alsworth Ross, *Russia in Upheaval*, edited by Rex A. Wade (2017)

Vol. 7
Donald Thompson, *Donald Thompson in Russia*, edited by David H. Mould (2017)

Vol. 8
Arthur Bullard, *The Russian Pendulum: Autocracy—Democracy—Bolshevism*, edited by
David W. McFadden (2019)

Vol. 9
David Francis, *Russia from the American Embassy*, edited by
Vladimir V. Noskov (2019)

Vol. 10
Pauline S. Crosley, *Intimate Letters from Petrograd*, edited by Lee A. Farrow (2019)

Vol. 11

Madeleine Z. Doty, *"The Bolshevik Revolution Had Descended on Me": Madeleine Z. Doty's Russian Revolution*, edited by Julia L. Mickenberg (2019)

Vol. 12

*John R. Mott, the American YMCA, and Revolutionary Russia*, edited by Matthew Lee Miller (2020)

Vol. 13

Carl W. Ackerman, *Trailing the Bolsheviki: Twelve Thousand Miles with the Allies in Siberia*, edited by Ivan Kurilla (2020)

Vol. 14

Malcolm C. Grow, *Surgeon Grow: An American in the Russian Fighting*, edited by Laurie S. Stoff (2021)

**Series General Editors:**

Norman E. Saul and William Benton Whisenhunt

# Trailing the Bolsheviki: Twelve Thousand Miles with the Allies in Siberia

Carl W. Ackerman

Edited and Introduction by
Ivan Kurilla

ANTHEM PRESS

Anthem Press
An imprint of Wimbledon Publishing Company
www.anthempress.com

First published by Slavica Publishers, Indiana University, USA, 2020

This edition first published in UK and USA 2026
by ANTHEM PRESS
75–76 Blackfriars Road, London SE1 8HA, UK
or PO Box 9779, London SW19 7ZG, UK
and
244 Madison Ave #116, New York, NY 10016, USA

Copyright © 2026 Ivan Kurilla editorial matter and selection;
individual chapters © individual contributors

The moral right of the authors has been asserted.

All rights reserved. Without limiting the rights under copyright reserved above,
no part of this publication may be reproduced, stored or introduced into
a retrieval system, or transmitted, in any form or by any means
(electronic, mechanical, photocopying, recording or otherwise),
without the prior written permission of both the copyright
owner and the above publisher of this book.

*British Library Cataloguing-in-Publication Data*
A catalogue record for this book is available from the British Library.

*Library of Congress Cataloging-in-Publication Data: Submitted*

ISBN-13: 978-1-83999-740-2 (Hbk)
ISBN-10: 1-83999-740-0 (Hbk)

ISBN-13: 978-1-83999-741-9 (Pbk)
ISBN-10: 1-83999-741-9 (Pbk)

Cover design: Tracey Theriault
Cover illustration from The Saturday Evening Post, June 25, 1921, 54

This title is also available as an eBook.

## CONTENTS

Editor's Introduction        ix
    Ivan Kurilla

Editor's Note        xxix

## TRAILING THE BOLSHEVIKI: TWELVE THOUSAND MILES WITH THE ALLIES IN SIBERIA

| | |
|---|---:|
| Introduction | 3 |
| I. From New York to Vladivostok | 7 |
| II. In the Land of "Nitchevo" | 15 |
| III. The Human Volcanoes | 26 |
| IV. In the Whirlpool of the North | 38 |
| V. The Fate of the Tzar | 52 |
| VI. At Czecho-Slovak Headquarters | 66 |
| VII. The Birth of a Government in Russia | 86 |
| VIII. American and Allied Exiles in Russia | 101 |

| | |
|---|---:|
| IX. Decisive Days in Siberia | 112 |
| X. Vagabonding Back to Vladivostok | 125 |
| XI. Japanese Activities in Siberia | 136 |
| XII. Bolshevism Outside of Russia | 149 |
| XIII. The Russian Co-operative Unions | 160 |
| XIV. The Future of Peace | 164 |
| Index | 167 |

# INTRODUCTION
## Ivan Kurilla

Carl William Ackerman (1890–1970) was a journalist, corporate public relations executive, author of several books, and for many years, dean of Columbia University School of Journalism. In 1918, as a correspondent of *The New York Times*, he traveled through Siberia, torn by Russian civil war, and was the first foreign journalist who reached Ekaterinburg after the murder of the former tsar, Nicholas Romanov, and his family, and while many uncertainties about their fate still prevailed. After his return to the United States, Ackerman became an ardent propagandist of the "Red Scare," and even brought to the American public the infamous "Protocols of the Elders of Zion," an anti-Semitic fake that he turned anti-Bolshevik by changing the main words. The book *Trailing the Bolsheviki*, published in 1919, was a result of his Russian travels, and one of the early firsthand accounts of the Russian Civil War read by the Americans.

Ackerman was born on January 16, 1890, in Richmond, Indiana, and after several years spent at Earlham College in his native town he moved to New York City to study at Columbia University, where he was awarded a bachelor of letters degree in 1913.

That same year, Ackerman began his journalism career as a United Press Association correspondent in Albany and Washington, DC. With the beginning of the World War, UPA sent him to Berlin in 1915. The journalist worked for two years in the German capital while the United States was keeping its neutrality. When America finally entered the war, Ackerman left Berlin and published his first book *Germany, the Next Republic?*[1]

In 1917, Ackerman worked briefly for *New-York Tribune* and then served as a special correspondent for *The Saturday Evening Post*. For that magazine, he gathered material in Switzerland, Mexico, Spain, and France concerning political events in the years 1917–18. In 1918, Ackerman published his second book *Mexico's Dilemma*.[2] While working for the *Post*, Ackerman served simultaneously as a confidential reporter to Edward Mandell House, President Wilson's adviser, and started an exchange

---

[1] Carl W. Ackerman, *Germany, the Next Republic?* (New York: Grosset & Dunlap, 1917).

[2] Carl W. Ackerman, *Mexico's Dilemma* (New York: George H. Doran, 1918).

of letters that ended only with House's death in 1938. At the end of World War I, Ackerman and House corresponded on such subjects as the League of Nations, press censorship, Russia, and Japan. On July 16, 1919, House wrote Ackerman: "I shall always regret that you were not in Paris during the Peace Conference. You would have been helpful in many directions and I constantly missed your not being here."

In 1917 and 1918, Russian news brought growing concerns and less and less understanding of the chaos that emerged after the abdication of Tsar Nicholas in February 1917, the seizure of power by the Bolsheviks that October, and the dissolution of the Constituent Assembly in January 1918. Ackerman got an assignment from *The New York Times* in late August and embarked to the Russian Far East, where he spent months, from September to December, getting his correspondences published on the pages of the leading newspaper. Upon his return to the United States, Ackerman turned part of his newspaper articles and his travel notes into a book manuscript that he published in 1919 by Scribner's under the title *Trailing the Bolsheviki: Twelve Thousand Miles with the Allies in Siberia*.

By that time, the journalist had become a fierce proponent of the idea that Bolshevism was a universal force that had already penetrated America. In the fall of 1919, Carl Ackerman toured the US for Philadelphia's *Public Ledger*, writing articles on industrial unrest that he described as the first signs of American Bolshevism. He eventually became one of the leading figures who created the "Red Scare" atmosphere in American society—the fear of the imminent Bolshevik revolt. The newspaper title and lead to one of his articles exposed his main idea: "Industrial 'Bad Spots,' Nest of Bolshevists, From Coast to Coast. Revolutionary Cancers Infect Many Sections and Produce Serious Situation That Necessitates Labor Conference at Washington. Class-War Propaganda and Un-American Ideas Spread by Unassimilated Radical Aliens. I.W.W.'s 100,000 Paying Members in United States in Touch With Reds Abroad Through Reports Smuggled Into This Country by Sailors."[3]

It was during that crusade against "Bolshevik hotbeds" in America that Ackerman published a rather unusual text. Its first part appeared in the October 27, 1919, *Public Ledger* issue under the title "Red 'Bible' Counsels Appeal to violence. 'Right Is Might' Is Cardinal Text of Doctrines Expounded in Guidebook of World Revolutionists." The second part was published the next day under the title "Reds Plot to Smash World and Then Rule with Universal Czar." Ackerman insisted that the document he extensively quoted was "the translation of twenty-four protocols written by one of the members of the inner cabinet of the soviet government."[4] In fact, the text was the infamous anti-Semitic fake "Protocols of the Elders of Zion," but creatively edited

---

[3] *Public Ledger*, October 7, 1919.

[4] Carl W. Ackerman, "Reds Plot to Smash World and Then Rule With Universal Czar," *Public Ledger*, October 28, 1919.

to change all the mentions of Jews to Bolsheviks.[5] We do not know whether that was Ackerman's own forgery or if he was just a tool of somebody else's manipulation. His publication cites some anonymous "prominent American diplomat" who presumably passed "the guidebook of the world revolutionaries" to the journalist.[6] In any way, that publication was one of the first English translations of the "Protocols." The text, however, very well fit Ackerman's mission to fight world Bolshevism on American soil (as he very probably defined his personal political goal in the post-war era).

A series of Ackerman's articles for *Public Ledger* appeared also in the form of a brochure. In the foreword, the editor explained that the journalist traveled for six weeks across the United States and found that "industrial conditions as a whole are fundamentally sound but that the cancer of Bolshevism, transplanted to America by alien agitators and spread by foreign-born labor, is infecting many sections from coast to coast. To meet this peril Mr. Ackerman urges the immediate mobilization of public opinion and vigorous action in defense of American ideas and institutions."[7]

Becoming an anti-Bolshevik crusader did not help Carl Ackerman's journalism career. For about a year he was a chief of *Public Ledger* foreign news service, but in 1922, he abandoned journalism for work in the sphere of corporate public relations. That same year, he and Colonel Edward M. House, who worked with Ackerman at the *Public Ledger*, played some role in the negotiations leading to the creation of the Irish Republic in 1922.

From 1921 to 1927, Carl directed as the president Carl W. Ackerman, Inc., a firm specializing in corporate public relations. During 1927–30, he worked for the Eastman Kodak Company, and in 1930, he published a biography of George Eastman.[8] Then he worked briefly for General Motors, but in 1931, he was appointed the dean of Columbia's School of Journalism (since 1935, Graduate School of Journalism), the position he held until his retirement in 1956.

During WWII, Ackerman criticized the Franklin Delano Roosevelt administration for restrictions imposed on the media. On October 20, 1942, Ackerman told the fourth accounting institute banquet that American newspapers were being subjected to a "freezing process by our government," and if the forces out to complete the pro-

---

[5] *Public Ledger*, October 27, 1919. See also Robert Singerman, "The American Career of the 'Protocols of the Elders of Zion,'" *American Jewish History* 71, no. 1 (September 1981): 53–54.

[6] Carl W. Ackerman, "Red 'Bible' Counsels Appeal to Violence: 'Right is Might' Is Cardinal Text of Doctrines Expounded in Guidebook of World Revolutionists," *Public Ledger*, October 27, 1919.

[7] Articles written for *Public Ledger* syndicate are reprinted in booklet form in Ackerman Papers, box 171.

[8] Carl W. Ackerman, *George Eastman* (Boston: Houghton Mifflin, 1930).

cess succeeded, "we may have freedom of speech but be deprived of the freedom to speak,"[9] the punch line widely quoted thereafter.

After the war, Ackerman wrote (but never published) a book titled *Eisenhower in Wonderland*, an informal history of Columbia University focusing on the years of Dwight D. Eisenhower's presidency.[10]

Carl W. Ackerman died on October 9, 1970, in New York City.

**Travel to Siberia**

The idea of travel to Russian Siberia was initially the result of Ackerman's intensive thinking about the future of the world after the World War. His first touch of the Russian theme took place in his article for *The Saturday Evening Post* "Germany's Policy in Russia," written in July and published in August 1918:

> Three journeys with the German Armies in Russia when they were commanded by Von Hindenburg furnished me an introduction and insight into the field marshal's aims and Ludendorff's methods.... The slumbering, silent, suffering masses of Russians are awakening.... Who knows and who can tell what a hundred million people want who have passed through the fires of war with Germany and a revolution against the Czar and Russia's past aristocrats? No one, perhaps, can formulate their hopes and aspirations, but it must be evident to the Allied world that they need counsel and assistance. Germany's policy has never been to help Russia, but the contrary. The Allied policy, if it is to be formulated with a possibility of success, must be helpful and constructive. There is a crisis developing in Russia with every hour and every day of time.... Whatever the United States and the Allies do, their policy must be constructive and certain of success.... I do not know whether the Allies should interfere in Siberia, Kola or through Turkey and the Black Sea; but whatever the policy is it must not be one of abandoning Russia when the approaching crisis develops. Whatever plans the United States and the Allies make must also be on a larger scale than Germany is capable of, because Von Hindenburg is again dreaming about Russia, and Ludendorf is planning.[11]

---

[9] Quoted from *The Daily Telegram* (MI), October 21, 1942.

[10] "Recent Acquisitions of the Manuscript Division," *Quarterly Journal of the Library of Congress* 29, no. 4 (October 1972): 334–36.

[11] Carl W. Ackerman, "Germany's Policy in Russia," *The Saturday Evening Post*, August 17, 1918.

INTRODUCTION                                                                        xiii

The editor called the text a "good article" and paid the young journalist five hundred dollars.[12] By the time of the article's publication in mid-August 1918, the AEF started to disembark in Vladivostok, Russia. Carl Ackerman did not wait long to plan his own participation. He offered his services to *The New York Times*, and by August 30, 1918, his contract with the paper was ready. Ackerman described the conditions in his letter to the managing editor of *The New York Times*, Carr V. Van Anda:

> I offer to go to Siberia as special correspondent of *The New York Times* for a period of six calendar months, the date of my sailing to be on September ninth, 1918, or as soon thereafter as possible, and the period of my service to begin on August twenty-sixth, 1918. I am to receive a salary of two hundred dollars ($200.00) weekly and necessary travelling and living expenses for myself, and such personal expenses as may be imposed upon me by any military expedition to which I may become attached. During this period I agree to write for *The New York Times* only and to take no other employment of any kind.[13]

During the course of his travels from October to December 1918, Ackerman visited Vladivostok, Chita, Irkutsk, Tomsk, Omsk, Cheliabinsk, and Ekaterinburg in Russia and Harbin and Pekin in China, and got almost fifty correspondences published in the newspaper, being the major source of the firsthand information about the Russian Civil War for the *New York Times* readers.

It would be wrong to say that Ackerman was well equipped for the Russian journey. Most importantly, he did not speak any Russian. That fact was not a problem for the editor as may be seen from Ackerman's mention of Van Anda's "statement in New York that I would not need to know the Russian language to cover the story here."[14] Most of his knowledge of the vast country he was about to travel was very probably the result of his reading of George Kennan's *Siberia and the Exile System*, published in 1891, summarizing Kennan's impressions from the early 1880s. Ackerman's first telegrams from Vladivostok started with the acknowledgment that "Siberia to most Americans has been a cold, bleak empire for the Czar's political exiles."[15]

While the journalist traveled a large part of his way with the American Red Cross train, the difficulties he faced in Civil War-torn Russia were still big ones. He wrote to Van Anda from "near Tomsk" informing him that "the further inland [he

---

[12] Editor to Carl Ackerman, July 13, 1918, Carl W. Ackerman Papers, box 140, Manuscript Division, Library of Congress, Washington, DC (hereafter Ackerman Papers).

[13] Ackerman to C. V. Van Anda, August 30, 1918, Ackerman Papers, box 122.

[14] Ackerman to Van Anda, Harbin, Manchuria, October 28, 1918, Ackerman Papers, box 122.

[15] Carl W. Ackerman, "Hustle in Vladivostok Where Our Soldiers Guard Vast Stores," *The New York Times*, October 15, 1918.

gets], the more difficult it becomes to send telegrams."[16] "The dollar which was worth 9.50 in October is worth only 7.40 today and in Omsk and Ekaterinburg I could not exchange dollars for rubles at any banks, Consulates or business houses," Ackerman reported on December 8. "In order to get back to Vladivostok I had to sell practically all of my civilian clothes in Omsk! Old clothes are worth more than dollars in Russia."[17]

The set of references that Ackerman brought with him to Russia was predetermined with his view of the world struggle between democracy and tyranny, and he witnessed the defeat of the former during his sojourn in Siberia.

In October, Ackerman reported on the establishment of the All-Russian government in Omsk, and seemed to be especially enthusiastic that "all Russia free of bolsheviki now supports all Russian provisional [government] located here [in] Russia's newest capital."[18] He interviewed the leader of the government, Nikolai Avksentiev, for the newspaper, and telegraphed his responses to *The New York Times*:

> Americans and Allies, by supporting this Government will be aiding that force in Russia which strives for order and democracy. While Russia knows it is the policy of the United States to favor Russian democracy, recognition of this Government will be the best thing America can do to insure stable democracy here and make it impossible for this revolution to end in a military dictatorship, as the French revolution ended with Napoleon.[19]

However, that government was soon overthrown by the coup led by Admiral Alexander Kolchak. The American journalist wrote in Ekaterinburg on November 27, 1918:

> Notwithstanding that after so many interrupting changes we are accustomed to look on the contemporary Russia as on a state of impossibilities, we must serious think about the change of Omsk, made last week. The official information of Admiral Kolchak from November 18 informs the world, that the All-Russian government does not exist more, and in consequence of this

---

[16] Ackerman to Carl V. Van Anda, near Tomsk, Siberia, November 6, 1918, Ackerman Papers, box 122.

[17] Ackerman to Van Anda, in Siberia en route from Omsk to Vladivostok, December 4, 1918, Ackerman Papers, box 122.

[18] Ackerman to *The New York Times*, eleventh (November 1918?), copies of dispatches cabled from Siberia to *The New York Times*, Ackerman Papers, box 170.

[19] Carl W. Ackerman, "Five Grand Dukes Slain in a Well by Bolsheviki," *The New York Times*, November 18, 1918.

begins the government of the Minister-Council, which gave over all power in his hands—to a dictator.[20]

Ackerman immediately telegraphed Kolchak asking for an interview: "I expect to arrive in Omsk about November Thirtieth ... I beg to ask if I may have the honor of an interview with your excellency which I may telegraph to New York."[21] On December 9, 1918, *The New York Times* published Kolchak's response to Ackerman's lamentation of the overthrow of the democratic body: "The council does not understand the psychology of the Russian people. The council does not consider the practical side of the situation, but deals in theories."[22]

The reality on the ground ruined the idealistic vision of the Russian Civil War that Ackerman maintained in the first weeks of his journey. In an article published in *The New York Times* on December 23, 1918, he described the situation from this newly acquired point of view:

> Divided between East and West, as America was between North and South during the civil war, Russia is today making a new start toward reorganization. Russia's civil war has reached a period where decisive battles are in preparation between the Bolsheviki in the east and the militarist and monarchist party in the west.... A distressing and disappointing feature is that Russia's civil war is not a fight for freedom, but a contest for power between anarchy on the one hand and militarism and autocracy on the other.[23]

It is worth adding that a year later, the commander of the American Expeditionary Force (AEF) in Siberia, General William Graves, whom the journalist befriended in Vladivostok, wrote to Ackerman a letter full of disappointment with Kolchak and all the "white forces" in the Russian East:

> I talked to a great variety of people ... in the towns between Omsk and Vladivostok. We did not find a single person who said that Kolchak had any popular support. My investigations at Omsk convinced me that Kolchak is simply

---

[20] "Justitia Fundamentum regnorum," Ekaterinburg, November 27, 1918, Siberia: Notes, Memoranda, Fragments, Ackerman Papers, box 141.

[21] Ackerman to Kolchak, telegram, undated (November 1918), Ackerman Papers, box 140.

[22] Carl W. Ackerman, "Kolchak Decries Siberian Council," *The New York Times*, December 9, 1918.

[23] Carl W. Ackerman, "Russia Wavers Between Anarchy and the New Siberian Autocracy," *The New York Times*, December 23, 1918. See also the original manuscript: Ackerman to *The New York Times*, en route to Vladivostok, sixteenth (December 1918), Ackerman Papers, box 170.

a name. His name is being used by the most disreputable lot of scoundrels that has ever gotten an opportunity to exploit a poor, starving, defenseless people.... How is one to expect Russia to be rebuilt when in hands of such people. Kalmykoff and Semenoff are still murdering people in great numbers.[24]

Among other themes that Ackerman studied in Siberia were the Czechoslovak corps and its hopes and positions, the role of the American Expeditionary Force in Siberia, the plans of the Japanese, the role of Russian Cooperative Unions in the future restoration of Russia, and the fate of the former Tsar Nicholas II and his family, who disappeared while in exile in Ekaterinburg.

He felt sympathy to the Czechoslovaks—whom he considered the most determined force fighting against Bolshevism—who waited in vain for military help from the Allies. Ackerman copied and sent to the United States many resolutions and complaints made by the Czechoslovaks about the United States' inactivity.

He wrote about Americans of the AEF as "American Siberian exiles," alluding to George Kennan's influential book. (Later, he changed the article title to "Vagabonds of Siberia" but kept the title for the book chapter, and also dedicated the whole book "To the American exiles in Siberia.") In his first correspondences, Ackerman still looked for Russia's place in the future:

> Long after this war Russia will be an international problem. The revolution in nineteen hundred and seventeen [has] made Russia almost an uncivilized country ... the work which the United States and the Allies have undertaken in Russia and Siberia may be expected to be practically endless for we cannot say today how long it may take and we cannot measure our aid by the tick of the clock. Long after this war the Allies will have to be crutches for Russians until they learn, as a nation, to walk again.[25]

Ackerman at first noticed the friendship between Russians and Americans:

In Vladivostok and Khabarovsk, the two chief cities where our men are encamped, there are numerous evidences of Russian-American friendship from the daily sight of Russian boys riding with a couple of soldiers in charge of an army wagon drawn by two teams of mules to the confession of a Siberian peasant that if any nation is to annex any part of Russia he hoped it would be the United States. We have come to Russia to help her people and we have

---

[24] Graves to Ackerman, Vladivostok, September 23, 1919, Ackerman Papers, box 28.

[25] The Americans in Siberia, Vladivostok, Siberia, October 21, 1918. Ackerman Papers, box 170 (articles written to *The New York Times* by Americans in Siberia, and miscellaneous typescripts).

done what we did not intend to do for we have "conquered" them. And this we have done despite our lack of knowledge of the country, of the language and customs of the people and in the face of an active anti-American propaganda; the suspicions of our older friends and the fear of thousands of Russians that we have ulterior motives.[26]

Disappointment in the American role grew during the travels. Ackerman used stronger language in his strictly confidential dispatch to Ambassador Morris and Colonel House written in Omsk:

When I observe that so far the United States has done nothing to help Siberia I mean that there are no evidences in Siberia that we have done anything for Russia or for the people.... Peace in Russia cannot be made at a peace conference in Europe. It can only follow the application and execution of a definite and separate Allied or American policy in Russia itself. Whether Russia is to emerge from this Civil War a democratic nation or a theatre of anarchy depends upon what the United States and the Allies do now.[27]

In his December correspondence to the newspaper, Ackerman lamented:

The United States has done nothing economically for Russia outside of Vladivostok.... Among neither the Cossacks afield nor the Russians does one find a very high opinion of America. I heard no favorable comment during my whole journey, while there was much criticism, which it is, perhaps, not wise to repeat. In Russia we have not made good. Perhaps it is not entirely our fault. The Allies do not agree fundamentally about what should be done.[28]

Besides writing newspaper articles, Ackerman cabled Colonel House urging the American government to announce a unified position toward Russia, and his opinion reached Secretary of State Robert Lansing in the first days of 1919. However, President Wilson refused to take any public stand.[29]

Ackerman fell victim to disinformation (due to his poor command of Russian) when he believed and transmitted to readers of *The New York Times* a fake story about

---

[26] The Americans in Siberia, Ackerman Papers, box 170.

[27] Ackerman to Ambassador Morris and Colonel House, Siberia, (November) 16, 1918, Memoranda for US Department of State, Ackerman Papers, box 141.

[28] Carl W. Ackerman, "Russia Wavers Between Anarchy and the New Siberian Autocracy," *The New York Times*, December 23, 1918.

[29] Carol Willcox Melton, *Between War and Peace: Woodrow Wilson and the American Expeditionary Force in Siberia, 1918–1921* (Macon, GA: Mercer University Press, 2001), 106.

the tsar's family. Ackerman published the first article about the fate of Nicholas II under the title "No Proof of Death of Czar and Family." Upon arrival at Ekaterinburg, the American journalist met with many people in that city, including the engineer Nikolai Ipatiev, the owner of the house where the Romanov family was held. The correspondence, dated November 21 and published on November 28, 1918, underlined that "here at Ekaterinburg ... None possessed proof that the family was executed.... All the reports of the Czar's execution at Ekaterinburg came from Moscow via Berlin."[30] Almost a month later, *The New York Times* published another correspondence from Ackerman, now under the title "Czar's Last Hours Told by Witness. His Plotting for Restoration of Monarchy Discovered by Soviet." This new article featured Parfen Alexeievitch Domnin, the tsar's majordomo, who "remained with his imperial master until the early hours of the morning of July 17, when the Czar was led away by Bolshevist soldiers."[31] Later, *The New York Times* published the story "How Nicholas Romanoff was Condemned to Death" on the first page.[32] Ackerman followed up with the theme of the tsar's fate on February 23, 1919. The title went: "Is the Czar Dead? Six Chances in Ten That He Was Executed by the Bolsheviki—Fate of his Family Also Doubtful."[33] The narration of the last days of Nicholas's life by some "Parfen Domnin" pretending to be the tsar's "majordomo" was, as we know now, fiction that was far from the real circumstances. Moreover, no person with such name or biography ever appeared near the Romanovs. Carl Ackerman seemed to stay intrigued by the fate of the Romanovs long after he returned home. Among his archival files, many magazine clippings from different decades may be found on "princess Anastassia," one of Nicholas's daughters. (In the twentieth century, about thirty people claimed to be "Anastassia"—evidently having miraculously escaped death—but all were proven to be impostors.)

Some of the Ackerman dispatches were factually inaccurate due to the shortage of reliable sources of information in the Civil War-torn country. So, he transmitted an opinion that "despite Germany's agreement [to] withdraw troops from Russia German Generals officers remain commanding Bolshevik armies, Czechoslovak staff here has information from front indicating that General Blucher remains as chief of Bolshevik General staff and that general Eberhardt still commands Bolshevik army

---

[30] Carl W. Ackerman, "No Proof of Death of Czar and Family," *The New York Times*, November 28, 1918.

[31] Carl W. Ackerman, "Czar's Last Hours Told By Witness," *The New York Times*, December 23, 1918.

[32] "How Nicholas Romanoff was Condemned to Death," *The New York Times*, December 29, 1918.

[33] Carl W. Ackerman, "Is the Czar Dead? Six Chances in Ten That He Was Executed by the Bolsheviki—Fate of his Family Also Doubtful," *The New York Times Magazine*, February 23, 1919.

on Samara."³⁴ He considered the German name of the Red commander—Blücher—the proof of direct German participation in the Civil War. In fact, Vasily Blyukher was a peasant's son whose grandfather was renamed by his landlord to celebrate the famous Prussian marshal.

And certainly, Ackerman could not even guess who one of his Siberian acquaintances was, to whose opinions he sometimes referred and whose business card he kept among his papers, where he was presented as Zinovy Alekseevich Pechkoff, "Chef des Services d'Information du Haut Commissariat de la Republique Francaise en Siberie."³⁵ Zinovy Peshkov was an adopted son of a great Russian writer, Maxim Gorky (Peshkov), but also an elder brother of Yakov Sverdlov, the head of the Bolshevik All-Russian Central Executive Committee and, according to Lev Trotsky and some later historians, the person responsible for the decision to murder the tsar's family.

## Book Writing

While Ackerman was still in Siberia (at the very end of 1918), a representative of the Chautauqua system offered him an opportunity to organize a lecture tour during the following summer. General Manager of the Coit-Alber Bureaus Louisa G. Alber expressed her trust that Ackerman "must know the truth about the Russian situation." She then proceeded with the list of possible questions to discuss:

> The newspaper reports that are being published relative to Russia are very conflicting, and the people are curious to know what the truth really is. Just what has the Soviet Government done to the different sections of Russia, and are the Bolsheviki half as bad as they are painted? Is the Bolsheviki Government likely to send an army into Poland and Germany? These are some of the questions the American people are now asking. I hope you can come back and answer them from the platform.³⁶

Ackerman received multiple invitations to speak about Russia in different locations, including Indiana University, Macmillan Publishers, and Brooklyn Chamber of Commerce. The interest in Russian affairs was obvious.

The American journalist was tempted to present his work as a continuation of the book written by George Kennan about Siberia. Ackerman met the patriarch of

---

³⁴ Ackerman to Robinson, November 22, 1918, Ackerman Papers, box 170.

³⁵ Ackerman Papers, box 122.

³⁶ Louisa G. Alber to Ackerman, December 28, 1918, Speeches and Lectures—correspondence concerning, Ackerman Papers, box 165.

Russian Studies in America in early March 1919 and discussed both the Siberian exiles and Russian Bolshevism. Kennan then wrote to Ackerman on March 3, 1919:

> It was a great pleasure to meet you at the house of Mr. and Mrs. Williams Saturday night and I learned from you a number of things that I had not previously understood. I enclose three or four articles that I wrote for *The Outlook* in the spring of 1917 almost immediately after the revolution. They have now only historical interest but they show how Bolshevism began in the Workmen's Council of Petrograd, I have written a number of articles on the subject since then.[37]

On March 14, 1919, George Kennan again wrote to the young journalist promising to lend him some of the books and materials about the current state of Russian affairs.[38]

Ackerman did not limit his stories to the pages of *The New York Times*. Upon return from Siberia, Ackerman planned also to publish a series of his stories in *The Saturday Evening Post*. He offered a "Schedule of Articles" that included titles with a brief outline of each article.[39] The response, however, was negative: "I am afraid that with the copy we are receiving from Captain Roberts we are 'out of the market' for Russian articles for the present at least."[40]

However, Ackerman managed to have at least some of his articles published there. If publishers of his book were not impressed by his theoretical generalizations, he put them in print in newspapers, thus giving start to his anti-Bolshevik crusade.

In the May 10, 1919, issue of *The Saturday Evening Post*, he published an article about Bolshevists under the title "The New Goblins." He started the text with a statement that the world, since the end of the World War, had turned into kindergarten, "Where all the inhabitants are pupils, whom the statesmen, like teachers, are trying to frighten into goodness with the warning that 'the Bolsheviki will get you if you don't watch out.'" Ackerman described the Bolsheviki as a world phenomenon—he did meet them in Germany and Austria, in Switzerland or Russia:

> In Siberia I traveled twelve thousand miles over abandoned trails, and upon my return to the United States I rode from Milwaukee to Chicago in a car of Bolshevist agitators on their way to Ellis Island and deportation! ... The new goblins travel, spreading their gospel of revolution wherever there is unrest,

---

[37] George Kennan to Ackerman, March 3, 1919, Ackerman Papers, box 29.

[38] George Kennan to Ackerman, March 14, 1919, Ackerman Papers, box 29.

[39] Carl Ackerman, Schedule of Articles Suggested for *The Saturday Evening Post*, Ackerman Papers, box 140.

[40] (Editor, *The Saturday Evening Post*, to Ackerman) April 3, 1919, Ackerman Papers, box 140.

discontent, dissatisfaction and disappointment. European Russia is a net of roads and channels of thoughts which the Bolsheviki control. Germany and Austria are in the midst of civil war with them. Siberia was once in their hands and may be again. India, Egypt, Rumania and the Balkans are threatened. In Norway, Switzerland, Sweden, England, Canada and the United States the Bolsheviki are propaganding.

Goblins are everywhere, and because I have but recently returned to this country from Asiatic Russia everyone I meet asks: "What are the facts about the Bolsheviki?"

The answer is simple and this is it:

... Fundamentally and essentially Bolshevism was a program for the destruction of civilization as it was known in Russia, where there was an autocratic government; where labor had no rights; where there were religious persecutions and pogroms, and where there was neither a local nor a national representative assembly....

The new goblins have left Russia and are on the warpath with propaganda. Bolshevism becomes not a Russian issue alone but a world political and industrial problem. Lenine's object at the Minsk congress was to Bolshevize Russia. To-day he seeks to Bolshevize the world.... Bolshevism has capitalized upon the world's discontent with the object of making everyone who desires readjustments and changes a Bolshevist. So we are informed by the wise statesmen of Europe that unless there is a League of Nations there will be a Union of Bolshevists. What they mean is that when governments fail nationally Bolshevism succeeds, and that if the governments of the world fail in uniting upon a world constructive peace program then the Bolshevists will attempt to unite Soviets upon such a plan. Bolshevism succeeds only when governments fail.[41]

Ackerman immediately offered Charles Scribner's Sons the opportunity to publish his book *Bolshevism and a League of Nations*, based on his Siberian travels. His title reflected his basic scheme of the world affairs as a great battle between two principles. The response he received (dated March 13, 1919) praised his idea and plan for the book, and he was offered a contract for publication. However, the editors decided:

> The present title does not seem to us a good one because it suggests a book that might have been written by a man who had had no first-hand contact with the Bolshevists;—even by one who had not left this country, It is an academic title in short. We think it should be amended so as to suggest the fact that the author is basing his views upon the very best of first-hand information derived from experience. We think too, that the tendency in the book should

---

[41] Carl W. Ackerman, "The New Goblins," *The Saturday Evening Post*, May 10, 1919.

be in the direction of giving as much of the experience as possible, as the fact that it has this experience for a basis is one of the great qualities of distinction that the book will have.[42]

After a discussion and at least two variants of the title being rejected, the editors agreed to a new one: "As to the title, we think Trailing the Bolsheviki and the sub-title, Three Thousand Miles With the Allies in Siberia are excellent. We think them better than the two latter ones you suggested to Mr. Brownell and we are announcing the book under this title and sub-title now."[43]

Ackerman asked the Russian Information Bureau in the United States for permission to include the Bolshevist Constitution in his book, and the director A. J. Sack provided the text:

> I am sending you here with a copy of the Bolshevist constitution. It was issued in pamphlet form by *The Nation*, and I was glad to get a copy for you. I am glad to hear that you are writing a book on your experiences in Siberia. Your articles in *The New York Times* were extremely valuable. I have watched them with great interest and I feel that, by writing these articles, you have served nobly not only the cause of democratic Russia but the cause of humanity as well.[44]

The agreement with the publisher on the book *Trailing the Bolsheviki* was signed and dated May 27, 1919.[45] On the stage of proofreading, the editor also asked to make Ackerman's anti-Japanese statements milder: "About the Japanese matter could you do this: apparently these actions of the Japanese were all under a party that is now out of power as you stated; but if you could make this statement more emphatic and pronounced the evidence against the Japanese would have a less alarming character. Every nation has a jingo emperialistic party, actual or potential."[46] On June 19, 1919, the publisher had already sent a copy of Ackerman's book to the author and to the people he suggested.[47]

At the request of the publisher, Ackerman prepared the list of "selling points" for his book:

---

[42] (Editor, Charles Scribner's Sons, to Ackerman) March 13, 1919, Ackerman Papers, box 140.

[43] (Editor, Charles Scribner's Sons, to Ackerman) March 31, 1919, Ackerman Papers, box 140.

[44] A. J. Sack to Ackerman, April 7, 1919, Ackerman Papers, box 139.

[45] Memorandum of Agreement…, Ackerman Papers, box 140.

[46] (Editor, Charles Scribner's Sons, to Ackerman) May 29, 1919, Ackerman Papers, box 140.

[47] (Editor, Charles Scribner's Sons, to Ackerman) June 19, 1919, Ackerman Papers, box 140.

# INTRODUCTION

1. Former President Taft has stated that if a League of Nations is not formed there will be a world Soviet of Bolshevists. This book explains the conflict between Bolshevism and a Union of World Governments.
2. This book is not pro-Bolshevist, anti or neutral but a clear, definite statement of what Bolshevism did to Siberia and what it proposes for the United States and Europe.
3. This book tells the inside story of the failure of the economic program of the Bolshevists who attempted to abolish all private ownership of property.
4. Why the Allies never invaded Russia, or assisted Russia after the Bolshevist revolution is related in this book by the author who was an American correspondent with all the Allied Armies in Siberia.
5. A part of the book contains an account of a vagabond journey twelve thousand miles in Siberia and Manchuria during the past Winter.
6. All the known facts about the mystery surrounding the death of the Tzar and his family are given in this book by the author who spent several weeks in Ekaterinburg, Russia, where Tzar was last imprisoned, making an investigation of his trial and reported execution.
7. The story of the operations of Japanese and American troops in Siberia is given with a narration of the part played by the Jingoes and the successful outcome of diplomatic negotiations in the far East,—the best indication that both Japan and the United States not only wish but intend to have peace in the East.
8. There are more than ten million refugees from European Russia in Siberia and the author describes their life in boxcars, caves and public buildings.
9. This book contains the constitution of the present government of Russia (The Russian Federated Soviet Republic).
10. The Covenant of the League of Nations as adopted in Paris and issued by the Department of State in Washington, is printed in full in the Appendix.
11. The author has been in eighteen countries during the war, from Mexico to Canada; from Belgium to Rumania and from Japan to Siberia and Russia and is author of "Germany, the Next Republic," published in June 1917.
12. An account of the conflict between the Russian Cooperative Unions and the Bolsheviki is given to prove that the Bolshevism as an "industrial democracy" has failed in Russia.
13. The writer contends that during the reconstruction period following the signing of peace in Paris there will be an international conflict between Bolshevism, which seeks to destroy all government, society and industry to build a new world and a Union of World Governments, or a League of nations, which proposes to reorganize and rebuil[d] the world by reform and readjustment.

14. The conflict between these two organizations is essentially a conflict between a revolution of action, which is Bolshevism, and a revolution of opinion, in which a League of Nations will lead. The author's conclusion is that Bolshevism has already been a failure in Russia and Europe and will not succeed in the United States.
15. This is the first book on Bolshevism which describes the failure of the Bolshevist's industrial reconstruction program upon which the Bolshevists have based their sole argument for world domination.[48]

Ackerman compiled a list of the persons to whom copies of the book should be sent "for advertising purposes." The first in the list was A. J. Sack, director of the Russian Information Bureau in New York City; the second in the list was George Kennan; and the last of the eighteen people was William H. Taft, former US president, whose idea Ackerman used in his description of the book.

An additional list of persons to receive copies of the book that should be charged to the author opened with the names of his Siberian acquaintances: Major General William S. Graves; Lieutenant Colonel O. P. Robinson; Ambassador Roland S. Morris; and continued with Colonel Edward M. House and other people.[49]

Most of the readers of the book did not like the bipolar scheme of world politics that the author considered so important.

One of the first reviewers in *The Sun* asked whether it was possible to get any truth about Russia. His opinion was: "It is difficult to access chaos; it can only be recorded."[50] A reviewer ridiculed Ackerman's comparison of Bolshevism to the League of Nations, and called Bolshevism just a "usual schism of post-revolutionary time." From a century's distance, we can judge his early understanding of the future fights of the cold war.

A reviewer in *The North American Review* also pointed out:

> There is no great mystery about Bolshevism itself ... It is the rule of the under dog. It is a form of anarchy that inevitably springs up after war, and before reconstruction ... That it is not only different from the League of Nations plan, but so strictly opposed to it that the one is the only alternative to the other, is an assumption that Mr. Ackerman frequently states, but never proves.[51]

---

[48] Carl W. Ackerman, Selling Points for Scribner's Book "Trailing the Bolsheviki," Book: *Trailing the Bolsheviki*, 1919, Ackerman Papers, box 179.

[49] List of persons to receive copies of "Trailing the Bolsheviki," Book: *Trailing the Bolsheviki*, 1919, Ackerman Papers, box 179.

[50] N. P. D., "Some More 'Truth About Russia,'" *The Sun*, July 13, 1919.

[51] *The North American Review* (February 1920), 288.

The newspaper reviewer of the book gave credit to Ackerman's description of the conditions in Siberia during the Civil War, but criticized his theories:

> The thesis by which he endeavors to bind all his chapters into a compact and united whole is that the world is confronted with the choice between Bolshevism and the League of Nations and that "these two international forces are working today for a new world." In carrying out this thesis he presents his observations in Siberia to show that Bolshevism failed in that country, and also that "the Allies, working as a nucleus of a League of nations, failed." The comparison of the representatives of several nations in Siberia and their attempt at cooperation with the scheme of the League of Nations is so far fetched and so strained that the reader at once begins to fear that Mr. Ackerman's ability to think is not equal to his ability to observe and report.[52]

Another reviewer concluded:

> Ackerman's discussion of the Russian political melee can be disregarded without loss. He is essentially the journalist, to whom the fate of the czar is immeasurably more fascinating than the development of political forms through experiments conducted in a nation of millions of souls.[53]

Ackerman took offense from the reviewers; in his papers, one can find a letter to the editors of *The New Republic* under the title "Books Half Read," where he responds to a review published in the magazine pointing out that the author had not read half of the book.[54]

Carl W. Ackerman's legacy is quite controversial. On the one hand, he left us with the unique description of Siberia during the Russian Civil War and provided the minutes of his conversations with Russian commanders and politicians, peasants and soldiers, and Russians and Czechs. Ackerman proved to be more insightful even in his predictions: his vision of a divided world would perfectly fit into the realities of the Cold War decades later. On the other hand, with his lack of background knowledge of the language and country he visited, having been interested in philosophy and politics rather than in fact-gathering journalism, Ackerman reported many incorrect facts, transmitted the news that we now would call fake, and even used infamous anti-Semitic sham when it seemed to support his anti-Bolshevik theses. He was an early

---

[52] "Notable Books in Brief Review," *The New York Times Book Review*, July 20, 1919.

[53] *The Dial* (NY), September 6, 1919.

[54] "Books Half Read," Ackerman Papers, Manuscript Division, Library of Congress, Washington, DC, container 179.

crusader who influenced the American vision of demonic Russia after the Russian Revolution and helped to maintain its image of a Constitutive Other of America.

## Suggested Further Reading

Ackerman, Carl W. *Germany, the Next Republic?* New York: Grosset & Dunlap, 1917.

Ackerman, Carl W. *Mexico's Dilemma.* New York: George H. Doran, 1918.

Davis, Donald E., and Eugene P. Trani. *The First Cold War: The Legacy of Woodrow Wilson in U.S.-Soviet Relations.* Columbia: University of Missouri Press, 2002.

Foglesong, David S. *America's Secret War Against Bolshevism: U.S. Intervention in the Russian Civil War, 1917–1920.* Chapel Hill: University of North Carolina Press, 1995.

Graves, William S. *America's Siberian Adventure, 1918–1920.* New York: J. Cape and H. Smith, 1931.

House, John M. *Wolfhounds and Polar Bears: The American Expeditionary Force in Siberia, 1918–1920.* Tuscaloosa: University of Alabama Press, 2016.

Kennan, George. *Siberia and the Exile System.* 2 vols. New York: Century, 1891.

Massie, Robert K. *The Romanovs: The Final Chapter.* New York: Ballantine Books, 1995.

McNamara, Kevin J. *Dreams of a Great Small Nation: The Mutinous Army that Threatened a Revolution, Destroyed an Empire, Founded a Republic, and Remade the Map of Europe.* Philadelphia: PublicAffairs, 2016.

Melton, Carol Willcox. *Between War and Peace: Woodrow Wilson and the American Expeditionary Force in Siberia, 1918–1921.* Macon, GA: Mercer University Press, 2001.

Mohr, Joan McGuire. *The Czech and Slovak Legion in Siberia, 1917–1922.* Jefferson, NC: McFarland, 2012.

Murray, Robert K. *Red Scare: A Study in National Hysteria, 1919–1920.* Minneapolis: University of Minnesota Press, 1955.

Pereira, N. G. O. *White Siberia: The Politics of Civil War.* Montreal: McGill-Queen's University Press, 1996.

Richard, Carl J. *When the United States Invaded Russia: Woodrow Wilson's Siberian Disaster.* Lanham, MD: Rowman and Littlefield, 2013.

Rosenberg, William G. *Liberals in the Russian Revolution: The Constitutional Democratic Party, 1917–1921.* Princeton, NJ: Princeton University Press, 1974.

Saul, Norman E. *War and Revolution: The United States and Russia, 1914–1921.* Lawrence: University Press of Kansas, 2001.

Singerman, Robert. "The American Career of the 'Protocols of the Elders of Zion.'" *American Jewish History* 71, no. 1 (September 1981): 53–54.

Smele, Jonathan D. *Civil War in Siberia: The Anti-Bolshevik Government of Admiral Kolchak, 1918–1920*. Cambridge: Cambridge University Press, 1996.

Toczek, Nick. *Haters, Baiters and Would-Be Dictators: Anti-Semitism and the UK Far Right*. New York: Routledge, 2016.

Unterberger, Betty Miller. *The United States, Revolutionary Russia, and the Rise of Czechoslovakia*. College Station: Texas A&M University Press, 2000.

Unterberger, Betty Miller. *America's Siberian Expedition, 1918–1920: A Study of National Policy*. Durham, NC: Duke University Press, 1956.

Ward, John. *With the "Die-Hards" in Siberia*. New York: George H. Doran, 1920.

# EDITOR'S NOTE

The original publication of *Trailing the Bolsheviki: Twelve Thousand Miles with the Allies in Siberia* included two appendices. The first was a translation of the Constitution of the Russian Socialist Federated Soviet Republic, reprinted in *The Nation* on January 4, 1919, with a preamble containing a resolution of the Fifth All-Russian Congress of Soviets, which was adopted on July 10, 1918. The second was the Covenant of the League of Nations. Both were significant for Carl W. Ackerman because he contrasted the two visions of the world's future as presented by Bolshevik Russia and the Wilsonian League of Nations. The two texts were not included in this reprint, but they are publicly available online.

We have kept Ackerman's spelling of personal and geographical names, but have opted for contemporary spelling in the footnotes (for persons) and in the index (for geographical names). While Ackerman's spelling is at times inconsistent, we believe that it reflects the style and haste of writing in a time of such historical significance.

# TRAILING THE BOLSHEVIKI

## TWELVE THOUSAND MILES WITH THE ALLIES IN SIBERA

BY
**CARL W. ACKERMAN**
Special Correspondent of *The New York Times*

NEW YORK
CHARLES SCRIBNER'S SONS
1919

COPYRIGHT, 1919, BY
CHARLES SCRIBNER'S SONS
Published June, 1919
COPYRIGHT, 1918, 1919, BY THE NEW YORK TIMES
COPYRIGHT, 1919, BY THE CURTIS PUBLISHING CO

# INTRODUCTION

One war is over and another conflict begins. Following the tracks of Thor is visible the trail of the Bolsheviki.

The armistice marked only a pause in the great world cataclysm—a pause where the contest ceased only long enough for the participants to change from nations to individuals. The Treaty of Peace, while recording the close of the war between the Associated Powers and the Central Empires, is but a sign to indicate the end of the War of Nations and the beginning of the period of reconstruction. The transition is from an international conflict of governments to a world contest between reconstruction forces—between those who believe in destroying the world to rebuild it and those who desire to accept the world as it is to remodel it.

The two contestants are Bolshevism, or class individualism and a league of nations, or a union of world governments. The essential difference between the two is that the former demands a revolution of action and the latter symbolizes a revolution of opinion and adjustment.

For five years I have been travelling as a correspondent within and without belligerent and neutral countries in Europe, Asia, and the Americas, following the developments of the war and studying the political and industrial causes and incentives of mass action. In Germany, in the old Hapsburg Monarchy, in Belgium, France, Poland, Rumania, and Siberia I followed the god of war and reported numerous events of fighting. This winter I followed the trail of the Bolsheviki over 12,000 miles in Russia, from Vladivostok to Ekaterinburg, where the Tzar is believed to have been done to death, and back again to New York via China and Japan. I met the Bolshevist vanguard in Switzerland and in the United States, and some of the exiles in Spain and Mexico. Over the face of the globe winds the serpentine trail of the revolutionists, a part of which I have followed and traversed.

From time to time on my journeys I have been in contact or in communication with those who have been dreaming and laboring for a world society of governments. With many statesmen and the chief executives of several nations I have discussed the problems and possibilities of international co-operation, and I have had the good fortune of knowing some of the men who wrote the first draft of a world constitution. In travelling and living with armies, refugees, and civilians I have had an opportunity of feeling the pulse of peoples under war conditions and the circumstances of reconstruction in no less than eighteen countries.

Looking back upon my contact with statesmen, soldiers, and non-combatants, I discern something of the development and the problems and programmes of these two international forces which are working to-day for a new world: Bolshevism and a league of nations.

Bolshevism is the Russian name for a revolutionary movement which has as its object the overthrowing of existing governments and society and the revolutionization of industry and commerce. Bolshevism is caused by industrial discontent, social unrest, and by the unsettled conditions in a nation passing through the transition period from war to peace. It is a political programme formulated and supported by those who have lost faith in political leaders and government. The Bolsheviki believe in razing the world in order to rebuild it.

The League of Nations is the name given to a group of world governments organized for the purpose of bringing about international co-operation, unity, and understanding in international, political, and commercial relations. The demand for such a society is due to the failure of alliances, spheres of influence, and the balancing of power. The universal desire of the public that governments co-operate in an attempt to minimize and limit the possibilities of international conflicts, was the foundation upon which the league was built. The fundamental object of a society of governments is to reconstruct the world upon a new basis; upon a basis of mutual understanding regarding international law, commerce, trade routes, and the maintenance of agreements. The League of Nations proposes to accept the world as it is and attempt through mutual discussion and exchange of ideas to rebuild, reconstruct, and revitalize it. The war ran a race with revolution and won in the Allied and neutral countries. It won the first lap of the race which ended with the signing of the armistice, but the second is beginning between a revolution of action and a revolution of opinion. The outcome is not visible to-day because it depends upon the speed with which opinions change. The mind of the mass moves rapidly, and there is peace both within or without a nation only so long as those who direct the public policies keep abreast or ahead of the opinions of the people. "The opinion of the world is the mistress of the world." The world-wide revolutionary movement of to-day is essentially only a universal sentiment in favor of a better world after this war. Four years of intense discussion of war issues has fed the minds of the people with new ideas and higher ideals. Thus far this great mass of humanity has not formulated these into a plan of action or a programme for realization. People are looking, as always, to their leaders.

A revolution of action develops when the mass mind moves too rapidly for statesmen and governments to change their opinions and laws, or when governments fail to sense the power of the will of the mass. Revolutions of action were successful in Russia, Germany, Austria-Hungary, Turkey, and Bulgaria when those who directed the governments and industries did not heed the desires of the people. There will be similar eruptions in other nations unless these compelling lessons of the war are applied elsewhere. The predominant force back of a union of world governments is the limitless longing of war-weary people that an attempt be made to solve international and national problems without bloodshed and destruction. On the other hand, the industrial crusaders of Bolshevism contend that the world can only be purged by fire and blood.

This is not a temporary question but the problem of a generation. In Siberia, after the revolution, both the Bolsheviki and the Allies, working as a nucleus of a league of nations, failed. Both reconstruction forces were unsuccessful. The experiences of the writer in this vast domain will serve as material for illustrations of the failure of Bolshevism and the difficulties of international concerted action. In Siberia Bolshevism and a union of foreign governments clashed for the first time. This is what makes Siberia the only laboratory at present available for an analysis of these two reconstruction forces. In trailing the Bolsheviki, I have followed and crossed the tracks of the revolution of action, not alone in Siberia, but in Germany, Hungary, Switzerland, and the United States.

"Give us peace and give us bread," said an old Russian peasant in the Amur. That is the world problem. Peace, bread, work, and opportunity are the demands of the people.

Peace will not come immediately after the ratification of the treaty in France. Peace will come only by slow stages of development. The long period of reconstruction which will follow the end of this war will be an era of constant conflict between the men and women who are to rebuild the world after their own ideas. No one doubts that the new world must be and will be different from the old, but there will be grave disagreements about the methods of reconstruction. There will be those who wish to tear down in order to rebuild and others who will seek to remake by gradual adjustment.

The pendulum of history has swung from reaction to revolution, but civilization has been advanced only when the pendulum swung backward and forward evenly over the arc of Time. The pendulum is now swinging from the extreme of war to the extreme of reconstruction. It is the task of the peoples and governments of the world to generate the gravity which makes the pendulum swing ceaselessly and regularly, ticking the hours of progress which make the days of happiness and the centuries of advancement.

CARL W. ACKERMAN<br>
New York City<br>
May, 1919

# Chapter I

# FROM NEW YORK TO VLADIVOSTOK

Eight thousand miles west of New York lies the city of Vladivostok, "Tzar of the East," under the empire, but today the political melting-pot of the Orient and an abandoned outpost on the trail of the Bolsheviki. It was a long journey from the United States to Peter the Great Gulf and this Siberian seaport and dismantled naval-station. Across the continent and the Pacific via San Francisco, the Hawaiian Islands, Yokohama, and Tsuruga, I travelled thirty-seven days before I saw the cliffs of Golden Horn Bay silhouetted against the dull gray sky of an October morning. The distance and the time were impressive and appalling. It seemed a long way to go to join the Allied armies in Russia as a correspondent and to follow the military vanguard on its ill-fated campaign against the Red army, but as the days and weeks passed, these elements became insignificant, because time and distance are not measured, after all, so much by hours and miles as by events, and the action or lack of it in Siberia was destined to bring the United States and Russia closer together than they were on the map.

Between New York and Vladivostok lies the continent, the Pacific and Japan, the Occident and the Orient—the East and the Far East—nations allied in a great war and still mysteries to each other. Riding from the Atlantic to the Western seaboard of the United States there was evident the preparation and development of a united nation for war in France, Flanders, and Italy. To Americans, Siberia was an incident, not an event; a playhouse, not a war theatre.

To those living in our Eastern States the war in Europe was the most vital part of their lives, although they may not have taken a direct physical part in any war activity. They followed the progress of events in France and Washington with such concentrated interest that the latest news was of more importance to their peace of mind than an essential meal. But the farther West one travelled, as the distance which separated Western cities from Europe increased, the interest in the war seemed to be linked to Europe by a rubber band, which snapped back when the strain became too great. It was a strain to follow the war developments in France as intently in San Francisco as in New York or Philadelphia. The vital news reached the West, but all of the color and detail were missing. Between the Atlantic and Pacific there seemed to be an invisible news-sieve which permitted only the biggest reports to reach the West.

It was not alone in respect to news that this was true. There was more food and more varieties of edibles, which became noticeable as soon as the Rocky Mountains were crossed. That State which is sometimes called the "Land of Perpetual Summer" was not Hooverized to the extent of those east of Ohio, and it was a curious but actual experience that the more food one obtained the less one felt the war.

Sailing on an old Japanese liner which had been lashed and rocked by the waves of the Pacific for more than a decade, from Frisco to Yokohama, when the war in France was rapidly approaching a climax, one felt that the Pacific Ocean was well-named by its discoverer, for the Germans were not able to disturb its tranquility. It was, indeed, a "subless" sea which only those who crossed the Atlantic during the U-boat warfare could fully appreciate. Instead of those tense days and uncertain nights, with their ceaseless rumor and semiconscious slumber, which were then the accompaniment of all trans-Atlantic journeys, there were days and weeks so devoid of war sensations, of submarine activities, of life-boat drills, and of passing convoys, that one was glad there was, at least, a pirateless Pacific.

Aboard the old *Nippon Maru*, the "swimming" Nippon, great abysses separated one from Europe. There was the calm and non-belligerency of the ocean, the lack of detailed and daily information about our armies in France, and the abundance of food with hundreds of varieties from California, Hawaii, and Japan. These great divides separated the traveller from the enemy. But as this vast gulf widened one became conscious of the fact that the half-hemisphere which separated New York from Siberia and eastern Russia was narrowing, and that East and Far East were meeting in Vladivostok. New York and the Eastern States seemed near to France and to the fighting because the Atlantic was bridged by human ties, by ships, news, and trade. The extreme Orient seemed far; Siberia was only a cold, bleak prison for the Tzar's exiles because these scores of interests and personal connections of a familiar Europe were lacking.[1] But now, at last, the Pacific was destined to be spanned by the same forces which linked the United States to England, Belgium, and France, except that the submarines did not appear to stain that placid sea of blue. While the "U-bootkrieg" severed the official lines between Washington and Berlin only to bind together more closely those human and national bonds between America and the Allies, it had by its very absence from the Pacific brought about the same results, and bound the United States, England, France, and Italy to China, Japan and Siberia through unobstructed trade.

A few miles off the Golden Gate the American pilot was dropped, and on the *Nippon Maru* I discovered the Far East and Russia in miniature! Here were the extreme types and the commonplace of the Orient and the Far Northeast. Monarchist, Bolshevist, and Social Revolutionist of Russia passed on the decks or in the hold the extremes of China, the lazy "coolie" who gambled day and night and the progressive Chinese merchant en route to Hong Kong with his Latin-American wife. Here were

---

[1] The American image of Siberia was determined by George Kennan's book *Siberia and the Exile System*, published in 1891. Ackerman visited Kennan in spring 1919, after his return from Russia, probably to share his impressions of the region once described by an old traveler.

Japanese professors, officers, and business men bound for Tokyo and Kobe with their compact brains stored with Western ideas; Western ideas of commerce and war. English and American professors en route to Manila and Shanghai; English bankers and American exporters; United States army officers and engineers; Italians, Brazilians, and Chilians [sic] were all bound for Russia, China, and Japan.

This steamer was only one of many which had been carrying Russians from every section of America as well as from France and England back to their native land via Siberia. The revolution opened the gates for the exiles and foreign refugees and the Bolshevist from the East Side; the Revolutionist from New Jersey and the Monarchist from Paris met on the Pacific en route to Russia to search for relatives or take part in political propaganda. These ships which sailed unheralded from our Western ports for Siberia and Japan were weaving a cloth of commerce and political interests over the Pacific. They were the shuttles sewing the coasts of the Far East and the West together.

In the air the wireless reported daily the events which followed in quick succession the landing of the Japanese and Allies in Vladivostok, and their march down the Usuri Valley in pursuit of the Bolsheviki. All fronts have a beginning in military action and there was action already in Siberia. It was a battle-front in the making.

Coming from Japan were other ships, which, steaming by in the distance, sent news of the "new front" not in bulletin form but in detail. They told of the progress of the Japanese troops in Siberia and Manchuria, of the towns and cities freed of Bolshevists. They described the cavalry charges, the counterattacks, the retirement of the enemy and, at the end of one message was a brief paragraph saying that the twenty-one Japanese soldiers and officers, killed in action, were being brought back to Nippon for burial!

And most of us had to look up the Usuri River on the map, for it was as new to us as the Marne to Americans before the war. Ignorance plays a surprising role in life and world events. A lack of understanding and knowledge especially of foreign countries and international politics is perhaps one of the causes of the Siberian debacle, which could not be sensed in the beginning by Americans and Allies because of their lack of knowledge of Russia. How strange the Far East is to the average American was evidenced one night on the ship when a Chicago merchant, en route to India on his first ocean voyage, to whom Siberia was a million miles away from his office in the McCormick building, looked down into the hatch, watching the Chinese play "fan-tan." It was a new game and a new experience to him and he rushed to the first cabin to spread the news that the "coolies are gambling with gold." Many of us, sceptical because of the thorough search by the United States Custom officials for gold before we left San Francisco, accompanied him to the lower deck to see the yellow metal and the yellow hands, but, alas! The "gold" was mere Chinese brass sen pieces, of which it is said it takes a wheel-barrow full to make a dollar, glistening like gold in the yellow rays of the electric lights! And our ideas of Siberia before seven thousand five hundred

American soldiers were landed there, under the command of Major-General William S. Graves,[2] was as glaring as this Middle Western merchant's knowledge of Chinese customs.

Travelling during the war one had more than the simple advantages of comfort over the days of Columbus. Ships in war-time were melting-pots of nations. Columbus had to wait until he sighted land or until he stepped ashore before he could learn the language, the customs, or the ideas of a new people. To-day one meets the citizens of all countries on the steamers, especially Russians on the ships which ply between America and Russia. Since the Russian revolution thousands of Russians have crossed the Pacific and these men and women who were residents of New York, Seattle, Chicago, and Newark have flocked to the land of their birth to become officials or business men. One of the Bolshevist commissars of Khabarovsk, the capital of the Amur, was a Chicago lawyer. Petrograd and Moscow were filled with political agitators from New York and New Jersey. In nearly every Siberian city were refugees from cities on our western coast. On the *Nippon Maru* were more of these Russian-Americans en route to their native land, Bolshevist, Menshevist, and Monarchist, plotter and peaceful citizen.

Walking the deck one evening I met a young Russian Jew from one of the communicating suburbs of New York. He had been in the United States three years, and was now en route to Russia to search for his family which he had left in a small town near Moscow.

"I don't know ver my vife iss," he said. "I halfnot heard about her or my children since April."

"You have an American passport?" I asked.

"No, a Russian."

"Were you in sympathy with the revolution?"

"Zertainly," was his quick answer. He was a keen, determined fellow and his English, while not perfect, showed that he had been utilizing every opportunity to improve it in his humble circumstances because he had been working in a junk-shop near Newark, and had saved five thousand dollars in three years!

"I tink, I mean 'I think,' it will be the greatest blessing there could be for the Russian people," he added. "You don't know what it was before. I do. I was born there. I lived there. I married there. It was hell. I left."

"And now you are going back?" I asked.

---

[2] William S. Graves (1865–1940) was a United States Army major general. He commanded American forces in Siberia during the Siberian Expedition, part of the Allied Intervention in Russia. In 1918, he was given command of the 8th Infantry Division and sent to Siberia under direct orders from President Woodrow Wilson. They landed on September 1, 1918. His troops did not intervene in the Russian Civil War despite strong pressure brought on him to help the White armies.

"To get my family," he replied, and we walked back and forth under the canvas awning over the promenade deck while he stared impatiently at the calm southern sea, his mind four thousand miles away, and I watched the rays of moonlight dance on the deck as the ship rolled silently and monotonously. Finally I asked him if he was a Bolshevist.

"*Niet*! I mean 'No,'" he retorted harshly.

"What does the word 'Bolsheviki' mean?" I asked.

"Maximum or majority," he replied. "There were two factions of the Social Democratic party. The Bolshevists and the Menshevists. The first desired the maximum programme of Karl Marx and the other the minimum."

"Are you a Socialist?" I questioned.

"*Niet*!" and then he paused. "I'm in business. I'm a partner in the junk business in Newark," he answered with pride. "I half taken my first papers out."

Another Russian passenger, a Monarchist, had come from Paris. He was being financed on his present journey by wealthy Russians in Washington. At various times in his life he had been school-teacher, army officer, and priest. He claimed to be the owner of considerable property near Petrograd, and was such a firm believer in the Tzar he could not imagine the "Little Father" dead. During the voyage he wrote essays in French to prove to an American lieutenant that there was more "Culture" in Russia than in the United States. He had neither patience for, nor interest in, any other faction in Russia than the Royalists, and he and the other Russians would get in such bitter arguments that they seemed to long for a landing in Russia so they could fight it out between themselves in their own country. But after they reached Vladivostok each went his way to fight with words, for they were either patriots or paid propagandists.

This ship controversy over Russia proved to be more than an amusing farce, and a rather accurate forecast of the situation in Siberia. There was about the same possibility of uniting our Russian passengers on a programme of relief or war or reconstruction as there proved to be possibilities of uniting the Russian factions. Revolutionists recognized no compromise. That was a plank in their political and industrial programme, and as for the Militarists and Monarchists, neither history nor war had taught them the lessons of concession.

Shortly before we left the United States the Allied governments had announced their decision to land troops in Siberia, and by the time we were at sea the Japanese, Americans, Englishmen, and Frenchmen were marched into the Amur in pursuit of the Bolsheviki. At that time the common impression was that the Bolshevists were German agents, and the object of the Allies, although rather cloudy, appeared to be to attack the Bolshevists through Russia—the back door to Germany. The Czecho-Slovak revolutionary army had been fighting since the latter part of May, and the Allies were entering Russia ostensibly to assist them, not in a campaign against Russia, but on behalf of the Russians!

I had my credentials to the Czecho-Slovak army issued in Washington when President T. G. Masaryk[3] was representing the National Council of Czecho-Slovakia in the United States. I had letters of credence to the Japanese, French, British, Italian, and Chinese forces, and was accredited to the A. E. F., but I had a confused idea of what might be the developments in Russia, because it was almost impossible to fathom the policies or the plans of the associated Powers. There had been more disagreement and mystery about the "Russian problem" than about any other phase of the war, and, as I read the declared intentions of the Allies before they landed their forces in Russia and studied the reports which I had taken with me aboard the ship, the difference of opinion between the United States and the Allies became more and more evident. Of the numerous proposals which had been considered by the associated governments there were two plans of action upon which the Powers were divided. Japan, England, and France were in favor of strong military intervention. Great pressure had been brought to bear upon Washington to permit the Japanese to intervene alone. Although there were indications that Japan would accept the task, if granted a free hand by the Allies and the United States, there were dangers ahead which the United States could not overlook. Washington, on the other hand, steadfastly contended that the best policy to adopt toward Russia was one of economic rehabilitation, and even after our troops were permitted to join the Allies in Vladivostok this policy was blindly followed. At the very beginning this was the gulf which separated the Powers.

When a war ends, no matter what the cause, reconstruction begins. For Russia the war ended in March, 1917, when the Tzar Nikolas Romanoff was overthrown and a provisional government proclaimed.[4] Because the war had not ended in Europe generally, few observers looked upon the new situation in Russia as being anything other than a reorganization for war. But the vital spark which fired the nation to revolution was partially caused by the war itself, and the one spark could not kindle two fires at the same time. Russia was the first reconstruction problem, and, whether the Allies as a unit recognized this or not, they were divided as to the methods and plans of action.

After twenty-eight days on the Pacific, associating with Russians, Japanese, Chinese, Americans, and six or eight other nationalities, I rickshawed from the dock to

---

[3] Tomáš Garrigue Masaryk (sometimes anglicized to Thomas Masaryk; 1850–1937), was a Czech politician, sociologist, and philosopher, and the first president of Czecho-Slovakia after it gained independence.

[4] Nicholas Romanov (1868–1918), Russian tsar Nicholas II from 1895 to 1917. The Provisional Government was established following the abdication of Tsar Nicholas II on March 2 (15), 1917, by the members of the State Duma (Russian parliament). The task of the Provisional Government was to organize elections to the Russian Constituent Assembly—but after eight months, it ceased to exist when the Bolsheviks gained power after the October Revolution on October 25 (November 7), 1917.

the Yokohama-Tokyo electric railway, and journeyed on to the capital of Japan, from which city I departed the following evening for Tsuruga.

From Tsuruga, a small inland harbor city of Japan, passenger-ships leave twice a week for Vladivostok. Being fourteen hours from Tokyo, on the Japan sea, a traveller would easily overlook the city, and, in so doing, would be making a fatal mistake. To see and know the Far East to-day one must visit Tsuruga to see one of the chief cities on the commercial route to Siberia from the Island Kingdom. To the Japanese Siberia is not a Russian problem but a Far-Eastern question, and, although Russia and Siberia may again be united, their interests, during the next ten years or more, will be divided. The reason is simple. In European Russia the problems of reconstruction will be essentially political, industrial, and social, and continental politics will play an important part. In Siberia will arise questions of influence, of development, and expansion, with the United States and Japan in the chief roles. So to an American Tsuruga is an important port.

These two passenger ships, and innumerable freight steamers, leave this port each week for Vladivostok. One of the passenger-boats, the largest, in fact, belongs to the Russian volunteer fleet; all others are Japanese. Ever since the beginning of the war millions of yen worth of supplies and ammunition have been shipped from Tsuruga, in Japanese bottoms, to the terminus of the Trans-Siberian Railway on Golden Horn Bay, and to-day there are other millions of yen worth of products awaiting transportation. Tsuruga is Japan's strategic commercial city as far as Siberia is concerned. It is the "shipping department" of Nipponese industries.

Vladivostok is two days by good weather from Tsuruga, and from four to ten when a typhoon sweeps through the narrow sea which separates the five hundred and eighty-one islands of Japan from Asia. I was fortunate the day I crossed, for it was calm and warm, and I was able to become acquainted with several Japanese merchants who were en route to Siberia and Manchuria with their families. One of these was the Siberian manager of Mitsui and Company, the largest and wealthiest business house of Japan, which is interested in almost every large enterprise in the Far East, from ship-building to mining and exporting and importing. He was a graduate of Columbia University, and had been a resident of New York and Washington nineteen years. Through him I met other Japanese commercial agents who were going to Russia on similar objects—to see to the expansion of Japanese business, and to make investigations and obtain mining and forestry concessions. During the two days we were together, I saw Siberia through Japanese eyes, and I was impressed by the oft-repeated statement:

"In Siberia, Japan and United States must work together. That's Mitsui's idea; Japanese business and American business must co-operate. We must not have competition. Competition no good to anybody. Competition makes trouble. Co-operation makes money and peace."

A Russian professor from the University of Kharkoff was sceptical of this programme. "The economic history of the world shows that where there are great commercially imperialistic nations there are colonies which are weaker nations," he declared. "Russia for the next decade will be a colony for Japan, the United States, England, France, and Germany. After that Russia as a colony will disappear, because these nations will fight among themselves over Russia, and our country will emerge as a free nation!"

Before I stepped from the *Hozan Maru* onto the dock of Vladivostok, this city had been temporarily abandoned by the Bolsheviki. As an outpost it was no longer important. The trail which had followed the Trans-Siberian Railway from Moscow and Petrograd to the Amur had been erased from the map by the echelons of Czecho-Slovaks and a few Allied soldiers, but the trail-makers of Bolshevism, although scattered, were still present in that country.

That phrase which is so common, "this is a small world after all," came to my mind when I was greeted on the pier by Americans; when I saw the Stars and Stripes waving from the flag-pole atop the headquarters of the American Expeditionary Force in Svetlanskaya No. 26. Automobiles manufactured in the United States were in use by all nationalities; "Yank" sentries were guarding war-supplies along the railroad-tracks. "Amerikansky wagons," or locomotives, with steam up, were in the railroad-yards. The armored cruiser *Brooklyn* was anchored along a temporary dock, and near by was a "hut" of the Y.M.C.A. Outwardly, Vladivostok did not appear much different from San Francisco, except that it was on a smaller scale.

Such were the first impressions after five weeks of travel. This was Vladivostok, founded when President Lincoln was making his second campaign for the presidency. This was Siberia, which was inhabited by Tartars as late as the sixteenth century. This was a part of the old Russian Empire, which had been ruled and misdirected for generations by autocrats. This was the old home of the exiles, of politicians, Jews, revolutionists, and democrats banished by Nikolas II and his predecessors.

From this base of Vladivostok, one of the few open ports of all Russia, I began my long journey north and into the interior, and as the days and weeks of travel multiplied I was impressed, not by the distance from New York, but by the vastness of the country itself, which stretches from the Pacific to the Baltic Sea over a continent twice as broad as the United States.

Thus, I began my explorations in the land of "Nitchevo," following the old trails and crossing the new ones of the Bolsheviki.

# Chapter II
# IN THE LAND OF "NITCHEVO"

Russia, as a nation passing through the period of reconstruction, is a "land of Nitchevo." Arriving in Siberia, "Nitchevo" is the first Russian word the foreigner learns. The Russians use it to cover a multitude of evasions and to answer a thousand and one questions. "I should worry," or "Nothing matters," expresses the national state of mind. Ask a droshky driver what he thinks of Bolshevism and he will answer: "Nitchevo." Question a poor refugee about conditions and the reply will be the same. Converse with a business man or a professor who has been struggling through the terrors of Russia's civil war, and the chances are he will say, "Nitchevo." There is something pathetic and discouraging about it. The revolution seems to have produced a sort of national coma where those who have suffered and hoped for two years or more have lost confidence in everything.

In trailing the Bolsheviki it is the philosophy of "Nitchevo" which impresses one as much as the lack of definite knowledge regarding the doctrines of Bolshevism and its workableness. The world may have been a stage in Shakespeare's time, but it is not now. To-day it is a kindergarten where all the inhabitants are pupils whom the statesmen are trying to frighten into goodness by the warning: "The Bolsheviki will get you if you don't watch out!" These new goblins of politics make children out of all of us and we ask with childish fear and curiosity: "What are the Bolsheviki?" "Why are they?" "What are they for?" "Will they get me?"

The trail of the Bolsheviki to-day is a long one, a sort of political caravan route winding and twisting over the map of Europe, Asia, and the United States, upon which the new goblins travel spreading their gospel of revolution wherever there is unrest, discontent, dissatisfaction, and disappointment. European Russia is a net of roads and channels of thoughts which the Bolsheviki control. Germany and Austria are in the midst of civil war with them. Siberia was once in their hands and may be again. India, Egypt, Rumania, and the Balkans are threatened. In Norway, Switzerland, Sweden, England, Canada, and the United States the Bolsheviki are propagandizing. Bolshevik goblins are everywhere and every one asks: "What are the facts about the Bolsheviki?"

The answer is simple and this is it:

Thirty-six years ago, in 1883, scores of political refugees from Russia met in Switzerland, where two years later, under the leadership of Plekhanow,[1] they formed the first Social Democratic organization for Russia, which was called the "Emancipation of Labor." Meanwhile the Socialism of Karl Marx became "legal" in the Tzar's empire and Socialist discussions were permitted; Socialist newspapers were established and Marxism became the foremost of the imports into Russia which were "Made in Germany."

In March, 1898, a congress of Socialists met in the city of Minsk, Russia, and the Social Democratic Working Men's party of Russia was founded. According to Professor James Mavor there were three groups represented at this meeting:

1. A group for the emancipation of labor.
2. A group which demanded the immediate improvement of the conditions of every working man, and
3. A group which believed in "limited centralization" of labor authority in which the mass of workmen should have no control of the party, but should be "disciplined by continuous agitation."

The leader of this third division was Nikolas Lenin, the present premier of Bolshevist Russia.

In 1903, Lenin, being unsuccessful with his work in Russia, officially launched the Bolshevist party in Stockholm. Two years later, during the great strikes in Russia which brought about the revolution of 1905, a "Council of Working Men's Deputies" was formed in Petrograd with the demand for a constitutional assembly. "At that time," says Professor Mavor, "there was the Mensheviki, the minority faction of the Social Democratic party, and a Bolsheviki, or majority faction."

Thus after twelve years of agitation the Bolshevist movement attained the dignity of a "faction" of Russian Social Democracy with Lenin the avowed and recognized leader. The name given to this faction was Russian, being derived from the word meaning majority. The Bolshevists were known as the section of the party which demanded the extreme measures to obtain the majority or major portion of the Socialist demands. The Menshevists and Bolshevists both believed in a revolution in Russia, but the latter believed in a continuous revolution and the establishment of a labor "general staff" and a labor army.

The Tzar was never really successful in his fight with the Bolsheviki, for the number of followers continued to increase both within and outside of Russia. Lenin remained the champion of uncompromising action while Trotsky, another Social

---

[1] Georgy V. Plekhanov (1856–1918), Russian revolutionary and a Marxist theoretician. He was a founder of the Social Democratic movement in Russia and was one of the first Russians to call himself "Marxist."

Democrat, and the present Bolshevist minister of war, devoted his efforts, by speaking and writing, toward the uniting of the Menshevists and Bolshevists.

In 1917, after the first revolution in Russia, which overthrew the Tzar and established the provisional governments, the Bolsheviki came into power, dominated Russia from Poland to Vladivostok, and made peace with Germany at Brest-Litovsk.

Such was the birth and growth of Russian Bolshevism; Bolshevism which Trotsky defined as a programme for the establishment of an industrial democracy. But throughout this period the Bolsheviki were concerned, not with the establishment of a socialistic state but with the revolutionizing of a nation. The theories and ideas of the new party were secondary. The primary object was to overthrow the existing government, industry, and society and the establishment of a proletariat state where labor was to be supreme, and where only those who did manual labor were to be recognized as laborers. Fundamentally and essentially Bolshevism was a programme for the destruction of civilization as it was known in Russia[2] where there was an autocratic government; where labor had no rights; where there were religious persecutions and pogroms and where there was neither a local nor a national representative assembly. Conditions in Russia were at that time entirely different from what they are to-day in the United States, and for this reason the Bolshevist demand for a "constitutional assembly" and "land and freedom" seized the thoughts and fired the imagination of the peasants and workers.

These are the historic facts about Bolsehvism and some of the theories or "ideals," but between the idealistic and practical state there is always a gulf which must be bridged. What did the Bolsheviki do when they had the machinery of government and industry in their hands and the physical power of the mass behind them?

The facts which I shall give about the actual workmanship of Bolshevism will be only those I observed personally in Siberia or those from disinterested witnesses such as representatives of the Russian Co-operative Union—that extensive organization of 20,000,000 Russians whose chief concern is business and education, not politics.

Bolshevism, considered as a practical programme, may be divided into three sections: (1) Politics; (2) industry and mines; (3) land distribution.

Without considering the methods which the Bolshevists used to obtain control of the government, for their means were revolutionary, and all political revolutions are alike, the facts are known about what they did after they came into political power. Almost their first act was to abolish the constituent assembly, and since they have been in control of Moscow and Petrograd and all of central Russia they have not called for another national election. The "demand" which they incorporated in their programme before the revolution for a "constitutional assembly" has been forgotten, or they have changed their ideas and no longer believe in such a congress,

---

[2] The text of the Constitution of the Russian Socialist Federated Soviet Republic, adopted July 10, 1918, was represented in an appendix to the original publication of this book.

being satisfied for the present with the "authority" which they receive from the local councils or Soviets. But they have not held elections for the councils. There has been no free, secret balloting by all citizens, only closed elections by working men. In politics the Bolsheviki have changed the methods of elections from universal suffrage to working-class suffrage only. They have not considered that all classes have a right to vote. They have opposed the right of representative government and substituted a class government, the very thing they condemned under the former Russian régime. The Bolshevist constitution explicitly excludes six classes of citizens from voting or participating in politics.

The second move of the Bolsheviki was to organize an army. This was in keeping with Article One, Chapter Two, Section "G" of the Russian Socialist Federated Soviet Republic which declares:

> For the purpose of securing the working class in the possession of the complete power, and in order to eliminate all possibility of restoring the power of the exploiters, it is decreed that all toilers be armed, and that a Socialist Red army be organized and the propertied class be disarmed.

And, a "Red army" was formed to maintain the Bolshevist government and their leaders in power in Russia, but the attitude of these leaders toward another revolutionary army was illustrated by the negotiations between the Czecho-Slovak National Council, and the Soviets of Russia during the summer of 1918. The Bolsheviki gave a written promise that their "comrades" from the former Dual Monarchy, could leave Russia via Vladivostok for France. That was when 50,000 Czecho-Slovaks were mobilized on the Dnieper River. After they started across the country, in small units, the Soviet attacked them! (In the chapter, "At Czecho-Slovac Headquarters," I have given all the details of the negotiations.)

This reference to the attitude of the Bolshevist army toward the Czechs, is made here to show the attitude of the "Reds" toward "fellow revolutionists" in Russia!

Considered from the standpoint of politics and army policies the Bolsheviki abolished the national assembly and never held another national election, and after making an agreement with the Czecho-Slovak echelons they broke it. These are the outstanding facts regarding the political aspects of Bolshevism. Bolshevism is revolutionary and so are its "treaties"!

Without having travelled across Siberia and several hundred miles into European Russia, I might have known something of the chaos which Bolshevism brought to the industries, but it's one thing to see a "dead nation" and another to picture it in one's mind. That great organism which we call "business" in this country, existed in Russia before the war and the revolution on a smaller and less intricate scale. There was a business life which affected every citizen, peasant, or factory employee. It was made up of a thousand and one arteries, veins, branches, and subdivisions which the people as a whole did not realize, just as we probably seldom think of the millions of factors which are linked together in our national business life.

When the Bolsheviki came into power they inherited what was left of this organism after it had been mismanaged and damaged by the military autocracy of the Tzar. They probably received not much more than a skeleton of the "business life"—the skeleton of factory buildings, railroads, depots, freight and passenger-cars, bank and office buildings, hotels, schools, and churches, but after they obtained control they decreed that all this belonged to the working men. That was the fundamental principle of Bolshevism. It was a political programme for the establishment of an industrial democracy. Here at last the dream was realized. Every working man was the owner and director of the factory, store, shop, or hotel where he had been or wanted to be employed. But what they had was only a skeleton which needed life. The buildings were of no use to the men or women unless there was work, unless they had some income either in money or food and clothing. The Bolsheviki tried to give the industries new life. They ran them on the new plan of four or six hours' labor per day, increased wages, but they found that factories were dependent upon outside sources for raw materials, and when the raw materials on hand were exhausted the Soviet government had to close the factories until raw materials could be obtained.

One example will serve as an illustration of what happened. In Moscow there are several great cotton manufacturing shops. The Bolsheviki decreed that these belonged to the working people, but after a few days of reckless management the supply of cotton was exhausted and the factories were shut down. The Bolsheviki local Soviet sent a purchasing commission of Bolshevist working men to the cotton-producing states of Russia to buy cotton from the Bolshevist cotton-planters. These cotton plantations had been socialized and each one belonged to the employees.

The Bolshevist factory men and Bolshevist cotton-growers met to discuss the arrangements for shipping cotton to Moscow. The cotton-growers asked the Moscow representatives what they would pay for cotton. The price was very much less than the cotton-growers could get in other markets, and they refused to sell. The Moscow laborers asked them if they did not believe in an industrial democracy. They certainly did, the cotton men answered, but cotton could not be sold at the low price which the Moscow Bolshevists offered.

The result was that the Bolshevist commissars could not buy the raw material which they needed for the factories so they appealed to the local Soviet, but the local council replied that it could not interfere with the rights of the local Bolsheviki.

At this point in the "negotiations" the Moscow buyers called upon the local representatives of the Russian Co-operative Union, which had been buying cotton from the Co-operatives who were members of the union, and selling it to other members, in Moscow and Lodz. The union could not buy for the Bolshevist government, however, because it recognized no government, and the Bolsheviki Soviet put the union men in prison, from which they were released afterward after pressure had been brought to bear upon the people's commissars in Moscow.

The final outcome of this practical demonstration of the inability of a Bolshevist industrial democracy to functionate was that the central Bolshevist authority in Moscow, represented by a bureau of business, asked the Co-operative Union to buy, ship, and sell the raw materials which were needed to give "life" to the new industrial nation.

Whatever "economic life" there is in European Russia to-day, is due not to the Bolsheviki, but to the Russian Co-operative Unions, but these unions are confronted with the problems of transportation because the railroads, too, are owned by the employees and they work, not for the general good of the community and the nation, but only for their own pleasure. In the meantime the factories remain closed; the workers who own them have no work. There is more forced idleness in Russia to-day than ever in the history of that country.

This same condition prevails as to food. The peasants do not bring food to the cities. Those who are Bolshevists sell only what they want, and those who are not followers of the Soviet "democracy" feed themselves and wait for better times. The working man who cannot raise his own food and work at the same time, starves.

These are some of the facts regarding industrial Bolshevism in Russia. In Siberia the conditions are similar because none of the governments so far organized in that country have been able to rebuild, reconstruct, or renew the industrial life of the country after the destruction of the Bolsheviki when they were in power, for, it is a curious development, of extreme Socialism, that that which the workers could not use, either because of a lack of ability or desire, they destroyed. I recall meeting the manager of a gold-mine near Ekaterinburg, an American who had lived at the mine nine years representing the foreigners who had bought and developed it. When the Bolsheviki controlled the local Soviet, they decreed him out of office, and decreed the mine the property of the miners. They were suddenly the owners of the gold-mine. Their dreams were realized. They were no longer laborers; they were owners!

One might have thought that workers suddenly made joint owners of a rich mine would have organized and developed it, but they didn't. The mine was their property. That satisfied them, but the machinery was made in France and was, therefore, a symbol of capitalism, "so they destroyed all the machines—machines which had been manufactured and brought to these shafts at an expense of 1,400,000 francs. Then they began working the mines in the most primitive fashion until the labor became too difficult, and one after another the miners drifted away!

Industrially, Bolshevism destroyed that spark of life which makes business not only a means of employment but of livelihood.

For more than ten years Trotsky had been campaigning in the Russian revolutionary newspapers in this country and abroad for the establishment of a Bolshevist state, and in nearly every leading article he stated that a revolution in Russia could never be a permanent success without the support of the peasants. To win them he added coals to the revolutionary fires labelled "Land and Freedom." But the first revolution guaranteed the peasants free land, and this battle-cry of Bolshevism fell on fallow soil. To-day the peasants do not have confidence in the Bolsheviki, because many of the local Soviets have decreed that any one owning property before the counter-revolution, or Bolshevist revolution, is a member of the old class system and, therefore, not a proletariat! Time after time in Siberia I met peasants in the market-places who had fled from European Russia because their small farms had been confiscated by the Bolsheviki on the ground that if they had been property owners they could not be recognized as having the right to hold property under the new regime!

These are some of the uncolored facts about the way Bolshevism has worked in Russia. There are to-day no indications of a representative government; no indications of a new economic system which is better or as good as the one now existing in the world. Nowhere can one find evidence in Russia that Bolshevism has solved the "industrial problems" or the problems of the working men. If Bolshevism was intended to be the creation of a new business life for the world it has failed in Russia. If Lenin expected it to be the beginning of a new social order in which the working people predominate he has succeeded, but at the frightful cost of universal chaos, individual suffering, nation-wide misery, and unemployment. Bolshevism has brought about a new order in Russia but the new nation is without life. In Siberia, as in Russia, the nation is dead.

With Russia passing through the pangs of still-birth, agitation grows throughout Asia, Europe, and the Americas for the application of Bolshevism to all nations, with the idea that if the present civilization of the world is completely destroyed and the existing society revolutionized the Bolsheviki of the world can rebuild it upon a new model. Grimm in Switzerland,[3] the followers of Liebknecht in Germany,[4] others in England and America are seeking to link sentiments with Lenin, with the international object of forming a World Union of Soviets to Russianize the universe. Hence the bogy story which appears ever so often in the press: "The Bolsheviki will get you if you don't watch out!" The new goblins have left Russia and are on the war-path (with

---

[3] Robert Grimm (1881–1958) was the leading Swiss socialist politician during the first half of the twentieth century. Grimm was the main organizer of the Zimmerwald movement and the chairman of the International Socialist Commission in Berne, 1915–17. He was the leader of the Swiss General Strike in November 1918, which demanded 48-hour work weeks, old-age pensions, and women's suffrage. He held various parliamentary seats and executive functions from communal to federal levels between 1909–55. In 1946, he became president of the Swiss National Council.

[4] Karl Liebknecht (1871–1919) was a German socialist and a co-founder with Rosa Luxemburg of the Spartacist League and the Communist Party of Germany. He is best known for his opposition to World War I in the Reichstag and his role in the Spartacist uprising of 1919. The uprising was crushed by the Social Democrat government and the Freikorps (paramilitary units formed of World War I veterans). Liebknecht and Luxemburg were both killed.

propaganda), and Bolshevism becomes not a Russian issue alone but a world political and industrial problem. Lenin's object at the Minsk congress was to bolshevik Russia. To-day he seeks to bolshevik the world.

Within thirty-six years Bolshevism has grown from a local Russian idealistic programme to a world-wide revolutionary programme. This is the fact. What are the reasons?

Those conditions which caused Bolshevism in Russia a decade ago did not exist in the United States or Europe. England, France, Switzerland, the United States, Germany, Holland, Denmark, and other countries had parliaments and congresses of one kind or another. There was a semblance, at least, of democracy and representative government in several of these nations. In all of these countries any one could own land or property. There were no religious restrictions; no pogroms outside of the Pale. There was no social-caste system in America. One man was as good as another before the law or the government.

This was not true in Russia. The abolition of serfdom in 1861 had not satisfied the peasants. The Tzar had not recognized the rights of equal suffrage. Factory employees were industrial slaves. Education was restricted. Religion was not free. The minds of the Russian people were in bondage and their bodies were servants of autocratic politicians and factory owners. Under these conditions one can understand why a revolution in that country might not swing the pendulum of life from one extreme to another. But a revolution is certain to have that result, because a revolution, too, is abnormal, and not until the pendulum swings backward and forward over an arc to bridge the two extremes—not until then are the conditions normal. It is the gravity of business which makes the pendulum move, which in turn gives life to civilization, and ticks off the hours and days of progress. Reaction and revolution are extremes which retard advancement.

Considering the conditions which produced the revolution and Bolshevism in Russia it may, at first, seem strange that Bolshevism should spread in other countries where the conditions on the surface are not at all similar. But there are underlying causes of this new movement which account for its sudden and extensive spread. Bolshevism has become very elastic. The Bolshevism we speak of to-day is not at all the same as that which was introduced in Russia nearly two years ago. Bolshevism of to-day has been tempered, but only slightly, by the mistakes and absurdities of the doctrine, and those who are advocating Bolshevism in other nations, especially the United States, are Bolshevist brothers of the Russian Bolshevists only as far as a revolution is concerned.

The causes of the Bolshevist movement in this country and abroad are threefold: (1) The difficulties confronting a nation during the transition period from war to peace conditions; (2) general industrial discontent and dissatisfaction kept alive and aggravated by propaganda, and (3) social unrest and injustice.

In the United States we do a great deal of loose talking. It is a part of our democracy. We juggle opinions and ideas, new and old theories, like the circus clown, and if one of them fall upon our feet we hop around with a wry face for a few moments and then forget about the pain. At present we are jabbering and juggling Bolshevism because it is a fad, or because it is new, or because it may be some industrial goblin. Some good Americans are getting bolsheviked themselves without knowing it, and others are adopting Bolshevism because they think it is the end of all trouble and dissatisfaction. A few, and only a very few, are Bolshevists because they believe in its theories, but those who have seen the theories fail in Russia are not tempted.

Bolshevism is a fad of gossip in the United States while in Russia it is a tragedy. No one who has seen any part of Russia since the revolution which overthrew the provisional government would desire to see the same torch applied to every other nation in the world. And still Bolshevism is openly talked about as an "international doctrine." What are the reasons for this success of Bolshevist propaganda? Why are we told that unless there is a League of Nations formed by governments there will be a "Union of Soviets formed by the people? Why have the Bolshevists remained in control of Petrograd and Moscow, if their programme is a failure? How has it been possible for the Bolshevists to hold out after the defeat of Germany, and after the Allies intervened in Siberia and Archangel?

These questions are not confined to those who believe in Bolshevism, but are asked by intelligent Americans who are in this kindergarten of the New World, but even these questions are readily answered.

The reasons for the success of various kinds of Bolshevist propaganda are that the word Bolshevism is used in the United States and Europe not only to name a political and industrial programme, but as a description of dissatisfaction and discontent. Almost any one who complains against the existing order is a Bolshevik. We are using the word more dangerously and ruthlessly than the Russians. Every one who wanted a radical change in Russia from the disorder and oppression of the Tzar was not a Bolshevist. A Bolshevist in Russia was only a man who believed in a continuous revolution; who disbelieved in representative government, and desired all authority placed in the hands of labor leaders. Obviously most of those whom we term Bolshevists in the United States are not Bolshevists at all. They are simply human beings who criticise present conditions and who expect and demand adjustments.

Bolshevism has capitalized upon the world's discontent with the object of making every one who desires readjustments and changes a Bolshevist. So we are informed by the wise statesmen of Europe that unless there is a League of Nations there will be a Union of Bolshevists. What they mean is that when governments fail nationally Bolshevism succeeds, and that if the governments of the world fail in uniting upon a world constructive peace programme, then the Bolshevists will attempt to unite Soviets upon such a plan. Bolshevism succeeds only when governments fail. Bolshevism can never succeed as an industrial programme unless those who direct our industries fail.

It will soon be two years since the Bolshevist coup d'état in European Russia. If Bolshevism is a failure, I am asked, how do you account for the continued presence of Lenin and Trotsky in Moscow?

There are two chief reasons: (1) The Bolshevist faction of Russia is comparatively united while every other political party is divided and none of the political parties will unite upon a common programme. The former leaders of Russia have left the country. They are in Paris, London, Tokyo, Washington, New York, Switzerland, and Spain. They have abandoned Russia to the Bolsheviki. (2) There is a government in Omsk directed by Admiral Koltshak, but he does not have the confidence of many Russians.[5] General Denekin is in South Russia, but his support is limited almost wholly to the Cossacks and the Monarchists.[6] My own opinion is, after travelling in both Europe and Asia since the first revolution in Russia, that at least seventy-five per cent of the people are, or would be, against the Bolsheviki if there were an election held where every one could vote, but this three-fourths majority to-day is not united.

I find many persons thinking that "there must be something to Bolshevism if it can defy the Allies longer than Germany."

Considering all the public promises the Allies have made to Russia, and the public expectations of military action, one might conclude that the Allies had really been fighting the Bolsheviki. But this is not true. The Allies have never been able to unite definitely upon a Russian programme. The Allies were not united in Siberia, and they did not land a sufficient number of troops to be able to take any effective military action against the Bolsheviki. The English and French sent small forces, not more than a thousand men, to Omsk and Ekaterinburg, but they did not take part in the fighting against the Red army on the Urals. At Archangel the Allied force has been very small, and there has been no real campaign against Trotsky's army. As a matter of record and fact the Allies at no time have really effectively and unitedly opposed Bolshevism in Russia.

---

[5] Alexander V. Kolchak (1874–1920), one of the leaders of the White forces during the Russian Civil War. He was a polar explorer and commander in the Imperial Russian Navy, who fought in the Russo-Japanese War and the First World War. During the Russian Civil War, he established an anti-communist government in Siberia and was recognized as the "Supreme Ruler and Commander-in-Chief of All Russian Land and Sea Forces" by the other leaders of the White movement from 1918 to 1920. His government was based in Omsk, in southwestern Siberia. In January 1920, during the White retreat before Red armies, Czecho-Slovak regiment captured him and handed him over to local Bolsheviks in Irkutsk in exchange for the free pass. The Bolsheviks executed Kolchak.

[6] Anton I. Denikin (1872–1947), one of the leaders of the White forces during the Russian Civil War, commander of the Southern anti-Bolshevist Front in European Russia. In emigration after 1920.

Throughout the world to-day there is revolutionary unrest. It is discernible everywhere, but this is not due to the propaganda of Bolshevism, but rather to the awakening of a new mass consciousness. This war has been fought by all classes and types of men and backed by every class of women. As a result of the four years of suffering, tension, discussion, debate, disagreement, and disillusionment the great body of humanity all over the world has come to the common conclusion that the New World must be different from the old. The mass mind has not developed the idea much further. Their programme is unformulated. The mass demands a better world. Humanity demands changes and readjustments. The people believe that as a result of their fighting and sacrifices there must be new world standards.

This is not a thing about which there is any disagreement. Every one whose finger is on the pulse of mankind feels it. But the Bolsheviki appear and claim that their programme of revolution and destruction is the only real reconstruction platform. They do not point to Russia and say: "See this is what Bolshevism will do for the whole world." They know their example in Russia will not appeal to the people outside that country. But they are wise in deceit. They are the only ones, they tell the war-weary public, who can make the future world a new world. They are half right. They can remake the world, but when they finish it will require generation after generation to bring the world ahead to what every one would consider an advance in civilization and life.

The world is, indeed, in the midst of a universal revolution which is developing in two ways. Revolutions may be of opinion or of action. The Bolshevist method is action. The method of representative governments and progressive industries is opinion.

Outside of Russia and a few countries in central Europe I do not anticipate a revolution of action, but in every other country a revolution of opinion and readjustment is inevitable. The one will lead to anarchy, chaos, and buffering, and follow the general lines of the Russian revolution, while the other will bring about rapid and radical readjustments in industry and politics, and start the pendulum of peace over the arc of time and progress.

You may recall when you were a child how you were frightened by goblins. The mere warning that "the goblins will get you if you don't watch out" was sufficient, but as soon as you were told the whys and wherefores of gnomes you ceased to fear them and they became only a passing fantasy of childhood.

This may be true of the new goblins, too. Attempts have been made to frighten the world into goodness by the warning, "the Bolsheviki will get you if you don't watch out," but the world is wise and inquisitive, wiser, indeed, than Russia was in November, 1917. And, as the facts become known, the people of democratic countries will cease to fear the morrow. The new goblins will become passing fantasies of this transition period from war to peace conditions unless the people of the world reach that dangerous and carefree state of Siberia, represented by the word "Nitchevo."

## Chapter III
## THE HUMAN VOLCANOES

About half-way between Petrograd and Vladivostok, on the Trans-Siberian Railway, lies the city of Omsk, white with its winter cloak of snow and black with throngs of people. Typical of all cities and towns in Asiatic Russia to-day, it is a community of contrasts and extremes; of homes and hovels; diamonds and rags. Misery is so universal it has lost its sting, and what happiness there is is found in the bottom of the vodka jug. Like Irkutsk, Tomsk, Tchita, Ekaterinburg—where the Tzar Nikolas the Second was reported killed—and Vladivostok, Omsk is a city in black and white; black and white on the outside, but red underneath—red with fear and suffering.

Through Siberia I trekked and travelled, in, about, and out of these living cities of silent masses during the winter of 1918–19. For two months I lived in the railway-cars—sometimes in the freight-yards where thousands of Russians had their only homes in near-by box-cars. For three weeks, while journeying from Ekaterinburg to Harbin, Manchuria, I did my own cooking, buying my supplies at the markets and stalls with the refugees. I went to theatres and churches. I explored the caves where the poorest live. Into the banks, the shops, and government buildings; through the public baths and filthy, overcrowded depots, the huts and the palaces I went, exploring city after city. Everywhere there were the same three colors, the black and white and the red. Each city was the same, from the Pacific to the Ural Mountains, each a human volcano where the exterior camouflaged but did not hide what was within.

Travelling in Siberia to-day is a task for Trojans, and most Russians are equal to it. Judging by the crowds at every railroad depot and the millions of human beings who live, day in and week out, in passenger and freight cars, one would think the population of that vast country was housed entirely on wheels, or that it was the supreme desire of every one to travel, despite the discomforts and inconveniences. In this respect, as in many others, Russia is on the move, seeking happiness which always exists at the end of the rainbow. Every train which departs from Vladivostok for the Amur or the interior of Manchuria or Siberia, every post, passenger, and goods train which leaves Omsk for Irkutsk, is packed with refugees. Every coach and every box-car is so overcrowded with men, women, and children, all of them standing, for there is no room for any one to sit down, that it is frequently impossible for the guards to close the doors. Even in mid-winter, when it is thirty and forty degrees below zero, people stand on the platforms and steps, wrapped in their heavy fur-coats. If the journey is a short one they survive; if a long one some may freeze to death and drop off, but no one worries about death. It is too common to excite worry, and it always makes room for the rest. I have seen people so crowded in freight-cars that when the conductor closed the doors to keep the Siberian winds from freezing every one to death I could hear women scream in agony. In the freight-yards of Omsk I saw as many as three families—seventeen men, women, and children—living in one small, four-wheeled box-car, and in Harbin I saw two trains which brought 1,057 Serbians from Odessa. When I visited the cars these people had been living in them seven months.

Arriving in Vladivostok on my way into Russia I rode to the depot in one of those four-wheeled Odessa carriages which the Russians call "izsvostcheks," bombarding the spectacled, whiskered, rag-covered driver from the rear with questions which my interpreter seemed to make him understand. He was an ex-soldier who had fought in East Prussia and Galicia until the March revolution, when he returned home. Asked why he didn't continue in the army and fight the Bolsheviki he was silent. Then, when he was pressed for an opinion as to what he would do if the Bolsheviki took Vladivostok, he answered "*Nitchevo!*" ("I should worry!")

At the station were throngs of Russians, old and young, intellectual and ignorant; strong and rugged for the most part, poorly clad, dark, and dirty. Each one lugged his worldly possessions, wrapped and tied in a colored table-cloth, shawl, or old coat. A line of several hundred persons was waiting at the third-class ticket-office. Another line was scrambling for baggage which had been stacked in the centre of the hall. Leading down the steps to the tracks was another crowd, waiting for the hour when it might rush through the barred doors to the filthy coaches of the ten-thirty train to Harbin or the later one for the Amur cities. An American, a Japanese, and a Czech soldier were standing on the outside as sentries, with nothing to do but stand and change guard every four hours. Sometimes they would separate a crowd of Chinese coolies who were fighting for an opportunity to carry the luggage of a foreigner who looked as if he might pay more than the regulation price, but otherwise they were idle spectators, alone in a foreign land, unable to understand what it was all about and longing for the end of the war—in Russia.

For several days I sauntered and drove about the city, up the steep streets, around over the hills, and back again to Svetlanskaya, the main thoroughfare, where the crowds paraded, the droshkies rattled over the cobblestones, and the automobiles raced by with the same feverish haste and recklessness which was common at the front. From the tallest and finest buildings waved foreign flags: American, French, Czecho-Slovak, British, Italian, and Japanese. From the street one could look down into the beautiful bay and see Allied and Russian ships at anchor or the sampans wiggling their way across the harbor, for Vladivostok is a city built on the slopes of the mountains, which descend rather steeply into Golden Horn Bay. In the distance were the cliffs which hid the former fortifications of the city in the days when Vladivostok was known as "The Tzar of the East," and up the bay, along the shore, were visible the dark gray gunboats and monitors which the crews had taken over as floating residences. An abandoned floating dry dock arose and fell with the tide in mid-channel.

In the cafes and restaurants the men gathered and gossiped and speculated. Information travelled mostly by rumor despite the numerous extra editions of the newspapers which the coolies sold, rushing excitedly through the crowds with their Manchu queues dangling against their backs. There were so many people in the streets, cafes, on the docks, jammed into tramways, and in the stores, that one wondered where they went at night, because the city was known to be conjested [sic]. Not only beds but sheltered floor spaces were at premiums. Walking about the city in the evening one learned that the people slept in shifts; those who could not find refuge at night slept by day in the depots and public buildings, the dark, damp cellars, and abandoned army barracks. It was not an infrequent sight to see men lying in gutters with the curb-stones as pillows or on the sidewalks where steps served as head rests.

Long before the Allies landed their troops in Siberia, Vladivostok was overcrowded. Being the eastern terminus of the Trans-Siberian Railway it was the chief outlet from Russia and Siberia for those many thousands of inhabitants who wished to leave their own country for the peace and happiness which they believed were to be found abroad. To Vladivostok came also those numberless Russians who had heard of the United States as the land of perpetual contentment, and who were en route there. Rumanians, Czechs, Serbians, Poles, Lithuanians, Big Russians and Little Russians, Indians, Chinese, Mongolians, Dutch, Americans, Scotch, Canadians, Japanese, Italians, French, Germans, and Austrians met Danes, Australians, Spaniards, Swiss, and Turks in this city. Never have I seen such a cosmopolitan, heterogenous community. It was as if the war and the revolution had shaken the whole world and dropped samples of every nationality in Vladivostok.

It was a curious war city. The two largest department stores were owned and managed by Germans, one of whom, a few months after the American soldiers arrived, appeared at the United States Consulate and subscribed for $25,000 worth of Liberty Bonds. The headquarters of the United States Expeditionary Force had been the home of the employees of one of these enemy concerns until Major-General William S. Graves arrived. The influence of Germany in Vladivostok was so great throughout the war that many Russians attribute the weakness of their own army to the intrigues of the Germans here in preventing war-munitions from reaching the front, and after the Allies landed it was a continuous performance, their search for German agents, many of whom were citizens of neutral countries. At lunch one day in the "Zolotoi Rog" cafe with several American army officers, I recognized a German whom I had encountered in Switzerland last winter; a man whom the Swiss police considered a spy. The United States Intelligence Service took steps immediately to establish his identity, but he disappeared in a motor-car and was never seen again in the city. A few weeks later he was located in Manchuria on the staff of a well-known army officer.

Because of the influence of German agents at this important port the vicinity of Vladivostok is cluttered with war-materials, valued by the Allied staffs at between $750,000,000 and $1,000,000,000. During the war scores of great warehouses were constructed to house the perishable goods, and when these were stacked to the rafters and it became impossible to erect buildings as fast as the supplies came, everything, from cotton to unassembled motor-lorries, were piled in open fields and lots and covered with tarpaulins. Outside the city, on the road to Khabarovsk, the capital of the Amur province and the first interior city I visited, are hills and fields of munitions and materials, rotting, rusting, decaying, and wasting. There is a hill of cotton shipped from the United States tucked under mounds of tarpaulins. There are 37,000 railway truck-wheels and heavy steel rails in such quantities as to make it possible to build a third track from the Pacific to Petrograd. There is enough barbed-wire to fence Siberia. There are field-guns, millions of rounds of ammunition, and a submarine; automobiles, shoes, copper and lead ingots, and these are only a few of the things which the Tzar's agents purchased from American factories to be used in the war against Germany, but which never came nearer than within 6,000 miles of the front, as near as San Francisco was to the Flanders battle-line.

Much of this waste of the Great War may be seen from the car windows travelling from Vladivostok to Nikolsk and Khabarovsk, but after the yards are passed and the abandoned factories and railroad-shops are left behind there comes into view the contrast between the dense cities and the vast, limitless fields. The horizon of the city is a sky-line of buildings and hills, while that of the valleys of the Usuri and Amur Rivers and the steppes of the interior is not a line but an indistinct indication of endless space. Travelling up the Amur railroad with the American commander on his first inspection trip, we passed through hundreds of thousands of acres of grain-fields, grazing-lands, and forests. Some places the oats and wheat had been cut but not harvested; elsewhere the farms were abandoned. There was so much grain it seemed to grow wild, like dandelions in Indiana. Forests were only nicked here and there along the railroad. Far into the interior they were primeval. Infrequently there were peasants' huts, log cabins, or rough frame houses painted yellow. For hours we travelled without seeing a living thing except golden pheasants on the wing. Sometimes at the village stations the general's train passed the "regular," which was regular only as a memory of the past, and we glimpsed the Rightfulness of travel. Men and women were packed so closely in box-cars they were more uncomfortable than steers riding from a Western ranch to Kansas City or Omaha. Chinese and Russians, brothers and sisters in misery, en route from Somewhere to Somewhere Else in search of peace, relatives, friends, business, or opportunity. Some were smugglers, others, business men, some peasants, and many of them political agitators. Bolshevist and Monarchist travelled together, disguised by the same attire and on the same mission.

Again at another station a train of Cossacks passed, young, reckless men, travelling with their sweethearts, their guns, and horses. They had the best of the rolling-stock. They feared God only and took their own part in everything. They swayed with the political winds and were anti-Bolshevist only because it was popular. They obeyed no laws but the mandates of their ataman, a twenty-eight-year-old "General." They ran a train of broken artillery, six-inch guns from England covered with tree-bows, up and down the line to impress the inhabitants.

From every station along the road waved the flag of the Flowery Kingdom, and with the exception of a few towns and bridges guarded exclusively by Americans, the Japanese troops were always present. From Lake Baikal to the Pacific it was the same. Everywhere their soldiers, merchants, investigators, agents, and prospectors dotted the country.

But that vast domain of tillable land was like a vision in a dream. With all the suffering in Vladivostok and Khabarovsk, for this Amur city was not an exception, it seemed strange that such fertile valleys should be so deserted, but the counter-revolution of the Bolsheviki bears the responsibility. Since the "Tzar" Lenin and his "Apostles" (a Petrograd poet has likened Lenin's cabinet to twelve modern disciples[1]) usurped the political power of European Russia, everything has been unsettled and topsy-turvy. There has been no inclination on the part of the people to stay on the land or return to it. There is no security. They cannot be certain that the farm they take or buy or receive, own or rent, will remain in their hands. Some peasants, many thousands of them, have remained on the land but mostly in districts far removed from the railroads.

In Khabarovsk, while idling through the market one morning, I saw a group of men gathered around an old peasant, a man crippled and calloused by hard work. In his twitching hands he held a deed to a piece of land near Samara. Physically broken down, he related his story, crying like a heartbroken child at the same time.

"When the Bolsheviki came to my house they said: 'Who owns this property?' I said: 'I do...'" The crowd was eager and silent. "'How long have you been here?' the commissar asked. 'Five years,' said I. 'Then get out,' he said. 'You had this long enough'... and he took my house, my cows, my geese, and my flour and grain, and...'" and he ended in tears while the interested villagers examined his "scrap of paper."

Returning to Vladivostok from the north I began, almost immediately, a two months' journey into the interior of Siberia, across the steppes to Omsk and over the boundary between Asiatic and European Russia to Ekaterinburg and Cheliabinsk, at that time the headquarters of the Czecho-Slovak armies on the Ural front. From the Pacific to these mountains, from which come many precious stones and ninety per cent of the world's platinum supply, it was a pleasant journey of six days before the counter-revolution. To-day the trip is made under the greatest hardships in from

---

[1] "The Twelve" is a long poem by a leading Russian poet-symbolist Alexander Blok (1880–1921). Written in early 1918, the poem was one of the first poetic responses to the October Revolution of 1917. In fact, it did not compare "Lenin's cabinet" to apostles, but rather described the Red Guard patrol on the street as being led by Jesus Christ.

three to four times that many days, depending upon the means of travel. Aboard a special train one can reach Omsk in nineteen days, while the "regular" or troop-train will take a month. Only about forty per cent of the locomotives can be used and on some divisions less. The best railway coaches have been commandeered by the various armies, domestic and foreign, and what is left for the "travelling public" resembles the dilapidated wooden cars one sees deserted in some American yards. The track, although badly in need of repair and attention, is still able to bear the burdens of flat wheels and heavy cars much better, indeed, than the passengers!

It is a thousand-mile journey across Manchuria, that province of China which the Tzar deemed his special sphere of influence, before one enters Siberia again. Manchuria to-day is a beehive of speculation and commerce. Long caravans, drawn by camel and oxen, move across the country with raw materials for Japanese and European markets. Through Harbin move the cars and wagons of manufactured articles, some of which ultimately reach Siberia, but by that time those things which cost a few kopecks in China sell for hundreds of roubles in Irkutsk and Omsk. Twenty cigarettes in a package sell for three cents in Manchouli Station, the border town of Manchuria. In Cheliabinsk they bring eighty cents. Sheepskin coats which the Harbin merchants dispose of in lots at seven dollars each, disappear from the market-stands of Irkutsk at five hundred per cent profit, this in spite of the fact that Siberia was one of the greatest fur-producing countries in the world. Sugar, which costs as much in northern China as in the United States, was two dollars a pound when I bought some at a railroad-station near Taiga. Chinese tea and rice are luxuries in the North. And salt! Salt is so precious in Russia that when I entered one of the shops of Ekaterinburg and asked to buy some, the old woman behind the counter looked at me in amazement.

"What," she asked, "salt? Are you crazy?"

Buying salt is like seeking other commodities which Siberia used to import, and I discovered it as soon as I crossed the line again into that empire of boundless possibilities and tragedies. The counter-revolution of the Bolshevists[2] so crippled the railroads and so disorganized the channels of trade that supplies from the outside are more scarce than German-made goods in France. Still those products which are produced in the country are cheap, cheap to an American who has been educated to a high cost of eating, but expensive to the Russians. Frequently I bought roast goose for eighteen and twenty cents a pound, butter for nineteen and twenty-five cents, and the best cuts of beef for about the same price, but this was at an increase of from fifty to one hundred per cent over the normal peace-time prices. And as for salt, coffee, vegetables, preserved and fresh fruit, they no longer exist as far as the Russian in the interior knows.

---

[2] Ackerman refuses to consider the Bolshevist seizure of power as a continuation or radicalization of a Russian revolution, but calls it "counter-revolution," according to his vision of a revolutionary path.

Economically Siberia may be divided into three districts. From Vladivostok across Manchuria to Manchouli Station there is an abundance of grain and meat. Harbin, the centre of this district, has all the food luxuries of the world. In the Baikal, the mountainous region around that lake which is almost as large as Lake Superior, there is such a scarcity of food that starvation is to-day more extensive than in any other part of Russia, not excluding Petrograd and Moscow. From Irkutsk, which is on the other side of the lake as one travels inland to the Urals, such food as butter, meat, bread, and fish is plentiful. But all Siberia, as far as household furnishings and every kind of clothing are concerned, is famished.

Arriving in Irkutsk early one winter morning, after awakening at dawn to see the sun's rays bring out in bold relief the snow-white mountain range which skirts the Baikal, I set out in a sleigh for the bazaar. Irkutsk is said to be the coldest city in Siberia, not because the temperature drops lower than seventy degrees below zero, but by reason of the heavy fogs and extreme dampness. As I rode from the station across the temporary wooden toll-bridge over the Angara River into the city proper, the fog was so dense I could not see the water nor the carriage in front. By eleven o'clock the city was still blanketed. By noon the sun appeared for its short irregular visit, and I went to the market-place from the American consulate, where I had gone to get warm as much as to inquire for telegrams.

Every Siberian city has its market-place, some even have two or three, but there is always a "big bazaar." Irkutsk had a big market which was typical of others I visited in Tomsk, Taiga, Omsk, Ekaterinburg, and Cheliabinsk. They were, in fact, not markets as we use the word. They were a collection of junk-shops. Over a vast square were several hundred stands and as many dilapidated frame shacks, temporary weather-beaten frame structures, facing narrow streets. To these stands every morning the businessmen and shopkeepers of the city brought their choice wares. Some of these they displayed on the rough tables or snow-covered ground. Some things were carried about by peddlers who mingled with the crowds bartering and exchanging. Walking about from avenue to avenue in search of a samovar which I needed to boil water for drinking purposes on my way in and out of the country (the water is so unhealthful in this country without sewerage systems that all drinking water must be boiled), I noticed that fully ninety-nine per cent of everything exhibited at the bazaar was second-hand, used or badly worn. Hardware, furniture, overcoats, stockings, underwear, table-cloths, stoves, dresses, jewelry, shoes, suits, books, guns, lamps, carpets, and beds were to be seen in numberless quantities, and every article looked as if it had changed hands several times before being brought to the stalls.

Everybody goes to the market, not only to buy and sell but to talk. The bazaars are the market parliaments. Here the peasants and city dwellers meet to discuss the war and politics, the Bolshevist, the Socialist, and the Monarchist propaganda, the policies of the Allies and the prices of food. There are no regular meetings, of course, and seldom are speeches heard, but rumors and pamphlets circulate, and the market-place discussions take the form of group debates. These are, indeed, crude efforts at democracy, but there is no representative government in Siberia and there is no other place where the people can gather to exchange ideas. So they make use of the markets for both business and politics.

Walking about the market of Irkutsk and sauntering through the bazaars in other cities, I noticed the presence everywhere of the three striking colors: the black, the white, and the red; the dark mass of people, the snow-covered streets and homes, the white nights, and the discontent, the fear, and the suffering. No lines of distinction were visible among the people. All were dressed alike in worn, torn garments. It was not unusual to see educated and cultured women standing in the crowds bargaining for a price for an old fur-coat or a piece of family jewelry. The first revolution destroyed titles and distinctions and made every one a Russian citizen, but the counter-revolution put an end to citizenship and made every one an animal.[3] And Siberia, despite the fact that the Bolsheviki are not in power, has not overcome the effects of the brief reign of terror which followed the usurpation of power by the followers of the Red army.

This was visible in Vladivostok, Khabarovsk, Tchita, and Irkutsk, but not until I reached Omsk did I feel as if I had climbed to the summit of the human volcanoes; not until I had explored the craters of suffering in that city, was I sure that I had seen the red of Siberia, the red which was brought by the Red army.

Omsk, like so many Siberian cities, is divided into an "old" and a "new" town, a condition due to the construction of the Trans-Siberian Railway as a strategic road. This line, which is to-day the backbone of the country, was built to serve a military purpose and not to benefit the cities or towns. The railroad does not pass through the chief cities, and the "old" towns of Omsk, Tomsk, Cheliabinsk, Ekaterinburg, and Khabarovsk are several versts from the railroad. Consequently new communities have grown about the stations and the "old and "new" cities are connected by shuttle-trains.

The train which brought me from Irkutsk arrived in the morning at "new town," and I stepped out upon the snow-covered platform of a low, white depot in front of which there was the ever-present black mass of humanity—men and women, wrapped in worn, winter clothes like mummies; Czech soldiers wearing the high, gray, fur hats of the Cossacks, marked with a small red-and-white ribbon, the national colors of Czecho-Slovakia; Russian officers and hundreds of soldiers. Following the crowd, which was so dense it moved with the speed of a cumbersome tank, I walked to the shuttle-train for Omsk proper, which was already crowded inside and out. From step

---

[3] The first revolution refers to the February (March) revolutionary events that culminated in the abdication of Tsar Nicholas II and the creation of a Provisional Government. Counter-revolution, according to Ackerman, is October (November) 1917, the Bolshevist seizure of power (traditionally called the October Revolution by Bolshevists and the October Coup by their enemies).

to step, with hundreds of others who were on the same mission, I searched for a place to stand or hold onto but with no success. Finally, as the whistle blew, I climbed with several others around the hangers-on on the steps, up between two cars, and found standing room on the bumpers. I had neglected to purchase a ticket, but I noticed that very few expected to pay their fares, and I waited developments, knowing that money was always a satisfactory substitute for any kind of a "billet."

After a ten-minute ride I climbed down from my uncertain foot-rest and walked through the station to the droshky stand, without being asked for my fare. This was what most of the others were doing and, inasmuch as this was a strange country and a strange world, I thought it best not to be an iconoclast but to follow the crowd. On later trips back and forth between these two stations, I discovered that each car had its conductoress, but that she was usually blockaded in some part of the coach and prevented from collecting the fifteen kopecks which the railroad "charged."

Riding to the centre of Omsk in an old sled (the picturesque, dashing troikas have disappeared), past the great stone railway office-building where the Omsk "government" was housed, past the railway cars where the French and Japanese missions were living, and through the wide streets, I noticed everywhere throngs of soldiers and civilians. It is said there are 100,000 Siberian troops in Omsk and 400,000 refugees. Certainly one obtains the impression that the figures are not exaggerated, for no city of a normal population of less than 90,000 could be so overcrowded as Omsk without showing it. There were no rooms to be had in the hotels, boarding-houses, or private residences. The government had been compelled already by circumstances to force the inhabitants to open their homes to the refugees, and still there was not a sufficient space of shelter for every one. Unemployed by day and idle at night, these inhabitants and strangers of Omsk present a typical Russian picture. The counter-revolution of the working men has not ennobled labor. It has made leisure supreme.

At noon I went to the Cafe "Delux," where the political strategists and officers gathered, where the business men came to bargain with each other, and the women of the night world had their dejeuner, but there was no room for a stranger and I went away to return in the afternoon when I might eat in peace with a young Russian cadet, my interpreter and guide.

Toward evening, after visiting the shops where only used articles were on sale—evening dresses, the relics of a past social life; silver services of noblemen, canes, and jewelled swords; after attempting to enter the opera-house where a company of Moscow players were presenting one of Tolstoy's dramas; after going through the Co-operative stores and seeking Russian money in exchange for the American dollars but finding the banks unwilling to buy American money, I set out in a farmer's sledge for the "new" station and my railroad car home, a compartment in an old sleeper, which I occupied as a guest with the American Red Cross contingent.

Omsk was the first Siberian city, in fact the only city in the world I had been in during the war, and my travels had taken me to eighteen countries in Asia, Europe, and the Americas, where our currency had no value. When I handed one of the bankers a twenty-dollar bill he looked it over and gave it back with the final remark that: "There is no demand for that money here." What a contrast that was from the situation in Vladivostok and Harbin only those who have had dealings with the money sharks of these cities can imagine.

The currency of Siberia is a collection of varieties of paper money and postage-stamps. No coins are in circulation, either gold, silver, or copper. Paper bills of the Tzar's Government sell at a premium and are almost unobtainable; the Kerensky, or provisional government, roubles rank next in value; then comes the Omsk and Siberian government paper money, and finally that of the Bolsheviki; but no one knows from day to day what the value of any of this money will be. The Omsk government did have 600,000,000 roubles' worth of platinum and gold as a reserve back of the notes of its treasury. This bullion the Czecho-Slovaks captured from the Red army at Kazan last summer, but no one knows whether that metal is still in Omsk, or whether some of the numerous officials who have been in office since have appropriated it. In October when American, English, French, and Japanese buyers were in the Urals seeking platinum for their respective governments, to be used in the manufacture of certain war-munitions, the Omsk government informed the men it was "unable to locate" more than forty pounds. What became of the other three or four hundred pounds no one seems to know.

The finances of European Russia are just as chaotic. From the *Primorsky Jizn* of Vladivostok I clipped the following despatch:

> The Bolshevik Central Committee official bulletin, gives the signed treasury statement of Finance Commissar Gukovsky[4] for the period from January to June, 1918. Total receipts from revenues of all kinds were 2,862,727,000 roubles. In the same time the total expenses were 17,602,727,000 roubles. The deficit is 14,740,000,000 roubles.

As a result of the instability of the currency there is universal speculation—outside of Omsk and the cities immediately back of the "front." In Vladivostok one out of every eight or ten stores has a sign in the window reading, "Money Changed," and the speculators approach every foreigner in each block. A Rumanian, who was in the business and had most of his transactions with the American and British soldiers because he could speak English, told me he averaged 400 roubles a day profit, all of which the inexperienced soldiers probably lost.

But the difficulties and exigencies of exchange did not trouble the refugees whom I saw living in caves as my sleigh crossed the wide, wind-swept plain which separated

---

[4] Isidor E. Gukovsky (1871–1921) was the people's commissar of finance of Russia from March to August 1918.

the city proper from the "new town." As I passed the barbed-wire stockade where Bolshevist and German, Magyar, and Austrian were imprisoned, I noticed a score or more of mounds above which the washing of the dwellers was stretched on wires in irregular lines atop rough posts. Shouting to the driver, a boy of fifteen dressed in a torn, man's sized fur overcoat and felt boots, to halt, I walked over to the dugouts, knocked at the board gate which served as a door for one of them, and walked down into the dirt room where a man and his wife with five children were seated or lying about a small iron stove. This hole was their home. Along one side was a straw bed, around the stove were a few cooking utensils. One of the five children had on shoes; three had no stockings; all of them were pale with hunger and weak from lack of exercise, for, with the rigors of the winter (that morning the thermometer registered forty-two degrees below zero at the American consulate), they had not a sufficient amount of clothing to permit them to leave their hearth.

I did not venture into the other "homes," but some of our Red Cross workers did and they found the same destitution, the same conditions, the same resigned expression on the faces of the people. I did not ask them what they hoped for in Russia. It was too evident, but I recalled the remark of a peasant to an American officer at Bira, in the Amur:

"Give us order and give us bread," he said, "nothing more."

That evening several of the nurses, American women who had volunteered to work in this desolate empire and who had been busy all day in the city, gathered in one of the compartments and sang the rollicking airs of American songs to the music of a guitar, and again there was the contrast. Life was always a series of contrasts in Siberia, and none was more graphic than the scene within this railway car and that within the thousands of box-cars in the same freight-yards where suffering refugees were huddled together unable to sense anything but the cold.

After midnight I left the car with several doctors, walked through the yards to the depot, and elbowed my way into the third-class waiting-room, stepping carefully over the bodies of sleeping men and women which covered the floor of the hall. In both the first, second, and third class rooms there was the same condition—everywhere the same sleeping, black mass of human beings.

In one corner a Red Cross official who accompanied me spied three children seated against the wall, practically naked. A young woman was lying beside them fast asleep, something the children could not do because of the "cooties" which they searched for like monkeys. A black-haired Turkestan soldier, who was a member of the military police, came up, noticing our interest, and addressed us in French. We asked him to awaken the woman and question her about the children. The private nudged her with his mace and asked in Russian if she was the mother of the three. Rubbing her eyes, raising her head, and frowning, she replied, curtly, "No!" and lay down to sleep again. Pressed for an answer as to where the mother was, she said, "Gone to town," and then, "Oh, she'll be back."

"Nitchevo," remarked the Russian. "There are lots of them like that."

On the walls of the depot, again in black and white, were thousands of posters put up by frantic mothers, fathers, brothers, and sisters in search of near relatives who had disappeared or who were lost in the trains. In these notices were descriptions and appeals, similar to but more tragic than the personal columns of the great metropolitan newspapers. If "Maria," "Tatiana," "Ivan," "Nikolai," or, "Alexievitch" arrived in Omsk; if "Mrs. A. Zemenov of Kazan," or "Katherine Rizoff of Kowno," or any one of a thousand-named refugees arrived in Omsk, the bulletins said, they will find relatives or friends living in this city or that. All day long the people read these signs. Even at night, under the white lights of the arc-lamps, the refugees perused them, for they were the sole means of personal communication—the only possible connecting links between separated families.

With Siberia cut off from European Russia by a "battle-line" running from Perm south along the Ural Mountains to the neighborhood of Orenburg, Omsk became the clearing-house for refugees within all that territory defended by the Czecho-Slovak echelons. To this city come men from the United States and Europe, from Poland and Petrograd, in search of their families whom they had left behind before the counter-revolution. To Omsk come the men, women, and children who have been fortunate in their escape from European Russia. Through this city have passed between 7,000,000 and 8,000,000 refugees to whom Siberia is no longer a place of exile but a land of temporary security and freedom from persecution, despite the congestion, the physical suffering, and mental anguish.

After sojourning several weeks here in the interior of Russia, and travelling 5,000 miles back to Vladivostok, I felt as if I had climbed to the summits, into the craters, and back to the bases of the human volcanoes, the cities of limitless distress; as if I had seen the fiery red of fear, the black mass of humanity, and the white land. Everywhere there was evident the terrible ruthlessness of the Bolshevist revolution,—which during its brief period of destruction in Siberia had made it impossible, for any of the governments thus far organized, to reconstruct, rebuild, renew, or revitalize.

In Siberia it seemed as if the world stood still and every one was doing his best to live until it began moving again.

## Chapter IV
## IN THE WHIRLPOOL OF THE NORTH

Before the revolution there were four ways of crossing Siberia: by first, second, and third class railway-carriages and fourth-class box-cars. To-day there are but two: box-cars and special trains. Almost every day both types of trains leave Vladivostok for "Somewhere in Russia," and after they depart no one can tell where they will ultimately arrive or when, despite the schedules. Railroading, like everything else in Russia, has been revolutionized—i.e., revolutionized in the wrong way. Travelling by box-car one fights for standing-room in a four-wheeled antiquated wooden car, painted railroad-red and about one-third the size of an American freight-car. If one is lucky in winter one gets a place near the stove in the centre; if unlucky one may be crammed into a corner without heat or light. By the box-car route one can travel as long as one can endure the un-ventilated interior and the company of Russia's unfortunates.

With the special train it is somewhat different. Instead of standing or sleeping in the ticket line for eighteen or twenty hours to purchase a fourth-class ticket, and instead of taking one's chances with the Russian trainman and his whip (and whips are not emblems of authority alone!), one applies to the Inter-Allied Railway Commission[1] in Vladivostok, and this commission, if it looks with favor upon the "mission," will grant a car or special train, whichever is needed.

The "permit" is only an invitation to travel because every general, commission, colonel, mission, society, and army has already confiscated the best cars, and what a new "mission" obtains is what others have left behind. The car the American Red Cross obtained for some of the doctors, nurses, and correspondents had been a "has been" for several years. The conductor claimed he had been living in it several months in the Vladivostok yards. Last spring, he said, his car had been ordered to Moscow but the Bolshevists arrived first, and he and his "wagon-lits" were sidetracked.

---

[1] The Inter-Allied Railway Committee was established in Vladivostok by the agreement signed by Russia (Omsk government), the United States, Japan, China, Great Britain, France, Italy, and Czecho-Slovakia on January 9, 1919, for the supervision of the Chinese Eastern and Siberian Railway systems. The chair of the committee was L. A. Ustrugov, the minister of communication of the Russian Omsk government, and the head of the Technical Board, John F. Stevens, an American engineer.

It does not really matter by what train one leaves the city because all are apt to make equally good time. There are no time-tables and the improvised schedules permit the trains to run when the tracks are clear, and it is fortunate that the Russian trainmen still have a sufficient interest in their work to take care in despatching trains. This appears to be about the only part of the railroad business which is not topsy-turvy.

Luck, however, plays a surprising role. If one is fortunate on the "special" one may arrive in Harbin, Manchuria, the first big station on the Chinese Eastern Railway, in twenty hours. If not it may require thirty-eight or forty hours. Travelling is a gamble. I made one journey between Vladivostok and Harbin in twenty hours with John F. Stevens[2] and Colonel George Emerson of the United States Railway Service Corps.[3] A second journey took thirty-six hours! One gambles with time, money, and patience, and if one can speak Russian fluently one gambles with the language, too. There was a time when one could go from Vladivostok to Moscow in nine days. Now it takes ten days to go to Irkutsk, which is about one-third the way.

It does not take long for one to become accustomed to railway travel in Siberia. It is bad business and is accepted as such.

You resign yourself to Fate; you get out your army blankets and your air pillow and make a bed; you see to it that your larder is well stocked. Then you forget everything else and trust to the revolution not to make any changes until you reach your destination, which is a fluctuating point on the map of Siberia. My destination was the Czech front, which was a movable line somewhere in the heart of Russia, and after I reached Irkutsk, a beautiful city with large modern buildings and great churches near Lake Baikal, one of the five largest lakes in the world, I was still at least a week from the front, its present location, but within a week it may move nearer or further away. Life and travel, alike, are unknown quantities in Siberia, and, I was travelling!

As far as Tchita there are two routes, one in Siberia proper and the other through north-central Manchuria. Originally there was but one trans-Siberian line from Tchita, and that connected with the Chinese Eastern Railway, but after the Rus-

---

[2] John Frank Stevens (1853–1943), head of a technical board of the Inter-Allied Railway Committee, was an American engineer who built the Great Northern Railway in the United States and was chief engineer on the Panama Canal between 1905 and 1907. In 1917, Stevens was selected to chair a board of prominent US railroad experts sent to Russia to rationalize and manage a system that was in disarray; among his work was the Trans-Siberian Railway. After the overthrow of the Provisional Government, Stevens remained in Allied-occupied Manchuria, and in 1919, headed the Inter-Allied Technical Board charged with the administration and operation of the Chinese Eastern and Siberian railways. He remained in an advisory capacity until occupying Allied troops were withdrawn; he finally left in 1923. After his return to the United States, Stevens continued to work as a consulting engineer, ending his career in Baltimore in the early 1930s.

[3] George H. Emerson, colonel, head of the Russian Railway Service Corps from 1917 to 1919; before that appointment, he was the general manager of the Great Northern Railroad.

so-Japanese War[4] the Russian Government began the construction of the Amur railway along the Siberian-Manchurian border, so that, in event of another war with Japan or any other nation in the Far East, Russian trains could be run to Vladivostok solely over Russian territory.

On the Amur railway to Tchita there is one chief town, Khabarovsk, where the American and Japanese troops were stationed in the old barracks of the Fifth Siberian Army Corps. Along the Chinese Eastern line through Manchuria our train, which reached Irkutsk after seemingly numberless delays, stopped at Harbin, Manchuria City, and Tchita long enough to permit us to glimpse the cities as a whole, and in some instances to examine and study the schools, the bazaars, the shops, and the churches; for Siberia has all the earmarks of civilization although this civilization is at a standstill. Every city of any size, and there are several with over 50,000 and 100,000 inhabitants, has its opera-house or theatre; its movies and cabarets; its cafes and midnight restaurants, and its banks, jewelry shops, fur stores, and Japanese curio stands. Cities like Harbin, Manchuria City, and Tchita, have their unpaved dirt streets, their log huts, and community cellars as well as their brick and stone business blocks.

No city is without its droshkies; those four-wheeled, opened, one-seated carriages drawn by Siberian ponies and driven by ex-soldiers, ex-vodka-drinkers, or ex-exiles. Russia, like France, can be distinguished from every other country in the world by its droshky drivers. They are an unchangeable quantity, with the same long, unkempt whiskers, the same curly fur hats and long lamb's-wool-lined coats and felt boots. Their faces betray their ignorance and their innocence, and still, with all their faults, they are the sponges of Russian public opinion. They are the most accurate reporters because they have no thoughts of their own; they repeat only what they have heard their passengers say or what they have been told. They disseminate news; they keep scandal alive; they absorb opinion, and they charge foreigners their maximum fare plus a generous profit. Their ambition is to make their gross receipts cover their expenses each day, and when that is done neither money nor influence will cause them to work an hour longer. They are men with fixed limits and they know their limit if nothing else.

To see these old, dishevelled men in their droshkies or their sleighs, and to see the thousands of miles of undeveloped, snow-covered land, is to see Siberia. These two, the people and the land, are the coarse, untrimmed dress of Siberia. Everything else—theatres, churches, and shops—is mere decoration!

We sauntered about Harbin, after running the gauntlet of the fur dealers along the line and without being disturbed by the Japanese troops guarding the railway. Through the narrow streets of the old city and the broad unimproved thoroughfares

---

[4] The Russo-Japanese War (1904–05) between Russian and Japanese empires for the domination on the Far East, and particularly for the control over Liaodong Peninsula in Manchuria. The Portsmouth peace treaty fixed the increasing influence of Japan and the Russian failure to maintain its dominance in Manchuria.

of the "new town," we journeyed in our droshky. In the streets were armed Chinese soldiers, the city police, while marching through the town were Japanese soldiers. Everywhere there were more Russians than all other nationalities combined. The stores were generously supplied with merchandise. Vodka, whiskey, and wines were for sale in shops throughout the town. During the day the restaurants were deserted. Even at eight o'clock one evening when we went to a so-called "modern" restaurant we found it cold and uninviting. Four hours later, at midnight, the crowd began to arrive, and we learned that "Harbin life," which is famous in the East, begins at the earliest hours of the day. After purposely dining very late one evening we went to the cabarets, four of them, and as we were leaving the last one about three o'clock in the morning some one called to us in English:

"What? You-all goin' home so soon?"

We looked around to see an American negro standing in the doorway of the cloak-room.

"What are you doing here?" we asked.

"Oh, I been battin' about this country fir twenty-five years. I go on at four o'clock," replied the negro. "I'm with the 'Lusiana Trio.' We sing after while. You-all better stay."

Here in Harbin were three American negroes on the stage of a cabaret, and their act began at 4 A.M.!

"How do you like it out here?" one of our party asked:

"All right. Me and mah pals er just pickin' up some uh de loose money aroun' here."

From the appearance of the city by day one would not think there was "loose money" in Manchuria, but by midnight money is spent lavishly on vodka, champagne, rich food, and the "life of the East." That there should be so much money here to be squandered was difficult for an American to comprehend.

Leaving Harbin we journeyed on by easy stages to Manchuria City, the last Chinese station. All along the line from Vladivostok to Manchuria we met the American railway engineers; the practical men and the experts from the United States who came to Russia with John F. Stevens to take charge of this railway line under the Kerensky government.[5] But at the time of my visit to Siberia they are men without a railroad. While they are scattered along the route of the Trans-Siberian they had no authority. They rode the trains, they attempted to introduce modern systems of train despatching, and for a few hours every day they controlled the telegraph wire, trans-

---

[5] Alexander F. Kerensky (1881–1970) was a key political figure in the Russian Revolution. After the February Revolution of 1917, he joined the newly formed Russian Provisional Government, first as minister of justice, then as minister of war, and after July 1917, as the government's second minister chairman. On November 7, his government was overthrown by the Lenin-led Bolsheviks in the October Revolution. He spent the remainder of his life in exile. "Kerensky government" refers to that Provisional Government.

mitting American messages and news. They were living for the day when they could assume control of the road and make it as efficient as they had made our own lines in the United States. But that day is always the day after tomorrow. (At this writing, although an agreement has been made, they are still inactive.) Should the time ever come, however, when the American engineers can take hold of the Trans-Siberian, there will be nothing about this line which they will not know.

Our train was passing through a small town one day when one of the Red Cross nurses opened the window to glimpse the station. Immediately there was a call in English:

"Won't you please come out here a moment. We haven't seen an American woman for nearly a year, and we have about forgotten what they look like."

It was an American engineer, alone in a small town in Manchuria, filling his place in Uncle Sam's worldwide war programme; a programme which will be, if it is not already, something of a world-peace programme also. And this engineer was beginning his second winter in Siberia, almost a voluntary exile.

In Manchuria and in Siberia a traveller to-day meets the representatives of two other American organizations, the Red Cross and the Y.M.C.A. It is a common sight to pass Y.M.C.A. freight-cars en route to and from the front, and in several cities along the line are American hospitals and relief organizations. Our army may not be very widely scattered in the Far East, but every other American organization is. Day after day we passed middle-aged and young men, riding in box-cars or in dilapidated second-class coaches—American men, most of them volunteers.

One meets, also, another class of Americans in this country—the Russians, Germans, Austrians, and Czechs who have lived in the United States. From Vladivostok to Irkutsk, at nearly every station, we met some one who could speak English, and who said that New York or New Jersey or Pennsylvania had been their home State before they returned to Siberia.

We were pushing our way through the crowded waiting-room of the Manchuria City station when some one called to us in English, recognizing us as Americans by our uniforms:

"She's a fine-looking girl, isn't she?"

We looked around to see a young Russian pointing to a Russian girl conversing with the station-master.

"Where did you come from?" That was our invariable reply to such greetings.

"Oh, I've been in Canada and New York seven years," was his reply.

At another very small village near Lake Baikal a young girl came to the train saying: "You Americans?" To our reply that we were, she said: "I been in New York in 'milliner' shop."

A few experiences such as these soon convince one that Siberia is not as far from the United States as many of us have imagined. I was walking through the railroad yards of Sema one afternoon, when I spied some German war prisoners in a box-car.

Climbing in I found seven Germans and Austrians; the tailors and shoemakers for a company of Cossacks.

"I have been seven years in Reading, Pennsylvania," said one of the men. "I have a brother there, Mathias Simon, but I haven't heard from him in thirteen months."

"Are you married?" I asked.

"Yes, I have a wife and baby in Budapest."

"Do you know that Austria and Germany have made peace."

"No!" he inquired, hopelessly astonished. "Then why don't they let us go home?"

With these words he echoed the wish of every war prisoner in Siberia. I met many hundreds of them in all parts of the country and their only question has been: "When do you think we can go home?" To some of them I have spoken about the war, asking:

"Well, when you do get back, will you be ready again for another war?"

Their answers have been a chorus of "Never again, if we have anything to say about it." In this respect Siberia has been a great pacifier.

From Manchuria City we moved on to Siberia, but not without having the customary experience with smugglers. In Manchuria everything from tobacco to liquor and food, and from clothing to raw materials, is plentiful. In Siberia many of the commonest articles are luxuries. And on every train there are smugglers, Chinamen and Russians, who carry everything they can across the border. Two Chinamen climbed on the engine of the Red Cross special train and arrived safely in Siberia. Although they admitted that they had smuggled tobacco and white flour, there was no one at the Siberian station to arrest them, and they proceeded on their way as if it were quite the ordinary thing to do.

It was only a short ride between the two border stations, and before we left Manchuria another correspondent and I were in the office of the station-master, on the second floor of the depot. While we were waiting there a train of box-cars arrived. Looking out of the window the official said:

"Another load of smugglers on their way!"

He seemed resigned to his position and to his helplessness. Smuggling in this part of the world is rapidly becoming legitimate, or perhaps legal, because it is now the custom of the country. In normal times smuggling was confined to tobacco, hides, sugar, and flour, but to-day the stakes are higher. Gold, silver, and platinum, firearms and other weapons bring the greatest rewards and the severest punishment. But the smugglers consider the game worth the gamble.

Tchita is one of the greatest trading centres in eastern Siberia, because years before the Siberian railroad was constructed the caravan routes of the East centred here. Even to-day one can see the caravans of camels and others of horses and ponies bringing in raw materials from Mongolia, Manchuria, and northern Siberia. In several places the Trans-Siberian Railway follows the old caravan routes, and from car windows may be seen the slowly moving columns making their way through the snow. The riches of the East still travel this way, because to most communities the railroad is unknown. Glance at the map of Siberia and you will see an empire at least twice as large as the United States. Imagine one railroad running from New York via Chicago to San Francisco, and no other railways in the United States, and you will have some idea of the hundreds of thousands of square miles of territory in Siberia without railway communication. In America the railroads cover the country like a fine net. In Siberia the railroad is scarcely more than a thread. And these caravans which pass through Tchita are the shuttles; the slowly moving shuttles between Tchita and hundreds of cities and towns 3,000 miles away.

Tchita, however, despite the fact that it was once the home of exiles, especially the revolutionists of the early nineteenth century, is to-day a busy city with modern business houses and schools. In Vladivostok and Khabarovsk I had seen similar evidences of progress and modern civilization, but Tchita seems to have been reserved for the greatest surprise.

I was walking about the city one day when I saw, what is now a very usual sight, hundreds of school children on their way to school. It is difficult for an American to comprehend Russia's educational system before the war, because only the children of the bourgeoisie could attend. Jewish children and those of the peasants and poor could not attend the public schools. Education was forbidden to them. But to-day, and only since the revolution of March, 1917, education is free to all and every schoolhouse and classroom is crowded. None of the schools of Siberia can accommodate all those who wish to attend.

Seeing the children of Tchita, bundled in their torn garments and furs, on their way to school, eager and happy, I followed with several other Americans and entered the gymnasium. One of our party, who spoke Russian, introduced us to the principal and we were escorted from classroom to classroom. Everywhere the condition was the same. The children were crowded in their seats. They were studying arithmetic, reading, and writing, and in one room we were shown the very limited number of instruments which were used in the physics and astronomical laboratories.

As we were about to leave, the principal led us to a large classroom in one corner of the big structure. It was a spacious, light room with various art objects, plaster casts and still-life studies arranged on a long table against the wall. In the centre of the room were some sixty girls standing before their easels, drawing or copying a plaster cast with intense interest in their work. Here in Tchita, Siberia, the last place in the world that I had expected to find such a thing, was an art school. One who has never been in Siberia, who has imagined it a wilderness and only a prison for political prisoners, can perhaps comprehend our astonishment. Art, of all things, in Siberia! What a mockery in the face of the revolution!

To pass from this scene to the snow-covered streets of the city and see a Russian soldier astride a horse, going from house to house with a telegram, in search of the man to whom it was addressed, was to pass from the sublime to the ridiculous. The soldier had a telegram for an officer whose address was unknown because there was no city directory or police register, and he was searching for him.

From Tchita to Irkutsk is the Switzerland of Siberia. It is said by all travellers that the Lake Baikal district is the most beautiful section of this great empire, and after one has made the journey by day in winter, one does not hesitate in joining those who have praised it. To awaken early in the morning while the train is skirting the shores of the lake, and to see the sun rise behind the snow-capped peaks of the mountains on the opposite shore, perhaps twenty-five miles across the placid blue lake, is to witness one of the most wonderful scenes in the world. Last winter I was in Switzerland. During the winter of 1916 and 1917 I travelled through the Transylvania Alps and the mountains of Bavaria. En route to the Far East I crossed the Rockies and the Sierra Nevada. For grandeur and mass, few of these mountain ranges can compare with the Baikal range, although the Swiss and French Alps are higher, and although the passes through Transylvania are picturesque and beautiful, I know of no scene to compare with that from the eastern shore of Lake Baikal on a clear winter morning before the lake is frozen over. Its massiveness may be comprehended when one realizes that Lake Baikal is one of the five largest lakes in the world; that it is 400 miles long and between eighteen and fifty-six miles wide, with a mountain range more than a mile above the lake stretching along the western shore like lace against a background of gold and blue clouds. Over the lake the sun appears, copper-gold in color, contrasting sharply with the silver sunrises and sunsets farther east in the birch forests.

Into this country some of the Allied troops have come. The Japanese flag flies from nearly every station from Vladivostok to Irkutsk. Here and there wave the colors of the Czecho-Slovaks, the simple red and white banner of the new nation whose army is locked in Siberia. From a few stations and public buildings flies the emblem of free Russia, the white, blue, and red. The French tricolor, the Union Jack, and the Stars and Stripes are not seen after one leaves Vladivostok, except on passing trains.

Between Vladivostok and Irkutsk the only evidences of a Russian army are the officers, and there are a sufficient number of these to command two new Russian armies. The privates have all disappeared into private life, excepting those who travel with the officers as orderlies or "guards of honor." Day by day our train passed special trains of Russian officers attached to this and that army several thousand miles away from the front, transporting artillery and automobiles from town to city and back again. What there is of a Russian army to-day is on wheels, and apparently there is no place to go. But when the Czecho-Slovaks stopped fighting the army, under Admiral Koltshak, was given new life.

With the Czecho-Slovaks this is not the case. Every one in Russia knows that it is the Czecho-Slovak army which kept the Bolsheviki forces out of Siberia. To the Czechs and to them alone belongs the credit for the order which exists in eastern and western Siberia, excepting, perhaps, in the few cities where the other Allies are stationed. The Czechs are not strutting on the war stage of the East. They are not even asking for praise. Their business is fighting, and they were doing their work quietly and splendidly before the armistice. Enter any Siberian city and call at the Czech headquarters. You will not find a general or even a colonel or major in charge. You may find a captain, but the chances are that a lieutenant and non-commissioned officer will greet you, because the Czech army is a working army and more attention is paid to work than to rank. Where there are thousands of Russian officers and dozens of privates there are thousands of Czech soldiers and a few officers. Most of the Czecho-Slovak army was at the front, the front which they made in a foreign country, in their fight for their own freedom and independence.

Travelling from Irkutsk to Ekaterinburg one passes through two important cities, Tomsk and Omsk. The former has been for many years the educational centre of Siberia. A large university is located there, where refugee students and professors from all sections of Russia have gathered since the Bolsheviki began to persecute the educated as well as the rich and professional citizens. The great white varsity buildings cover several acres of ground and compare favorably with many prominent American universities. It resembles, perhaps better than any university I have seen, the famous old institution in Geneva, Switzerland.

The attitude of the Bolsheviki toward the educated classes was illustrated for me by a professor of the University of Moscow, who had been and is still a representative of the Russian Co-operative Unions, and an instructor on their general board. Throughout the war and the revolution he has been travelling in Russia from Wilna to Vladivostok and from Archangel to Tashkent on business for the unions. After the Bolshevist revolution he appeared in Tashkent as Professor "Z," of the University of Moscow, but he had not been there many hours until he learned that his life was in danger because he was a "professor," and therefore an "intellectual," and a member of the "old regime."

He was arrested and taken before the local Soviet on the charge of carrying on propaganda as a "professor."

"But I am not a 'professor,'" he told the commissars. "I am an instructor in the Co-operative Unions. Here is my card."

Those who could read scanned his credentials but looked at him sceptically because he wore eye-glasses. Finally they released him, being convinced that he was only an "instructor," and the Red revolution officially recognized "instructors" as workmen!

Tomsk, being an educational centre, has exerted a deal of influence upon Siberian and Russian politics. During the time the Siberian Government, with headquarters in Omsk, controlled the country, several important political meetings and conventions were held there. Tomsk is the home of Premier Vologodsky of the All-Russian

Government and the present premier acting under the dictator, Admiral Koltshak.[6] Tomsk is also, next to Ekaterinburg, the most beautiful city in this part of Russia.

Omsk has gained its fame and importance only as a seat of the government. After the convention held at Ufa during the summer, when all of the local governments of Siberia, Archangel, and the Urals formed the All-Russian Government, Omsk was selected as the temporary capital and the directory and cabinet opened offices there. The National Assembly, which was controlled by the industrial workers of the left wing of the Social Revolutionists, by men with very extreme views, held themselves somewhat aloof of the central government, and made Ekaterinburg the seat of the national Parliament.

From Omsk one journeys to Ekaterinburg, the city which became famous with the discovery of the platinum and gold mines near by and the Ural stones, such as alexandrites, emeralds, rubies, sapphires, aquamarines, etc. Ekaterinburg is also one of the largest industrial cities in the Ural Mountains. It is a city of palaces built by mine owners, millers, and stone merchants. Until 1905 the chief government mint was located here, and to-day the low brick buildings, enclosed by a high brick wall, still stand, deserted and goldless.

Politically, in addition to its importance as the former meeting-place of the National Assembly, it is the present headquarters of the Czecho-Slovak National Council in Russia.

In Ekaterinburg I remained until Thanksgiving Day, walking and riding about the beautiful city in an old sleigh which I hired daily at the station, paying from ninety to one hundred roubles per day for its use!

The city was renowned before the war as the platinum centre of the world. From the Ekaterinburg mines came ninety per cent of the world's platinum supply, and after the city was captured by the Czecho-Slovaks American, English, French, and Japanese officials came here to bid against each other for this valuable metal which was of such supreme importance during the war. But that which made Ekaterinburg famous was not the mines nor the great monastery founded by Katherine the Great, but the residence of Professor Ipatieff[7] in which the Tzar, Nikolas II, and his family were imprisoned until they mysteriously disappeared in July, 1918.

---

[6] Pyotr V. Vologodsky (1863–1925), Russian politician. On June 20, 1918, after the collapse of Soviet power in Siberia, he became head of the Provisional Siberian Government. On November 4, 1918, he was appointed chair of the All-Russian Council of Ministers; he resigned on November 18, 1918, after Kolchak took power, but was convinced to stay as the chairman of the Council of Ministers of Russia. He resigned from his position as chairman on November 22, 1919, and emigrated to China the following winter.

[7] Nikolai N. Ipatiev (1869–1938), Russian military officer, engineer and activist; owner of so-called Ipatiev house in Ekaterinburg, where Tsar Nicholas II and his family were held and finally murdered in 1918. He emigrated after the Civil War.

During my stay in the city I devoted a great deal of time to the investigation of the Romanoff's fate, and the story of the circumstances of his imprisonment and trial (related in Chapter V) throw an interesting search-light upon the methods of the Workingmen's Union of Soldiers, Sailors, and Cossacks in handling the "aristocracy."

This section of Siberia, from the Pacific to the Urals, is the whirlpool of Russia. Gone are the days when the proud armies of the Romanoffs march through capitals and villages singing:

"Who were our grandmothers?"

"Our grandmothers were the white tents."

"And who were our grandfathers?"

"Our grandfathers were the Tzar's victories."

Chaos rules Russia to-day with greater power than the Romanoffs possessed in their regal days, for not only is Russia at the mercy of universal chaos, but the Allies and the Great Powers are seemingly powerless.

That Russia's civil war is not ended, and that it will be extremely difficult, if not impossible, for peace in Russia to be made at any European conference, are two impressions which become convictions as one travels to-day through Siberia to European Russia—to Ekaterinburg and Cheliabinsk, the headquarters of the Czecho-Slovak armies. From Vladivostok to the Ural Mountains Russia assumes her common dress of chaos; the garb the Tzar cut and the revolution sewed for the land and the people. Everywhere the people ask: "When shall we have peace in Russia?" and from all sides comes the answer: "I don't know," or "Nitchevo."

Russia is the supreme tragedy of the war. The invasion of Belgium in 1914 was ruthless and criminal, but Belgium had friends who came to her help; neighbors who knew the danger and who understood conditions in that heroic country. The sympathy for Belgium which was so universal and real, even in the United States, was a source of wonderful help to the Belgian people. But as for Siberia and Russia, during their days of trial the world looked on with cold pity. But while the rest of the world hesitated the Bolsheviki worked to further disorganize and disgrace Russia. Trotsky stated recently, according to the Siberian newspapers, that Russia's civil war would last fifty years. If this is a good forecast; if Russia is to be another Mexico, except on a grander scale, then Russia's civil war is not only not ended but it is just beginning, and the overthrow of the Tzar and the Red army reign of terror are the prologue and preface to one of the greatest and most tragic national dramas in history. And who to-day can doubt Trotsky's statement when there is no more a recognized central government even in Siberia, and when bands of revolutionary generals and soldiers seize cities, towns, and provinces and exact tribute; when in European Russia the Bolsheviki and the Allies fight near Kieff; when General Denekin and his army of Cossacks march across southern Russia; when the Czecho-Slovak armies hold the Ural Mountain front, and when a dictator rules in Omsk who is not recognized by leaders in all other parts of Siberia? What is there but chaos, chaos everywhere, when hundreds of thousands of refugees live in box-cars and are shuttled from freight-yard to freight-yard; when factories are closed because of strikes or a lack of raw materials; when any one and every one can have a special train or car without paying for it or without buying railway tickets; when the educated stand at street-corners selling their old clothes to pay their living expenses; when banks are robbed and people murdered with the guilty escaping prosecution and arrest? Russia is in that sad state where civilization is a mockery.

And the pity of it is that no one seems to know what should be done to help Russia, or, if there is some one person or some great nation which knows, either power or decision is lacking. Russia to-day, is a prostrate patient, baffling the greatest political specialists in the world. Some advocate an army, others maintain that an efficient and effective army is impossible. Some leaders believe in Allied military intervention, but soldiers throughout the world are weary of fighting. The militant spark which makes men fight is dimmed. The war is over in Europe and the common masses here do not understand why the war does not end in Russia.

Opposing these military specialists are others who believe that Russia should be left alone to work out her own destiny; to fight a fratricidal war until the strong survive and the weak perish. Others believe that Russia should be fed and clothed and rehabilitated economically. No two nations agree, while the Russian people look first to Omsk, then to Moscow and Petrograd, or Washington, Vladivostok, Paris, or London, expecting all the while to see the sun rise on a new era but witnessing daily the same red sunset, ending a day of terror and forecasting another day of strife and suffering.

From Vladivostok to Ekaterinburg, Asiatic Russia takes on its real appearance, as an empire without order.

But this is not new. Russia has been disorganized and disturbed long before the revolution. The revolution only raised the curtain for the whole world to see the spectacle. There was bribery and corruption before; the government was disorganized; people were dissatisfied; the railroads were overburdened; there were traffic tie-ups, crowded prisons, plots and complots. The story of Russia to-day is not new; it is only a new version, but, what makes it important, perhaps more important to-day than ever before, is that the United States and the Allies promised to help Russia and the Russian people want to know where that help is and when it may be expected. They also wish to know what kind of aid is to be forthcoming: economic, political, social, moral, or military. One soon learns how keen is this Russian wish when one traverses that part of Russia along the Trans-Siberian Railway between Irkutsk and the present front. Perhaps that part of the world which is fifteen thousand miles away does not wish to be disturbed by the situation in Russia, but the fact remains that here, in this part of the world, several million people are interested in knowing whether or no[t] the Allies intend to keep their promises. It does not matter so much what is being said and thought about Russia in the other section of the universe as it does what this country is saying about the Allies and America. And it is the opinion and sentiment of central Siberia that I shall give in twelve statements which I heard during my journey in November and December from Irkutsk to Ekaterinburg and back again. This is to be a statement of what others think of us. In the words of the latest song hit in Moscow:

"Forget your fireplaces, the fires have gone out."

Think about Russia!

In a few sentences these are some of the expressions one hears in Russia to-day about America, Russia, and the Allies:

1. Russia can never help herself to order. There never will be a strong government in Russia until the Allies establish such a government and maintain it.
2. Without military aid from the Allies the Bolsheviki will never be overthrown.
3. If all foreigners would get out of Russia and let the Russian people alone there would soon be order here.
4. A military dictatorship is the only solution of Russia's present problems.
5. The Russian people want a monarchy. A Socialistic government is not the wish of a majority of the people.
6. The Social Revolutionists made the first revolution a success, and Russia's salvation lies in their hands.
7. Give Russia food, household supplies, clothing, raw materials, and other supplies, distribute them without favor and at reasonable prices, and Russia will work out her own destiny.
8. Let the Japanese come in.
9. Keep the Japanese out of Russia.
10. Reorganize the Russian army, supply it with war-materials, and the new army will save Russia.
11. But don't give Russia to Germany.
12. Some nation will get Russia if the Allies do not come in now. What has become of the Allied promises to help Russia?

These are twelve main varieties of opinions expressed among inhabitants and foreigners of Asiatic Russia to-day. I believe this represents, also, the chief views of Russians of all Classes and from all parts of the country, excepting the Bolsheviki, because Siberian Russia does not represent to-day what it represented before the Bolsheviki uprisings. Siberian-Russian opinion is the opinion of Bolshevikiless Russia, because in every city of Asiatic Russia to-day are political leaders, officers, merchants, landowners, peasants, traders, doctors, lawyers, and laborers from Petrograd, Moscow, Libau, Riga, Kowno, Wilna, Brest-Litovsk, Kharkoff, Kieff, Odessa, and elsewhere. They have come here to escape the Bolsheviki and, if they can, to help Russia to overthrow the Bolsheviki. I met men and women from all parts of European Russia on my two trips across central Siberia. These people are living in Omsk, Ekaterinburg, Tomsk, Tiumen, Taiga, Irkutsk, Cheliabinsk, Marinsk, and other cities, awaiting the day when Russia makes peace with herself and they can return to their homes. "To our homes," and not "To the front," is the cry of the Russian people today. If the wish of these people could be expressed in a few words it would be this: "Let us live at home in peace."

How this wish can be realized is the problem of Russia. How the people can be helped to attain it is the problem of the United States and the Allies—the nucleus of a league of nations.

## Chapter V
## THE FATE OF THE TZAR

The fate of the former imperial family of Russia is one of the great mysteries of the war. The last place in which they are known to have been imprisoned is Ekaterinburg, that beautiful snow-white city with broad thoroughfares and palaces—the jewel of the Ural Mountains.

To Ekaterinburg Nikolas II, his wife, daughters, son, physicians, and servants were removed under a strong Bolshevist guard from Tobolsk, a city 300 versts from the nearest railroad-station to which they had been taken from Petrograd for "safety."

It was April, 1918, when a committee from the Ural District Soviet of Workingmen, Cossacks, Soldiers, and Sailors called upon Professor Ipatieff, the owner of one of the largest and finest homes in the city, demanding that he give up his residence immediately. They did not state their reasons but ordered him out.

The Ipatieff palace was built on one of the main thoroughfares of the city, not far from the spacious white residence of the "Platinum King" of the world. Mr. Ipatieff was an engineer and a leading citizen of the community. His house was of cement and stone construction, also painted white, and modern in every respect. This residence, which was destined to be the last known prison for the Tzar and his family, was within a stone's throw of the British and French consulates. In front was a wide, open square, in the centre of which stands one of the numerous cathedrals of the city. To the left as neighbors the Tzar had some of the poorest citizens. They lived in uninviting log or frame huts. To the right, across the side street, was a large two-story red brick residence surrounded by a brick wall. From the upper windows of this house one could see into the small garden in the rear of the Ipatieff residence, even after the Bolsheviki built a twenty-foot board fence around the "Tzar's house." It was in this garden that the former imperial family was permitted its only recreation and fresh air during the eighty days the members were imprisoned there.

After receiving the Bolshevist command Professor Ipatieff moved without delay. He was an "intellectual" and an "aristocrat," and realized that the quicker he left the safer he would be. This was about the 25th of April. Within a few days the Tzar, the Tzarina, and their daughter Mary arrived, accompanied by one of the physicians who had attended the Empress, who suffered from heart trouble and rheumatism. The Tzarevitch and other daughters were delayed because of the illness of the boy, but within a week the family was united inside the white house and board fence, guarded by some twenty Bolshevist soldiers of the Red Guard, said to have been recruited especially from the mines and factories near by.

The former royal family entered the house under heavy guard through the main entrance on the public square, which led directly into the rooms on the second floor. Professor Ipatieff had been living in these rooms, while on the first floor lived his servants, who used the side-street entrance.

Entering the house, the Tzar and his wife were "escorted," if not ordered, through the reception-hall and past one of the private rooms already filled with soldiers, to the large drawing-room which Professor Ipatieff used when receiving guests. All of the furniture and carpets remained as he had left them.

Suspended from the ceiling was a large crystal electric chandelier, imported from Italy, and on the walls hung valuable oil-paintings. The furniture of carved oak was modern, expensive, and comfortable. To the left, as the Tzar entered, he saw another room the other side of an arch. This room was assigned to him as a study. The Tzarina's wheel-chair, which had been brought from Tobolsk, was placed before one of the wide plate-glass windows looking out upon the inside of the high board fence through heavy iron bars which had been fastened in the walls outside the windows. Directly in front of the former imperial leaders, as they stood at the entrance to the reception-room, were two large oak doors leading into the dining-room. To their left were the kitchen, pantry, bathroom (one of the few private bathrooms in the city), and another room which was later used by the former Empress's maid.

The Bolshevist commissars of Ekaterinburg led the royal couple through the dining-room into two smaller rooms facing the side street. One of these was assigned to the Tzar, his wife, and son as a bedroom. The other was designated as the living and sleeping room for the four daughters, although no beds or cots were provided.

Alone for a few brief moments in these rooms the Tzarina walked to the window, drew aside the portieres and looked with a fainting heart through iron bars upon the rough interior of the board fence which obstructed entirely what was once a beautiful view of the cathedral square and the "Platinum King's" palace, not more than 200 feet away and now occupied by soldiers of the Red army. But these the former Empress could not see. Above the fence were visible only the vast, free, pale-blue heavens.

Turning to the Tzar and asking for a pencil, she again drew the curtains aside and wrote on the frame of the window "April 30, 1918," the day of her arrival and the first day of her eighty days of suffering and anguish in Ekaterinburg, prisoner of her husband's former subjects.

During my sojourn in the city I had several opportunities of going through the house with Czech officers and Professor Ipatieff. From numerous sources I learned what transpired in this house between the 30th of April and July 16, but I doubt whether even the details, which these witnesses give, fully describe the terrible torture which the Romanoffs were forced to endure. The account of one eye-witness, the former Tzar's personal valet, I shall give in detail, because, unabridged and uncensored, it is one of the greatest known indictments of "revolutionary red justice."

This account of the Tzar's last days under the Bolsheviki was written by Parfen Alexeivitch Dominin, who for twenty-two years served the Tzar as his majordomo, accompanied him into exile, and remained with his imperial master until the early hours of the morning of July 17, when the Tzar was led away by Bolshevist soldiers.[1] In his manuscript report, in simple Russian, filled with the devotion of a life-long servant, is presented, as far as I was able to learn, the only single, complete, and authentic account of the Tzar's life in Ekaterinburg. Dominin describes the Romanoff family life, tells of the illness of the Tzarevitch, of the Empress's tragic pleas for mercy on her knees before the Soviet guard, and gives details of the evidence presented at the secret midnight trial, where Nikolas Romanoff appeared, undefended and alone, dressed in his soldier's garb.

Dominin states that the indictment presented against Nikolas charged him with being a party to the counter-revolutionary plot to overthrow the Bolsheviki, and with secretly corresponding with Generals Denekin, Dutoff,[2] and Dogert,[3] who were endeavoring to liberate him and who had sent him word to be prepared to be freed.

Dominin's manuscript, in Russian, which is here given in verbatim translation, contains a supplement with the Tzar's abdication manifesto, written in October, 1905, during the Russo-Japanese War, which was printed but never promulgated.[4]

Parfen Dominin, who is sixty years of age, now lives in seclusion. He was born in a village in the Costroma Government and began serving the Tzar in 1896. His manuscript reads:

> Beginning with the first days of July, airplanes began to appear nearly every day, over Ekaterinburg, flying very low and dropping bombs, but little damage was done. Rumors spread about the city that the Czecho-Slovaks were making reconnoissances and would shortly occupy the city.
>
> One day the former Tzar returned to the house from his walk in the garden. He was unusually excited, and after fervent prayers before an ikon of Holy Nicholas the Thaumaturgist, he lay down on a little bed without undressing. This he never did before.
>
> "Please allow me to undress you and make the bed," I said to the Tzar.

---

[1] There was no such person as Parfen Dominin in Nicholas II's entourage, neither by name nor by description of his activities. The whole story of Parfen Dominin appears to be false.

[2] Alexander I. Dutov (1879–1921), one of the leaders of the counterrevolution in the Urals; ataman of the Orenburg Cossacks, who supported Kolchak. Lieutenant general (1919). After the Civil War, he emigrated to China and was killed there by Cheka agents.

[3] No such general or person existed.

[4] No proof of such a manifesto was ever found.

"Don't trouble, old man," the Tzar said, "I feel in my heart I shall live only a short time. Perhaps to-day—already"—but the Tzar did not end the sentence.

"God bless you, what are you saying?" I asked, and the Tzar began to explain that during his evening walk he had received news that a special council of the Ural District Soviet of Workingmen, Cossacks, and Red army deputies was being held which was to decide the Tzar's fate.

It was said that the Tzar was suspected of planning to escape to the Czech army, which was advancing toward Ekaterinburg and had promised to tear him away from the Soviet power. He ended his story by saying resignedly:

"I don't know anything."

The Tzar's daily life was very strict. He was not permitted to buy newspapers, and was not allowed to walk beyond the limited time.

All the servants were thoroughly searched before leaving and upon returning. Once I was forced to take off all my clothing because the commissary of the Guard thought I was transmitting letters from the Tzar.

Food was very scarce. Generally only herring, potatoes, and bread were given, at the rate of half a pound daily to each person.

The former heir to the imperial throne, Alexis Nikolaievitch, was ill all the time. Once he was coughing and spitting blood.

One evening Alexis came running into the room of the Tzar, breathless and crying loudly, and, falling into the arms of his father, said, with tears in his eyes: "Dear papa, they want to shoot you."

The Tzar whispered: "It's the will of God in everything. Be quiet, my sufferer, my son, be quiet. Where is mamma?"

"Mamma weeps," said the boy.

"Ask mamma to calm herself; one cannot help by weeping. It is God's will in everything," the Tzar replied.

With ardor Alexis pleaded: "Papa, dear papa, you have suffered enough already. Why do they want to kill you? That is not just."

The Tzar replied: "Alexis, I ask you for only one thing. Go and comfort mamma."

Alexis left. The Tzar knelt before the ikon of Holy Nicholas, praying for a long time. During these days Nikolas became very devout. Often he would awaken during the night because of some nightmare. He would not sleep any more, but spent the rest of the night in prayers.

From time to time the Tzar was permitted to meet his wife, Alexandra, or, as he called her, Alice, but his son he could meet whenever he desired. Once Alexandra Feodorovna came weeping into the Tzar's room, saying: "It is necessary in any case that you should put all your papers and documents in order." After this Nikolas wrote all night.

The Tzar wrote many letters, among them those to all his daughters, to his brother Michael,[5] to his uncle, Nicholas Nicholaievitch,[6] General Dogert, Duke Gendrikoff,[7] Count Olssufieff,[8] the Prince of Oldenburg,[9] Count Sumarokoff Elston,[10] and many others. He did not seal his letters, as all his correspondence was controlled by the Soviet censors. Often it happened that his letters were returned by the commissary of the Guard, with the pencilled remark: "Are not to be forwarded."

For many days Nikolas Alexandrovitch would not eat. He would fall down and only pray. Even for a man who had not the gift of observation it was evident that the former Tzar was greatly troubled and feeling heartsick.

On July 15, late in the evening, there appeared suddenly in the Tzar's room the commissary of the Guard, who announced:

"Citizen Nikolas Alexandrovitch Romanoff, you will follow me to the Ural District Soviet of Workingmen, Cossacks, and Red army deputies."

---

[5] Grand Duke Michael Alexandrovich of Russia (1878–1918) was the youngest brother of Nicholas II. When Nicholas abdicated on March 2 (15), 1917, Michael was named as his successor instead of Nicholas's son, Alexei. Michael, however, deferred acceptance of the throne until ratification by an elected assembly. He was never confirmed as emperor and, following the Russian Revolution of 1917, he was imprisoned and murdered.

[6] Grand Duke Nikolai N. Romanov of Russia (1856–1929), a grandson of Nicholas I of Russia, was commander in chief of the Russian armies on the main front in the first year of the war, and was later a commander in chief in the Caucasus. Nicholas spent the first two years of the revolution in the Crimean Peninsula, sometimes under house arrest, taking little part in politics. There appears to have been some sentiment to have him head the White Russian forces active in southern Russia at the time, but the leaders in charge, especially General Anton Denikin, were afraid that a strong monarchist figurehead would alienate the more left-leaning constituents of the movement. He and his wife escaped just ahead of the Red Army in April 1919, aboard the British battleship *HMS Marlborough*.

[7] Alexander S. Gendrikov (1859–1919), count, colonel, founder, and member of the Main Council of the monarchist and anti-Semitic Union of the Russian People.

[8] Dmitry A. Olsufiev (1862–1937), Russian politician and public figure, big landowner; participated in Russo-Japanese War of 1904–05. A founder of the Union of October 17, and member of Russian State Council. He emigrated after the revolution.

[9] Duke Alexander Petrovich of Oldenburg (1844–1932) served as adjutant general to Alexander III of Russia, and also as commanding general of the Imperial Guard. At the outbreak of World War I, Nicholas II of Russia appointed Alexander, a medical doctor, as supreme chief of the medical service of the military and naval forces. A member of State Council. After the revolution, he emigrated.

[10] Felix F. Yusupov, prince (since 1885), Count Sumarokov-Elston (1856–1928), Russian general, head of Moscow military district in 1915. After his son played the leading role in murdering Grigory Rasputin, Prince Yusupov was removed from the tsar's court. After the revolution, he emigrated.

The Tzar asked in a pleading tone: "Tell me frankly, are you leading me to be shot?"

"You must not be afraid, nothing will happen until your death. You are wanted at a meeting," the commissary said, smiling.

Nikolas Alexandrovitch got up from his bed, put on his gray soldier blouse and his boots, fastened his belt, and went away with the commissary. Outside the door were standing two soldiers, Letts, with rifles. All three surrounded him, and for some reason began to search him all over. Then one of the Letts went ahead. The Tzar was forced to go behind him, next to the commissary, and the second soldier followed.

Nikolas did not return for a very long while, about two hours and a half at least. He was quite pale, his chin trembling.

"Old man, give me some water," he said.

I brought him water at once. He emptied a large cup.

"What happened?" I asked.

"They have informed me that I shall be shot within three hours."

During the meeting of the Ural District Soviet a minute of the trial was read in the presence of the Tzar. It was prepared by a secret organization named the Association for the Defense of Our Native Country and Freedom. It stated that a counter-revolutionary plot had been discovered, with the object of suppressing the workmen's and peasants' revolution by inciting the masses against the Soviet by accusing it of all the hard consequences resulting from imperialism all over the world—war and slaughter, famine, lack of work, the collapse of transportation, the advance of the Germans, etc.

The indictment further stated that to attain this the counter-revolutionists were attempting to join all the non-Soviet political parties, Socialists as well as imperial parties. The evidence presented at the trial showed that the staff of this organization could not carry out its intentions fully because of a divergency of views regarding the tactics between the Left and Right parties. The evidence presented showed that at the head of the plot stood the Tzar's personal friend, General Dogert.

The evidence presented against the Tzar shows that in this organization were working also such representatives as the Duke of Krapotkine,[11] Colonel of the General Staff Ekhart, Engineer Llinsky, and others. There are reasons for believing that Shavenpoff[12] was also in direct connection with this orga-

---

[11] Pyotr A. Kropotkin (1842–1921) was a Russian activist, scientist, and philosopher who advocated anarchism.

[12] Probably Boris V. Savinkov (1879–1925), a Russian writer and revolutionary. As one of the leaders of the Fighting Organization of the Socialist Revolutionary Party, he was responsible for the assassinations of several high-ranking imperial officials in 1904 and 1905. After the February Revolution of 1917, he became assistant war minister in the Provisional Gov-

nization and that he was supposed to be the head of the new government as a military dictator.

All these leaders had established a very strong conspiracy. In the Moscow fighting group were 700 officers who afterward were transferred to Samara, where they were to await reinforcements from the Allies with the purpose of establishing a Ural front to separate Great Russia from Siberia. Later, according to the supposed plot, when results of the famine should show, all those sympathizing with the overthrow of the Soviet would be mobilized to advance against Germany.

The evidence presented shows proofs that certain Socialist parties were taking part in the plot, including the Right Social Revolutionists and Mensheviki, working in full harmony with the Constitutional Democrats. The chief of staff of this organization was in direct communication with Dutoff and Denekin.

The testimony stated that during the last few days a new plot had been discovered, having for its object the rescue of the former Tzar from the Soviet with the help of Dutoff.

Besides this, it was proved at the trial that the Tzar conducted secret correspondence with his personal friend, General Dogert, who urged the Tzar to be ready to be freed.

In view of this evidence, together with the troublesome situation caused by the decision of the Ural District Soviet to evacuate Ekaterinburg, the former Tzar was ordered to submit to execution without delay because the Soviet believed it harmful and unjustifiable to continue to keep him under guard.

"Citizen Nikolas Romanoff," said the Soviet chairman to the former Tzar, "I inform you, you are given three hours to write your last orders. Guard, I ask you not to leave Nikolas Romanoff out of your sight."

Soon after Nikolas returned from the meeting his wife and son called upon him weeping. Often Alexandra fainted and a doctor had to be called. When she recovered she knelt before the soldiers and begged for mercy. The soldiers answered that it was not within their power to render mercy.

"Be quiet, for Christ's sake, Alice," repeated the Tzar several times in a very low tone, making the sign of the cross over his wife and son.

After this Nikolas called me and kissed me, saying:

"Old man, do not leave Alexandra and Alexis. You see, there is nobody with me now. There is nobody to appease them, and I shall soon be led away."

Later it proved that nobody except his wife and son, of all his beloved ones, was permitted to bid farewell to the former Tzar. Nikolas and his wife and son

---

ernment. After the October Revolution of the same year, he organized an armed resistance against the Bolsheviks. Savinkov emigrated in 1920, but in 1924, he was lured back to the Soviet Union, arrested, and either killed in prison or committed suicide.

remained together until five other soldiers of the Red army appeared with the chairman of the Soviet, accompanied by two members, both working men.

"Put on your overcoat," resolutely commanded the chairman.

Nikolas, who did not lose his self-possession, began to dress, kissed his wife and son and me again, made the sign of the cross over them, and then, addressing the men, said in a loud voice: "Now I am at your disposal."

Alexandra and Alexis fell in a fit of hysterics. Both fell to the floor. I made an attempt to bring mother and son to, but the chairman said:

"Wait. There should be no delay. You may do that after we have gone."

"Permit me to accompany Nikolas Alexandrovitch," I asked.

"No accompanying," was the stern answer. So Nikolas was taken away, nobody knows where, and was shot during the night of July 16, by about twenty Red army soldiers.

Before dawn the next day the chairman of the Soviet again came to the room, accompanied by Red army soldiers, a doctor, and the commissary of the Guard. The doctor attended Alexandra and Alexis. Then the chairman said to the doctor:

"Is it possible to take them immediately?" When he answered "yes," the chairman said: "Citizen Alexandra Feodorovna Romanoff and Alexis Romanoff, get ready. You will be sent away from here. You are allowed to take only the most necessary things, not over thirty or forty pounds."

Mastering themselves, but stumbling from side to side, mother and son soon got ready.

"To-morrow get him out of here," the Soviet chairman commanded the guard, pointing at me.

Alexandra and Alexis were immediately taken away by an automobile truck, it is not known where.

The morning of the following day the commissary again appeared, and ordered me to get out of the room, taking with me some property of the Tzar, but all the letters and documents belonging to the Tzar were taken by the commissary. I left, but had great difficulty in procuring a railway ticket, because all the stations and trains were overfilled with soldiers of the Red army, tossing about evacuating the city and taking along all precious objects.

An epilogue and supplement to the manuscript, also written by Dominin, follow:

The Cheliabinsk newspaper *Utro Sibiri* states that the Tzar's execution was certified to by a special government declaration at a place ten versts from Ekaterinburg. On July 30 a tumulus was found containing metal things belonging to each member of the family of the former Tzar, and also bones of burned corpses, which may be those of the Romanoff family.

As hostages, Grand Duchess Elena Petrova, Countess Henrikova, and a third, whose name I don't know, were taken away. The total hostages were about sixty. The Bolsheviki fled in the direction of Verknoturie.

The Academician Bunakovhky,[13] a member of the Russian Historical Society, found accidentally in the secret division of the senate archives the proof sheet of a "collection of laws ordered of the government," dated October 17, 1905, in which was printed the following manifesto:

Disturbances and riots in the capital and many parts of the empire are filling my heart with painful grief. The welfare of the Russian Emperor is indissolubly joined with the welfare of the people, and the affliction of the people is his grief. From the disturbances which have now arisen may proceed deep disorder among the population, a threat to the unity and integrity of our state.

In these days, when the fate of Russia is being determined, we consider it the duty of our conscience to fuse our people into a close union and join all the powers of the population for the height of the state's prosperity.

Therefore we have decided to abdicate the throne of the Russian Empire and lay down the high power. Desiring not to be separated from our beloved son, we surrender the succession to our brother, the Grand Duke Michael, and bless him upon the ascendance to the Russian throne.

Nikolas Romanoff.
(Countersigned) Minister of the Court,
Baron Fredericks.
October 16, 1905. Novy Peterhof.

Written with a red pencil on the text was "Hold up printing. Manager of Typography Kedrinsky."

He tells me the following details regarding the delay in printing the manifesto, Dominin wrote. At eight o'clock on the evening of October 16 I received from a courier a packet from the minister of the court, Baron Fredericks, asking me to publish the manifesto in the next number of the Collection of Laws. As the manifesto was not received in the usual way, through the minister of justice, Kedrinsky, in giving the manifesto to a typographer to prepare the printing, simultaneously informed Shthegtovioff[14] by telephone.

---

[13] Probably Bunyakovsky; however, there was no Russian academician-historian with either variant of the surname. The whole story of the manifesto appears to be a fake.

[14] Probably refers to Ivan G. Shcheglovitov (1861–1918), a Russian politician who served as the Russian minister of justice and last chairman of the State Council of the Russian Empire.

At first the minister of justice only asked for the holding up of the printing, but at eleven o'clock the functionary for special commissions from the minister visited Kedrinsky and asked for the original of the manifesto and ordered the proof sheet transmitted to the secret archives of the senate.

Thus the Tzar spent the last days as a Bolshevist prisoner, disappearing within a few hours before the Czecho-Slovak troops freed the terror-stricken city of Ekaterinburg, according to the testimony of his faithful servant.

From Professor Ipatieff and other witnesses I obtained additional details of the conditions in the house during their imprisonment. Although the Tzar, his wife, and son were provided with beds and were supposed to have the private use of the room, it frequently happened that the Tzarina's physician was forced to occupy the same chamber. In the adjoining room the four daughters slept on the floor, with scarcely any bedding. At times the Tzar was forbidden to see his wife, and they were seldom permitted to talk except in the presence of a soldier. Although the family ate in the spacious dining-room of the Ipatieff home food was prepared by the Red army men and was very meagre. For the family only five plates, knives, forks, and spoons were provided, and on more than one occasion the soldiers would help themselves from the erstwhile imperial table. When any member of the family bathed it was forbidden to close the bathroom door, and in the frame of the door both at the top and sides are literally hundreds of bayonet marks showing that on many occasions soldiers stood on guard at the door with drawn bayonets. In fact, so many bayonet jabs are still visible in the walls and ceilings of some of the rooms that it seems certain, beyond a doubt, that the guard in the house always had bayonets attached to their loaded rifles.

After examining the walls of the house I concluded that the soldiers must have tried bayonet practice from time to time in the various rooms, but whether this was done when members of the Tzar's family were there one cannot say. Whenever any member of the family walked in the garden soldiers stood on the balcony leading from the dining-room and looking out over the garden. Professor Ipatieff, who was in Ekaterinburg, living nearby throughout the Tzar's imprisonment, stated that the soldiers often aimed their rifles at the Tzar when he was walking. With their fingers on the triggers of their rifles and eyes on the sight-points they would follow his movements.

The Tzar was not permitted to receive any newspapers, and many of the letters which he wrote, and which were sent to him, were never delivered. Nikolas himself wrote scores of letters to his friends, but they were usually simple statements about the health of the family. The day before his trial for participation in an alleged counterplot against the Bolsheviki he was permitted to write letters to his relatives and friends, but as far as known none of these were sent by the Ural District Soviet.

That the Tzar, however, was in communication with the outside world through various secret channels is quite certain. One of the nuns in the monastery of Ekaterinburg, for instance, informed me that one day she received word from Odessa saying that the Tzarevitch was ill, and asking her, in behalf of "friends of the Tzar," to take milk, eggs, and butter to the Tzar's house. By this name the Ipatieff residence became known as soon as the Tzar arrived, and to-day any one in Ekaterinburg can tell you where the "Tzar's house" is. All of the droshky drivers know, as the taxi-drivers in Paris know the location of Napoleon's tomb.

This nun—a simple, kindly faced, quiet, and patient old woman—related to me one afternoon her experiences in delivering fresh eggs and milk. She would not tell me how she received word from Odessa, nor why any one in Odessa should know quicker than the people of Ekaterinburg that the Tzarevitch was ill—that he was so ill that he often spat blood.

At the beginning of July, however, when she began to take food to the Tzarevitch, the Bolshevist commissar permitted her to take butter, eggs, and milk to the Tzarina personally. Often, she said, she would take a bottle of cream, sugar, and sweets to the house, but it was not long until the Bolsheviki either became suspicious or were revengeful. One day they seized everything she had for their own use, telling her to get out and never return. The following morning she appeared as usual and was permitted to send in the eggs and milk.

On several occasions during the visits she had very brief "audiences" with the members of the family. Naturally she would not tell me whether she carried news to the Romanoffs, but from other sources I learned that it was through this monastery that some of the Tzar's friends in Crimea were able to "keep in touch" with the Tzar.

It is known, also, that the former Emperor on a few occasions received letters and news through a member of the Soviet Guard, who, despite his position, was still loyal to the "Little White Father." Another route by which news travelled to and from the Tzar, was through signals from the attic of the brick house across the street from the Ipatieff residence, which I have described. A private telephone in this house was connected with the office of a certain prominent business man. The man in the attic and this merchant communicated with each other day and night, and I remember learning from one of them some of the secret phrases they used in talking, so that if any one should by chance overhear them the Bolsheviki could not understand. When the observer under the roof of the house across the street saw the Tzar in the garden he would phone, "the baggage is at the station," and then messages would be communicated to the Tzar.

Throughout the time the Tzar and his family were imprisoned here efforts were being made to release him. On more than one occasion the Tzar received a message stating that he would soon be freed. General Denekin, who is now commanding the Cossacks near Kieff, an old and intimate friend of Nikolas, was endeavoring in every possible way to save his former imperial master. General Dutoff, another friend of the Tzar, operating in the Urals, was seeking to deliver his friend. The Czecho-Slovaks, despite their revolutionary tendencies, were bent upon snatching the Tzar from the Bolsheviki. There were independent Russian and foreign business interests in Ekaterinburg which wanted him released. More money was spent trying to free Nikolas Romanoff than the Bolsheviki ever used in guarding and transporting him or maintaining an organization to prevent his escape.

Thus, in advance of the Tzar's trial before the secret night session of the Ural District Soviet, there was being waged in Russia and Siberia a bitter and ceaseless contest between the friends and enemies of the Tzar. Ekaterinburg was the centre of the intrigue and the Tzar himself was playing no unimportant part.

After the trial, where the Tzar was condemned to death, the Moscow wireless station sent out an official communication addressed, as are all messages from wireless towers under control of the Soviet, "To all, to all, to all!" announcing that the Tzar had been executed in Ekaterinburg, but that the family had been removed from the city to a place of safety.

But was Nikolas II killed? If so, how and where? This is where the real mystery of the Tzar begins. From this date until to-day the world has speculated. Evidence of all kinds has been published to prove his death and to announce that he is still alive.

It has been said that "votes should be weighed and not counted." So is it with regard to facts. Weighing the evidence regarding the Tzar himself I should say that six-tenths of the weight indicates that he is dead; four-tenths that he may be alive.

The Tzar was tried, condemned to death, and taken from the court room back to the Ipatieff residence. Some maintain that he was executed immediately in the basement or the first floor of this house. Other citizens declare that he was taken outside the city and shot. Some think he was murdered in the house without trial.

To show how the testimony differs I shall refer to the published statements of Prince Lvoff.[15] He declared in Vladivostok and Japan that he and the Tzar were kept in the same prison and had the same jailers. That cannot be true as far as Ekaterinburg is concerned, because I could not find a person in Ekaterinburg who had heard that Prince Lvoff was in the Ipatieff residence as a prisoner. He was confined for four months in the prison of Ekaterinburg, but the Tzar was never there. Prince Lvoff and many others declare the Tzar and his whole family were killed in the Ipatieff house, and they point to the bullet-holes in the walls of the room. The nun from the monastery who took eggs and milk to the Tzarevitch told me that she is positive none of them was executed in this house, and that the Tzarina, the Tzarevitch, and the daughters were taken away in a motor-truck which she saw standing in the grounds of the Ipatieff residence on July 15. She believes the Tzar is dead, but that the family is still alive. On the other hand, one of the priests from the same monastery, who held short services upon a few occasions in the house for the imperial family, assured me that "the whole family is alive and well."

---

[15] Georgy Y. Lvov (1861–1925), prince, Russian statesman, and the first post-imperial prime minister of Russia, the head of Provisional Government from March 15 to July 21, 1917. He was dispatched to the US by the Siberian Provisional All-Russian Government in 1918, and later moved to France.

While I was in Tiumen, the chief city between Omsk and Ekaterinburg, one of the members of the Russian nobility, who was an intimate friend of the Tzarina, received a message from the "interior of Russia by courier saying, 'Your friends are all well.'" When I questioned the American, British, and French consuls, who were in the city throughout the Bolshevist occupation, as to their opinions, they stated frankly that they did not know whether the Tzar was dead or alive, and they were still conducting their investigations. Professor Ipatieff, who is now living on the first floor of his house, surrounded by most of the furniture which was used by the former imperial family, showed me through the house on two occasions and described in detail how the whole family was brought from the second floor to the main floor by way of the servants' stairs, lined up against the wall and shot. A member of the Judicial Investigating Commission believes the family was killed in this house, but the only evidence any of them possess is the bullet-holes in the walls and floors and the finding of certain property of the Tzar and Tzarina in the ashes of one of the stoves. I saw the room in which they were supposed to have been killed en masse, but I was not convinced by the evidence presented there for these reasons:

(1) If the whole family was executed in this room, then seven persons were killed. The bullet-holes were in the walls and some "blood clots." There were no pools of blood, and it seemed doubtful to me that seven persons should die a horrible death and leave only small "blood clots" in the bullet-holes and small bloodstains on the floor.

(2) If they were executed in this room, then the soldiers' rifles could not have been more than five feet from the victims, because the room is very small. If killed here the bodies must have been removed, because they were not found in this room nor in the house. By removing seven bodies from such a room, in midsummer, when it was very hot and sultry, the members of the family surely did not wear very heavy clothing, and it seems that bloodstains should have been found in other parts of the house, but none were found.

(3) It is stated that the bodies were burned after execution in this house. This I believe is impossible, because none of the stoves in the house are large enough. The house was heated, as are most Russian houses, by Russian stoves built in the walls, and the opening to each stove is not more than a foot wide or deep. Still, in one of these stoves the investigating commission found a military cross which the Tzar once wore, corset staves and a large diamond belonging to the Tzarina. The stove in which these things were found was in the bedroom of the Tzar's daughters. This stove was never used by the Bolshevist guard, and it is plausible that the Tzar or Tzarina burned these things themselves at the last hour so that the Soviet would not find them. This might be substantiated by the fact that the investigating commission, after having the ashes examined, failed to find traces of any human bodies.

I do not believe the evidence that the whole family was executed here is convincing. I think the Tzar may have been shot in this room, but, on the other hand, there is the testimony of the Tzar's personal valet, Parfen Dominin, that the Tzar was taken away from the house early in the morning of July 16 by a small Soviet guard. Dominin himself remained in the house until the morning of the 17th. If any one was shot in that house that night; if twenty shots were fired on the first floor, the valet would have heard them, because he was in the living-room of the Ipatieff residence, which was almost directly above the room where the bullet-holed wall stands to-day, and no Russian house is sound-proof.

After examining carefully all of the evidence presented by Professor Ipatieff I made an investigation of the testimony that the Tzar was taken away and executed. The Bolsheviki claim that this is what happened. They maintained he was executed outside the city, before a firing squad. But was he? Is it not possible that the Tzar was kidnapped after he left the house, surrounded by only three Red army soldiers? Considering all of the efforts which were being made in and about Ekaterinburg to save the Tzar, does it seem possible that his friends, who were numerous in the city and watchful, should permit three soldiers to take him away? Is it not possible that some of the disloyal Bolshevist soldiers, who were accepting bribes and transmitting secret messages to and from the Tzar, were among that guard?

I asked these questions because they came into my mind while I was in Ekaterinburg, and because I asked many Ekaterinburg citizens the same. In reply I received all varieties of answers and various degrees of speculations. The fact is that no one knows, but all have their opinions. Professor Ipatieff maintains that the questions are without justification. The priest thinks that the Tzar was "saved." The nun thinks he was killed afterward. The valet states the same. The investigating commission is divided. The Allied consuls don't know. And still there is the testimony of a prominent Russian merchant of Ekaterinburg that he saw the Tzar and his family in the private office of the railroad depot master on July 20!

Ekaterinburg is divided. Since the latter part of July, for seven months the city and surrounding country has been searched, and no remains of the bodies, no authentic traces of the family, have been found.

Some day, when it is possible for investigators to go into European Russia and question other witnesses, the puzzle may be solved.

Nikolas II, the former Tzar of all the Russians, and his family may be dead. They may still live. Who knows?

But, dead or alive, the whole story of the Tzar's relationship with the Bolsheviki shows the results of the Bolshevist abolition of the courts and the substitution of soldier tribunals. Laws to the Red army are elements of the "old regime," and have been as ruthlessly done away with as have the "intellectuals" and "aristocrats."

Chapter VI

AT CZECHO-SLOVAK HEADQUARTERS

An abandoned army, an army on wheels, an army in the wilderness—all these describe the Czecho-Slovak army in Siberia and Russia, and, although I had seen thousands of Czech and Slovak troops along the Trans-Siberian Railway and in the cities and towns near by, it was at their headquarters in Ekaterinburg that I learned the details of their break with the Bolsheviki, and the story of the beginning and the development of their campaign against the Red army and of their relations with the French, British, and American officials. In the "Tzar's house" Major-General Gaida,[1] commander of their Eastern army, had his headquarters. The National Council and other Czecho-Slovak government bureaus were housed in the "Amerikansky Nomera," once the leading hotel of the city, and about town were the intelligence bureaus and supply departments. Ekaterinburg was a Czecho-Slovak city throughout the time these brave soldiers fought the Bolsheviki and held the Ural front, barring the advance of the Red army into Siberia.

Their campaign in Russia is another tragedy. Courageous patriots, they were, 50,000 of them, who were concentrated in the Ukraine Republic in May, 1918, when at a mass-meeting they voted to leave Russia via Siberia for France to fight with the autonomous army of Czecho-Slovakia against the combined armies of the Central Powers. Happy and free, lovers of liberty and Austro-Hungarian revolutionists, they started across Siberia only to be attacked by the Bolshevist army under orders from

---

[1] Radola Gajda, born as Rudolf Geidl (1892–1948), was a Czech military commander and politician. During the conflict between the Czecho-Slovak Legion and Bolshevik government, Gajda commanded the area between Novonikolaevsk (Novosibirsk) and Irkutsk. His aggressive tactics helped to defeat the Bolshevik forces and connect all units of the legion. The most successful operation was the capture of Perm (December 24, 1918). Gajda enjoyed widespread popularity amongst his troops and throughout the White movement. He was promoted to major general and nicknamed "the Siberian Ataman" and "the Siberian Tiger." He later accepted an invitation from Alexander Kolchak to become a commander in his army, but was dismissed on July 5, 1919. After involving himself in the unsuccessful mutiny of the Socialist Revolutionaries ("esers") against Kolchak (November 17, 1919), he escaped from Siberia and boarded ship to Europe. Later, he participated in Czecho-Slovak politics, was the leader of the Czech Fascist party, but took an anti-German position in the 1930s. After the Munich agreement of 1938, Gajda, as a gesture of defiance, returned all French and British honors and medals.

Leon Trotsky, minister of war in Moscow and chief militarist officer of the Russian "proletariat" army. Attacked by the Bolsheviki, despite the "agreement" which had been signed guaranteeing them unrestricted passage across Russia, they turned, and, like fighting falcons, beat back the Red army, freed Siberia of Bolshevism, and established an eastern front in the Ural Mountains at the request of official representatives of the United States and Allies. The Czecho-Slovaks crossed the trail of Bolshevism in Russia, and, if they had had the support which was promised them, the situation in Russia to-day might—in all probability would be—different. The trail might have been broken in European Russia as it was in Siberia.

When I left the headquarters of Ekaterinburg and the G.H.Q. of the western army under General Syrový[2] at Cheliabinsk in December, the Czecho-Slovak forces were still the mainstay of the "Ural front," although they were being withdrawn gradually, after seven months of continuous, ceaseless fighting, to make room for the new Russian army organized by Admiral Koltshak.

At the offices of the Czecho-Slovak National Council I obtained a copy of the official version of the break between the Czecho-Slovaks and the Bolsheviki. This statement, which was submitted to the Allied governments, is interesting in all its detail because, in addition to the light it throws upon the activities of the two armed forces in Russia, it illustrates pertinently the oft-repeated assertion of the present Bolshevist leaders of European Russia that "agreements" made by the Bolsheviki are lived up to only so long as they serve the purpose of Moscow and Petrograd!

This diplomatic document, entitled "The Czecho-Slovak Incident," follows:

> An authorized and verified translation of the official version of the incident given by the Temporary Executive Committee of the Czecho-Slovak army, into whose hands the direction of military operations and political negotiations was placed by the Assembly of Czecho-Slovak Soldiers at Cheliabinsk, May, 1918. See signature and seal below.
>
> The principle of the neutrality of the Czecho-Slovak army as regards the internal conflicts and battles of Russia was definitely expressed and recognized both in the agreement and treaty made by the Czecho-Slovak National Council[3] with the temporary government of Russia, and in that arrived at

---

[2] Jan Syrový (1888–1970) was a Czecho-Slovak Army four-star general and later prime minister. During the Russian Civil War, Syrový was the chief commander of the Czecho-Slovak corps in Russia. In January 1920, he played some role in giving Admiral Kolchak away to the Irkutsk socialist government, which resulted in Kolchak's execution. He made a career in Czecho-Slovakia and was appointed prime minister during the Munich Crisis in 1938. After World War II, Syrový was sentenced to twenty years in prison (freed in 1960) for alleged collaboration with Hitler, which he refused to admit.

[3] The Czecho-Slovak National Council was an organization founded by Czech and Slovak émigrés during World War I to liberate their homeland from Austria-Hungary. The leader

later with the government of the Ukraine Republic, the Ukraine National Council. To this principle both political and military leaders adhered to firmly, and succeeded in implanting it so deeply in the minds of the soldiers, that, in spite of the attempts made right and left to induce them to break it, not a single section of the army could be induced to do so.

Later, when the Ukraine National Council was defeated and gradually driven out of the governments on the eastern side of the Dnieper and later out of Kieff and the rest of the Ukraine, the commander-in-chief of the Soviet forces, Colonel Muravjof,[4] and Mr. Kocubinsky,[5] the minister of war of the Soviet Government of the Ukraine, recognized the strict armed neutrality of the Czecho-Slovak army. (See official order to the Czecho-Slovak Army Corps No. 12, January 28, 1918, published in the *Czecho-Slovenny Dennik* (Czecho-Slovak Daily), the official organ of the Czecho-Slovak National Council).

Prior to this, when on January 12, 1918, the Ukraine Central Council adopted the "Fourth Universal," which expressed the desire of the Ukraine Government to live on terms of friendship and harmony with all neighboring states, and especially with Austria, it was decided at a meeting of the Czecho-Slovak National Council, at which Professor Masaryk himself presided, to declare the Czecho-Slovak army in all parts of the former Russian state as a part of the autonomous army of the Czecho-Slovaks in France. This proclamation was published on February 10, 1918, after the arrival of the Bolsheviks in Kieff. Soon after that, simultaneously with the success of the peace negotiations of the delegates of the Soviet and Ukraine Governments

---

of the Council, Tomáš Masaryk, traveled to Russia in 1917 and established a Russian branch of the council, which was crucial in organizing the Czecho-Slovak Legion in Russia. During the closing weeks of the war, the Czecho-Slovak National Council was formally upgraded to a provisional government and its members were designated to hold top offices in the First Czecho-Slovak Republic.

[4] Mikhail A. Muravyov (1880–1918), Russian officer, revolutionary, and Soviet military leader. After the February Revolution, he organized volunteer units to continue the war, joined the Left Socialist Revolutionaries, became close to Kerensky but was disaffected with Provisional Government. During the October Revolution, he defended Petrograd against the forces of Kerensky. In January 1918, he led Red Guard units against the Central Rada of Ukraine. After his forces took Kiev, they performed mass terror against the offices of the imperial army and pro-Ukrainian elements. Then his forces fought against the Don Cossack forces of General Kaledin. He had been named commander of the Eastern Front, fighting the Czecho-Slovak Legion; however, early in July 1918, he rebelled, proclaimed peace with Czecho-Slovaks and war against Germany, and was shot during an attempt to arrest.

[5] Yury M. Kotsiubynsky (1896–1937) was a Bolshevik politician, activist, member of the Soviet government in Ukraine, and one of the co-founders of Red Cossacks Army of the Ukrainian Republic.

with the representatives of the Central Powers at Brest-Litovsk, definite steps were taken to arrange for the departure of the Czecho-Slovak army to the French front.

The first movement was to be the concentration of all our forces on the eastern side of the Dnieper, and this was to be carried out on the basis of an agreement made with the Ukraine-Soviet Government, which at one time planned to establish a front against the Germans in the Ukraine. (See *Czecho-Slovenny Dennik*, No. 102.) In the meantime, however, the Germans began to threaten the Czecho-Slovaks from both flanks, and they were obliged to retire into the territory of Great Russia. Again this retirement was made in complete agreement with the Soviet authorities in the Ukraine, an arrangement having been reached with the Czecho-Slovak National Council and the commander of the Soviet forces of the South Russian Republics, Antonov-Ovsejenko.[6] On the basis of this agreement an order was issued to the Czecho-Slovak Army Corps (No. 26, March 16, 1918) to turn over to the Soviet forces all superfluous arms and other military equipment, while Antonov on his part issued an order to all revolutionary forces of the South Russian Republics (No. 92, March 16), from which the following is a literal extract:

"Our comrades of the Czecho-Slovak Army Corps, who fought so bravely and gloriously at Zhitomir, Kieff, Grebyonka, and Bachmac, defending the way to Poltava and Kharkoff, are now leaving Ukraine territory, and are turning over to us a part of their military equipment. The revolutionary army will never forget the fraternal assistance rendered by the Czecho-Slovak Army Corps in the battle of the working people of the Ukraine against the thieving bands of imperialism. The military equipment given up by the Czecho-Slovaks the revolutionary army accepts as a fraternal gift."

On the basis of this agreement, Antonov consented to the departure of the Czecho-Slovaks from the Ukraine, and the staff of the Soviet army of Great Russia also agreed to our departure toward the East, and issued the necessary orders to the railway officials who were to attend to the details of the transport on behalf of the Soviet Government. Agreement to our departure from Russia via Vladivostok was also expressed in telegrams sent by Lenin and Trotsky.

In Penza, however, a new set of negotiations was begun. The Council of People's Commissioners in Moscow demanded the complete disarmament

---

[6] Vladimir A. Antonov-Ovseyenko (1883–1938) was a prominent Soviet Bolshevik leader and diplomat. An active participant of the October 1917 revolution, Antonov-Ovseyenko was put in charge of the Red Army in Ukraine and southern Russia on December 21, 1917. The army subsequently captured Kharkov, where Soviet power in Ukraine was proclaimed. In 1918 and 1919, Antonov-Ovseyenko oversaw the defeat of Ukrainian nationalist and White Army forces in Ukraine, ensuring the creation of the Ukrainian Soviet Socialist Republic.

of the Czecho-Slovak army. As the result of the negotiations between the Czecho-Slovaks and the Moscow authorities a telegram was sent from Moscow on March 26 signed by Stalin,[7] in which a certain number of arms were to be left to each echelon to provide protection against attack by counter-revolutionists. In this same telegram the promise was made to help in every way possible the Czecho-Slovaks as long as they remain on Russian territory, provided they maintain an honest and sincere loyalty. Further, the Penza Soviet was ordered to appoint reliable commissioners who were to accompany the Czecho-Slovak echelons to Vladivostok, see that their unity as an organization was unimpaired, and at the same time keep the Council of People's Commissioners informed as to the progress of the transport. In this same telegram it was stated that telegrams with necessary instructions would be sent by the Council of People's Commissioners to all interested parties.

Our army maintained an honest and sincere loyalty. But meanwhile the Soviet Government proceeded to break its word at every step. The Penza Soviet named but one commissioner, who went on ahead to Vladivostok with the first echelon, and there sat down and did nothing. In spite of our repeated requests that other commissioners be named, the Penza authorities absolutely refused to do this, giving as an excuse the lack of suitable men.

The local Soviets one after another put all sorts of obstacles in our path. In Samara, but 400 versts beyond Penza, the local Soviet demanded that we give up more of our arms. These demands were repeated in Ufa, Zlatoust, Omsk, Irkutsk, Tchita, and so on all along the line. The representatives of the Czecho-Slovak National Council, as well as the commanders of the various echelons, used every possible means to prevent the movement of our transports from being halted. In Samara the echelons gave up 138 rifles apiece, leaving only thirty to an echelon; in Omsk each echelon gave up a machine-gun, and in Irkutsk more rifles, until there was left but twenty to an echelon. The negotiations of these loyal Soviets, being in clear opposition to the orders of the Council of People's Commissioners quoted above, often had the appearance of bargaining at the bazaar, and for the Czecho-Slovak soldiers was insulting in the extreme, and had the effect of increasing every day mistrust in the Soviet Government, and in creating a disgust for them which ever grew stronger.

One great reason for this lack of confidence and disgust was the attitude assumed by the Soviet authorities, both local and central, toward those who

---

[7] Joseph V. Stalin (Jughashvili, 1878–1953) was a Georgia-born Soviet revolutionary and political leader. After the Bolshevik Revolution, people's commissioner on nationalities and a member of Bolshevist Party Bureau, then a member of the Revolutionary Military Council. After the death of Lenin, Stalin governed the Soviet Union as its dictator from the mid-1920s until his death in 1953.

had deserted the Czecho-Slovak army and joined the ranks of the Red army. There were not many of them, and they were bad soldiers and men of weak characters. They went over to the Soviet army for mercenary reasons. The munificent salaries, the opportunities to at once assume a position of high rank, fear of the French front, petty personal spite ... these were the motives that led these men to desert their comrades. Our soldiers knew these men, and were glad that they were rid of them. The Soviet Government welcomed these deserters and supported them in every way possible. At Penza the Soviet named some of these deserters as their representatives on the commission which had charge of receiving the arms given up by the Czecho-Slovaks. Other deserters holding documents from the Soviet political or military authorities insisted on coming into the Czecho-Slovak echelons to carry on agitations for the Red army, and to determine if we did not have some arms hidden away.

These deserters, who called themselves social revolutionists, internationalists, and communists, often declared that the holding up of our transport and all the obstacles put in our path were for the purpose of causing dissension within our ranks and gaining as many recruits as possible for the Red army. They declared that this was the reason why the Soviet Government wished a part of the troops to go by way of Archangel; that somewhere on the way in a region where no food was to be had they planned to halt us and compel us from very hunger to join their ranks.

The Czecho-Slovak National Council exercised all its influence with the army to keep them from taking stock in these tales, and to induce them to keep their patience, and as good soldiers not to make any reply to the unfaithfulness and insulting behavior of the Soviet Government.

The atmosphere was therefore highly charged with electricity when the Cheliabinsk incident occurred. At Cheliabinsk, besides the Czecho-Slovak eshelons, there stood several trains filled with prisoners on their way home to Austria and Germany. The relations between the Czecho-Slovak soldiers and these prisoners was good, as it was uniformly whenever they came in contact with one another on the road. The soldiers did carry on an agitation amongst them against Austrian and German imperialism, and laughed at them for returning to serve once more under Austrian and German officers. But at the same time they felt sorry for them, and often shared their food with them. On May 14, one of these prisoners threw a piece of iron out of a train that was just leaving, wounding one of the Czecho-Slovak soldiers. The soldiers immediately surrounded the car from which the iron had been thrown, and demanded that the guilty prisoner be given up to them. When this was done, they immediately killed him. In the course of the investigation of this affair, the local Soviet called as witnesses the members of the guard which had been on duty at the station. But instead of hearing their testimony, they put these men under arrest. A deputation which was later sent by the Czecho-Slovaks to demand the release of the guard was likewise put under arrest. This illegal imprisonment of their fellows was more than the soldiers in the echelons at Cheliabinsk could stand, and, led by their commanders, they marched into the city, released their imprisoned comrades, and returned immediately to their trains. No attack by force was made, the whole proceeding was conducted in an orderly and quiet manner, hardly a shot being fired.

The local Soviet proceeded to describe this action on the part of the Czecho-Slovaks in lurid colors in telegrams sent out in all directions. Believing the information thus imparted to them, the Council of People's Commissioners issued an order to completely disarm all Czecho-Slovak echelons. At the same time orders were issued to the Soviets of all cities where our echelons were then located to proceed against them by force. Accordingly, almost on the same day the Soviet forces, composed for the most part of Magyar and German prisoners of war, fell upon the Czecho-Slovak echelons, which were almost entirely disarmed. At the attack made upon echelons of the Sixth Czecho-Slovak Regiment at Marianovka, near Omsk, the Czecho-Slovaks suffered losses amounting to ten killed and ten severely wounded. The staff of the First Regiment, whose echelon was attacked at Zlatoust, defended itself with stones against the machine-guns and rifles of the Bolsheviks, but lost six men killed and ten severely wounded, and was compelled to make its way across the Urals on foot. Similarly the staff of the Second Artillery Brigades was attacked at Imokentjeska,[8] near Irkutsk, when they had already given up their arms. Machine-guns placed in the windows of the railway-station opened up a heavy fire upon the Czecho-Slovaks, but in spite of the fact that the men had no arms except a few hand-grenades, they succeeded in clearing the station of Bolshevist forces and in capturing their machine-guns. A fourth attack was made at Serodobsk, south from Penza. All of these attacks were made on May 27 and the following two or three days immediately after the issuance of the order from Moscow to disarm the Czecho-Slovaks at any cost.

Prior to these events, but after the first incident at Cheliabinsk, the Assembly of Czecho-Slovak Soldiers met for its annual meeting and decided that in view of the tense situation existing between the Soviet Government and the Czecho-Slovaks, vigorous measures must be taken immediately in order to secure the rapid passage of the trains toward Vladivostok. Accordingly delegates were dispatched to all echelons with instructions to proceed ahead at any cost, and an executive committee was appointed to see that these plans were carried out. The executive committee in formulating its plans counted

---

[8] Must be Innokentievka, a village near Irkutsk (now part of the city).

## AT CZECHO-SLOVAK HEADQUARTERS

on the probability of an armed conflict with the Bolshevik forces, but felt confident that they would be able to force their way through to Vladivostok in spite of any resistance that might be offered by the Soviet forces. The reason for their confidence in the successful outcome of their new plan lay not only in the well-known weakness of the Red army, but also in the fact of their knowledge that the people at large were sick and tired of the Bolshevist rule, and that therefore they would not turn a hand to help the Bolshevists in any possible conflict with the Czecho-Slovaks. Furthermore, the Czecho-Slovaks, from their intimate knowledge of political conditions throughout Russia, judged that the feeling against the Bolshevists was strongest in the very regions where most of their echelons were located, namely in the Urals and western Siberia. The executive committee, therefore, in planning their action, took cognizance of these facts and planned to take advantage both of the weakness of the Red army and of the strong popular feeling against the Bolsheviks to force their way through to the East. That their action would be accompanied by or followed by the overthrow of the Soviet Government and the establishment of a new government in western Siberia never entered into their calculations, although later, when the fall of the Soviet Government was an accomplished fact, the Czecho-Slovaks were the first to welcome the new government and to lend it their moral and armed support.

The plans of the executive committee for the forcing of the passage to Vladivostok had not been thoroughly worked out when the events of May 25 brought things to an issue. By its cowardly attacks upon the Czecho-Slovak echelons the Soviet Government began a warfare against the Czecho-Slovaks, the object of which was, according to the command of Trotsky, to disarm and disband the Czecho-Slovak army corps, place them in prison-camps, and there try to enlist them in the ranks of the Red army or to put them out at hard labor. In short, they wished to destroy entirely the Czecho-Slovak army, that important moral support of the revolutionary movement of the Czecho-Slovakia and the other oppressed nationalities of Austria-Hungary.

After the first order to disarm completely the Czecho-Slovak echelons, there still remained the possibility of diplomatic negotiations. But after the attack made upon the echelons on May 25–26, the soul of each soldier cried out for revenge for the blood of their innocent comrades. And so there was nothing left but war, a war which has already resulted in the seizure of almost the entire Siberian Railway by the Czecho-Slovaks and the fall of the Soviet Government all along the line.

The Czecho-Slovaks are convinced that the action taken against them by the Soviet Government was dictated from Berlin through the German ambassador in Moscow, Count Mirbach.⁹ This conviction is based on the opinion, very widely spread throughout Russia, that the Soviet Government are the paid agents of Germany. This conviction grew stronger as repeated attempts were made to disarm the soldiers, for the men could not but see in this disarmament real danger, knowing as they did that the Central Soviet Government was really powerless, and that in most places the chief strength of their armed forces consisted in armed German and Magyar prisoners. For example, in Omsk the commander of the forces of the Internationalists, composed of prisoners, was an Austro-Hungarian officer, a Magyar by race. This officer, Ligeti by name,¹⁰ had all the Czecho-Slovaks and other Slavs who were serving in the Red army disarmed, so that Omsk was really in the hands of this Austro-Hungarian officer. In Ishim the Red army was composed entirely of Magyars. In Petropavlovsk the men who came to negotiate with the Czecho-Slovaks in the guise of Czech communists afterward proved to be the representatives of the German section of the Internationalists. The commanding officers of the Red army were in many cases Germans and Magyars, judging by the orders and the curses in those tongues that were heard on all sides during the battles. When the echelon was attacked near Irkutsk, there was heard the command: "Schiessen."

The conviction that the Soviet Government wished to destroy our forces was also strengthened by the constant holding up of the transport, for which no adequate cause could be found. At first the delay was blamed upon the Amur railway, where transportation was reported to have been halted. The advance of Semenov upon Irkutsk was given as an excuse. But the Czecho-Slovaks soon learned that transportation on the Amur railway had been soon resumed, while the advance of Semenov existed more in the imagination of the Soviet authorities than in reality. Amongst other excuses given was that of a lack of locomotives on the Amur road, but all the while German prisoners were being merrily transported toward the west, and there were plenty of locomotives for them.

---

⁹ Count Wilhelm von Mirbach-Harff (1871–1918) was a German diplomat. He was appointed German ambassador to Russia in April 1918 and was assassinated on July 6, 1918, at the German embassy in Moscow by two members of Socialist Revolutionary party at the request of the Central Committee of the Left Socialist Revolutionaries, who tried to incite a war between Russia and Germany.

¹⁰ Károly Sándor Ligeti (1890–1919), Magyar revolutionary participant in the Russian Civil War, poet, head of the Hungarian party organization at the Federation of Foreign Groups of the Bolshevist party, and commander of a Hungarian international squad. He was shot by Kolchak soldiers in June 1919 near Omsk.

On April 20 the people's commissioner for foreign affairs, Tchitcherin,[11] sent the following telegram to the Siberian Soviets: "Transport German prisoners as rapidly as possible toward the west. Hold back the Czecho-Slovak echelons."

It was only after a long and tedious session of negotiations that there was secured an order for the renewal of our transport toward Vladivostok. One day, about May 15, a member of the Czecho-Slovak National Council was officially informed that the trains would now be moved. On the very next day, however, he learned through private conversation with the railway officials that another order had been issued in Irkutsk to stop the movements of the Czecho-Slovak trains. He finally learned that this command had issued from the commander of the Soviet forces at Irkutsk, General von Taube,[12] a German, whose adjutant had issued the order by "mistake."

The Seventh Czecho-Slovak Regiment captured a German engineer, who had been commandeered from Moscow to destroy the bridges and tunnels on the railroad beyond the Baikal. In Troitsk the commanders of the Soviet artillery were all Austrian officers.

From all these facts even an uninterested onlooker may picture to himself the news which had been spread about the Czecho-Slovak army. Inasmuch as the warfare is still being carried on on all sides, it has not been possible to gather all the evidence from the Soviet offices, and unfortunately in many cases the Bolsheviks succeeded in carrying away with them or destroying all their papers before our men took possession. Later, however, there will be certainly found many proofs of the truth of the assertion made by the president of the Cheliabinsk Soviet and the military commissioner in that town, who informed our representatives in confidence, shortly before the outbreak of hostilities, that the cause of all the acts against the Czecho-Slovaks was the German ambassador at Moscow.

Translation certified to be accurate and is hereby authorized.
(Signature) (Seal) Prozatimni Vykonny Vybor.[13]

---

[11] Georgy V. Chicherin (1872–1936) was a Bolshevist revolutionary and Soviet politician. He served as people's commissar for foreign affairs in the Soviet government from March 1918 to 1930.

[12] Baron Alexander A. von Taube (1864–1919), nicknamed "Siberian Red General," was an imperial Russian general from a family of Baltic Germans, and one of the first generals who supported the Bolshevik Revolution. In spring 1918, he was appointed chief of staff of the Red Army in Siberia, and organized a resistance to Czecho-Slovak corps on the west and Ataman Grigory M. Semenov on the east. He was captured by White soldiers in September 1918, and died in jail in Ekaterinburg in January 1919.

[13] Provisional Executive Committee.

The Czechs were opposed, however, not only by the Red army but by prisoners of war of the Central Empires. Both Germany and Austria attempted in April to mobilize their citizens who were in Russia in order to bring them back to central Europe to take part in the fighting on the Western front. At various depots, which the Czecho-Slovak armies took over during their march across Siberia, they found copies of telegrams of which the following is an example:

Telegram from Berlin No. 772,650, 1918.

To all German, Austrian, and Hungarian prisoners of war in Russia:
1. Every one who distinguished himself during his captivity by some work for the benefit of his country has the right to look for a betterment of his conditions.
2. All who obey this order will receive after their return home a month's furlough and will be sent to the front only after four months, if it is necessary.
3. He who is not working in Russia for his country, will after his return be severely punished. It is an indisputable fact that it is better to work for our own culture than abroad.
4. He who behaves unworthily in captivity and betrays his country will be punished with all severity. For the discovery of traitors 300,000 marks have been appropriated. Officers who have not received their salaries will get them upon their return home.
5. Special officers will care for the return of prisoners. I order all commandants of trains to trouble themselves in providing quick transportation.

(Signed)
William II.
Charles I.
Berlin, April 28, 1918.

The Czecho-Slovak version of the incidents which led to war with the Bolsheviki differ from the explanations given by the various Soviets. For instance, in the railroad offices of the trans-Baikal railway was found the following statement, No. 2,640:

From Russia to Vladivostok are moving sixteen echelons of Czecho-Slovaks, at the disposal of America, ostensibly to be sent to France. In view of the hostile attitude of international imperialism and threats of a foreign landing at Vladivostok, the central executive committee of Soviets in Siberia considers the concentration there of these forces dangerous and inadmissible. It has therefore applied to the Omsk military committee with the demand that the further movement of these troops be stopped until there is further communication with the Soviet of the Peoples' Commission in Moscow.

To our question Comrade Stalin answered in the name of the Soviet of the Peoples' Commission as follows:

"In the name of the Russian Republic there can be no other armed detachments than those of the Soviets, and he advised the local Soviet to disarm them. The central Siberian Government cannot be satisfied with this decision. They protested again to the Peoples' Commission and demanded that the echelons be sent to Archangel, because the concentration in Vladivostok, where there are large stocks of arms and many thousands of unarmed soldiers, will place them at the disposal of international imperialists, and may turn out to be the decisive blow to the Soviet authority in Siberia, especially at the moment of the advance now being prepared by Semenov. Therefore, the central Siberian Government categorically demands of all local Soviets and railway servants the immediate disarmament and suspension of the movement of the Czecho-Slovak echelons. Their arms must be delivered up in full to the staffs of the military district. The soldiers must be detained where they are disarmed until the question of their destination is settled. We have again put this question to the Soviet of Peoples' Commission.

"When will you answer our statement about the impossibility of sending the Czecho-Slovaks to Vladivostok? We categorically demand that they be sent over Archangel.

(Signed)

President, Central Siberian Executive Committee, Yakolev,[14] Secretary Klinov."

This shows the difficulty which arose in Siberia as well as in Russia because of the fact that there was no responsible central government, and only local governments scattered throughout the country each one with different ideas about the conduct of national affairs. That there should eventually be a conflict between the Czecho-Slovaks and the Russian Soviets was obvious because of this very fact that a Soviet in Siberia would not be bound by what the Soviet in European Russia might do.

The Bolsheviki, however, have always maintained that the difficulties with the Czecho-Slovaks arose, not from any faults of the Bolsheviki, but because of an unwarranted attack by several of the Czecho-Slovak echelons upon local councils. There

---

[14] Nikolai N. Yakovlev (1886–1918), Bolshevist political exile before the revolution; chairman of the Soviet of Workers' and Soldiers' Deputies in Tomsk; chairman of the Central Executive Committee of the Siberian Soviets.

is extant the following document signed by the People's Commissariat for Military Affairs and Member of the Supreme Military Council Podvoisky:[15]

> Supreme Military Inspector of the People's Commissariat for Military Affairs. Dated Zlatoust, May 30, 1918. Railway car of the Supreme Military Inspector.
> The Czecho-Slovak echelons sent by the Soviet authorities to Vladivostok on the Zlatoust-Cheliabinsk line, insolently raised a mutiny against the Russian Soviet Republic. They have thereby placed themselves in the ranks of the greatest enemies of the republic, and no mercy will be shown them if they do not return to reason.
> Endowed by the workmen's and peasants' government with plenal powers in military matters I order the Czecho-Slovak echelons confronted with a bloody penalty of being shot in masses by the Soviet troops, to leave their echelon and take up quarters in barracks, as directed by the local military authorities, until further instructions, which will follow on completion of the labors of the mixed commission, and with the representatives of the French military commission about which all the Czecho-Slovak echelons have been informed by the Czecho-Slovak representative, Professor Max, whose telegram is enclosed herewith.

The telegram, which was enclosed, was as follows:

> Iz to Moscow No. 702. To commanders of Czecho-Slovak Echelons, President of the conference, Military Commission of Cheliabinsk.
> In view of the regrettable occurrences, the conflicts between the Czecho-Slovak echelons and the local Soviet authorities, the Czecho-Slovak National Council in order to avoid such deplorable cases orders all commanders of Czecho-Slovak echelons to deliver, without debate, all their arms without exception to the official representatives of the local Soviets. The duty of assuring the safety of the Czechs rests entirely upon the Soviet institution of the Russian Federal Republic. Whoever does not obey this order will be considered a mutineer and outlaw.

---

[15] Nikolai I. Podvoisky (1880–1948) was a Russian revolutionary. From November 1917 to March 1918, he was people's commissioner of war affairs. From January 1918, he was chairman of the All-Russian collegium for organization of the Red Army. From March 1918, he was a member of Supreme Military Council, then chairman of the Highest military inspection, and a member of the Revolutionary Military Council.

May 21, 1918, P. Max,[16] Manager of Operations, Section of Military Commission.

In the meantime, however, the Bolsheviki made extensive preparations for an attack upon the Czechs. The feeling between the two sides was very bitter and all that was needed was an incident to start the war. Even the Bolshevist version of the incident which brought on the war shows that the actions of the Czecho-Slovaks were due directly to attacks made upon one of their echelons. Leon Trotsky, the Bolshevist minister of war,[17] sent his attorney Sedkovkin to the Moscow telegraph office to talk with the district military commissioner Sedlutsky at Cheliabinsk. Their conversation, which was written out by the operator at Cheliabinsk, who received and transmitted the questions and answers, was as follows:

> By direct wire Moscow-Cheliabinsk. Speaking from Moscow Trotsky's attorney, M. Sedkovkin. Speaking from Cheliabinsk District Military Commissar Sedlutsky.
> With you is speaking Sedkovkin, authorized by Comrade Trotsky. Kindly tell me all you know about the Czecho-Slovak formation and the object of their action. Explain everything in detail.
> On May 16 there arrived in Cheliabinsk station an echelon of Magyar prisoners. According to data, a stone or stove-leg was thrown into a truck of Czecho-Slovaks. A fight took place between the Czechs and Germans, enhanced by their national antipathies, as a result of which one Magyar was killed. The next day a delegation of Czechs went to the committee of investigation in order to explain the murder, which delegation was arrested. In connection therewith the Czechs became excited and at six o'clock on the evening of May 17, having armed, they entered the town, occupied all corners and streets, placed a company at the building of the Executive Committee and left parts of companies on other streets. Beside that, they occupied the station and arrested there the commandant and several commissaries. They did not enter the Executive Committee. They presented a demand for the immediate release of those arrested. I was personally among them, and they

---

[16] Prokop Maxa (1883–1961) was a Czech and Czecho-Slovak diplomat, politician, and organizer of Czecho-Slovak legions. He was a professor at the Business Academy and an ally of Tomáš Masaryk. During the First World War, he organized Czecho-Slovak legions in Russia and supported Masaryk's conception of the Czecho-Slovak state. From 1917 to 1918, he was the vice chairman of the Czecho-Slovak National Council in St. Petersburg. Later, Maxa was a deputy of the Czecho-Slovakian Assembly, and represented Czecho-Slovakia as an ambassador in the Netherlands (1920–21), Poland (1921–24), and Bulgaria (1931–39).

[17] Leon Trotsky, born Lev D. Bronstein (1879–1940), was a Marxist revolutionary, theorist, and Soviet politician. After March 1918, he was people's commissar of army and navy affairs.

continually demanded the release of the arrested ones, and when I explained to them that their action was directed against the Soviet authorities, they declared that they were not acting against the Soviet, but only wanted the release of the arrested delegation. We categorically demanded that they go away in order to avoid bloodshed, for we might lose control of our Red army, and they might start firing, but it led to nothing. To avoid bloodshed, and in view of the discipline of the Czecho-Slovaks, and the unreadiness of our Red army, it was decided to release those arrested. After this they returned, singing, to their cars. Our Red army was ready, and occupied part of the town behind the river. At the time of the occupation of the town the Czechs disarmed the guard of the Military Commissary, rummaged among the papers, broke the telephone wire, stole a part of the arms, disarmed a part of the Red Guards, and took from them two machine-guns. They instituted searches of pedestrians, took away their arms, and even the revolver of the President of the Executive Committee. On the part of the Czechs there were three killed and two wounded by provocatory shots; on our side there no losses, for it was forbidden to shoot. There are altogether with us about 8,400 Czecho-Slovaks, of whom 1,600 are armed and they have six machine-guns.

The next day martial law was proclaimed and order was restored.

On May 18 we invited the Czechs to surrender the stolen arms, and they gave up the rifles already taken from the Red Guard, and two machine-guns, but as regards most of the stolen arms, the commanding officers promised to return same but asked leave to wait a day or two, as the mass of soldiers was insubordinate and did not trust them, since, according to pledges given by the Soviet of Peoples' Commissaries, they were to travel to Vladivostok but are detained here, and if they were forced to give up their arms now, while still in a state of excitement, they would not obey the order. We wanted to disarm them, but have not sufficient strength, and they are, in addition very watchful. Local government and district Soviets and Ekaterinburg cannot give forces, as they have been sent from us to Orenburg. It is desirable, by all means, to move the Czechs to Siberia, for in future a halt of over a month in the echelons, not knowing when they will go on, in the end may cause in their minds a violent fermentation, and to get entangled with them, when the Cossack action is not yet liquidated, would be undesirable.

After their outburst they posted proclamations, stating that they will not oppose the Soviet authority, and that they had acted because we had arrested them wrongfully.

At present all is quiet. At Ekaterinburg it has been decided not to disarm them, in view of lack of sufficient forces, which have been sent to Orenburg and which await instructions from the Soviet of Peoples' Committee. That is all I can say at present. Tomorrow will inform you more in detail, if necessary, as I have perhaps omitted something to-day. The whole matter is under investigation.

Good, thanks. If you have any information, inform us. Keep in touch with us. Arrange regular attendance at the telegraph.

Good, will inform you of everything. Good-by.

Correct translation<br>
Adjutant of Second Czecho-Slovak Shooting Regiment,<br>
I. Mesar.

It was after this conversation that Trotsky sent the following telegram to all Bolshevist representatives along the Trans-Siberian Railway:

All Soviets on the railways are obliged, on pain of grave responsibility, to disarm the Czecho-Slovaks. Each Czecho-Slovak on whom is found arms on the railway line is to be shot on the spot. Each echelon, in which a single armed man is found, must be thrown off the trucks, and the men confined in a prisoner-camp. Local military commissariats are enjoined to execute this order at once. Any delay will be equivalent to dishonorable treachery, and will call down on the culprit severest punishment. Simultaneously, reliable troops, who are commissioned to teach the mutineers a lesson, are being sent against the rear of the Czech echelons. Those Czecho-Slovaks who lay down their arms will be treated as brothers; every support will be given them. Trotsky.

Siberia and central Russia became almost immediately the scene of military operations between the two contending forces. The Bolsheviki, who were masters at propaganda because it was propaganda which had been their main weapon for a decade before the revolution, placarded Russia with appeals from local Soviets to peasants, workmen, and Cossacks. An appeal dated May 28, 1918, and posted on Omsk is an indication of the nature of the propaganda carried on in Russia by the Bolsheviki. It reads as follows:

Comrades: Surely not because of the pretty eyes of the compromising Socialists and the upstarts from the ranks of the Co-operatives have the Japanese and Czecho-Slovak leaders, who are in the service of the French bourgeoisie, thrown their detachments into the fight with the workmen and peasants authority. The imperialistic bourgeoisie for friendship, gratuitously, does nothing! It has its own interests. In its own interest, Franco-Japanese capital seizes Siberia just as the German capitalists have seized the Ukraine. The same object is pursued by the Franco-Japanese capitalists. The riches of Siberia are necessary to them.

But simultaneously it is imperative to them to lay a steel grasp on the people of Siberia, and with machine-gun fire to force the working class, the peasants, and Cossacks of Siberia, to again enter the ranks of the imperialistic army, to again litter with their corpses the field of battle, and to again become the marionettes of capital.

Indifferent attitude to the position of the Soviet authority leads you to this. We summon you to protect the Soviet authority.

Not for a moment should you forget that before you are only two ways: Either resistance to the adventures, a desperate resistance, and the strengthening of the Soviet authority; or the yoke of the Skoropadskie-Sazonoffs, lackeys of the imperialistic bourgeoisie, and fresh colossal sacrifices of blood for strange interests, for the interests of the still militaristic bourgeoisie. There is no other way out!

During all of this time the Allies were playing tag with the Bolsheviki and dilly-dallying with Russian policies. Although the representatives of the Allies, meeting in Rome in the spring of 1918, had indicated their sympathies for the oppressed nations of Austria-Hungary, they had not advanced to the point where they were willing to take sides in Russia in the dispute between the Czecho-Slovaks and the Bolsheviki. Officially the Czechs were under the command of the French, because France was the first to finance the Czecho-Slovak revolutionary movement and because French officers were the first to assist the Czechs in Russia. At the very beginning of the difficulties in the neighborhood of Cheliabinsk, official representatives of the Allies were involved. Even after the fight at Cheliabinsk and in Omsk the Czecho-Slovaks had not changed their plan of going on to Vladivostok and France, but because of the unfortunate attacks by the Bolsheviki a new agreement had to be drawn in order to guarantee the Czecho-Slovak forces unrestricted travel to Vladivostok. The Czechs believed that the attitude of the Red Guard was due to the influence of the Germans.

At the very beginning of the controversy the Omsk Soviets appealed to United States Consul Thompson for support.[18] Mr. Thompson pointed out that he could not confer with his government because the Bolsheviki had prohibited the use of cipher telegrams, despite the assurance of Consul-General Poole, which he had obtained from Foreign Minister Tchitcherin. The Soviet, however, again requested the American consul to appear at a conference between the Soviet and the French-Czech delegates at Isilkul.[19] At this meeting, however, the lack of confidence on both sides in any

---

[18] Alfred Ray Thomson (1889–1943), US consul, served under the US Consul General Maddin Summers gathering information in Samara, Omsk, and Irkutsk. Later he was consul general in Dresden (1938).

[19] Isilkul is a railway station west of Omsk.

agreement was so evident that the conference could not possibly come to a successful conclusion. Even Major Guinet,[20] who was representing the French Government, was so in doubt about the attitude of his government and the Allies, that he sent the following telegram to the Czechs:

> Your action forces the French Mission to wash its hands of this affair. It will be a disgrace for the Czechs to become involved in Russia's difficulties. If the Czechs persist in their activities everything must end between them and the French Government. The Czechs must take no action whatever until the French Mission arrives in Isilkul.

The conference was continued for two or three days, but the difficulty which developed here was the one which was present in every phase of the negotiations in Russia. The Allies were not united upon either a Russian policy or upon their attitude toward the Czecho-Slovaks, and while the French representative informed the Czechs on the night of May 31 that the French Government would "wash its hands of this affair," he stated the following day to the Bolsheviki delegates at the conference:

> The Czechs are courageous troops. Armed, they know they can attain their end, and complete their journey. While en route they have no desire to shed blood. Their aim is to reach France. Concessions from both sides are imperative. You possess some strength and they possess some strength. Safety is necessary to them and must be guaranteed. At present it is only a question of time. It is premature to talk of the surrender of arms. This question must be referred to the coming conference at Cheliabinsk. Otherwise the Czechs will take Omsk, and arms in hand will secure their onward progress.

While the Soviet adjourned to discuss the question and decide upon their action the French and Czech delegates received a telegram from Isilkul ordering them to leave. Before the meeting could be adjourned both sides agreed that the truce should remain only until both sides were notified.

Thus the war was on. The Bolsheviki were united. The Czechs were united. The Bolsheviki had the support of the Germans and Austrians while the Czecho-Slovaks, for the moment, were without moral assistance or political support or the military co-operation of any of the Allies. It was not until June 22, three weeks after their break with the Soviet, that the Czechs were given their first intimation that they might rely on the assistance of the Allies. On that date Major Guinet received the fol-

---

[20] Alfons Guinet, captain of French artillery who got a brevet promotion to the rank of major during his stay in Russia. In April 1918, he was sent to Samara and further east by the head of the French military mission.

lowing message, which had been brought by courier from Perm to Cheliabinsk, dated May 18, and which he delivered to the Czecho-Slovak National Council:

> The French ambassador informs Major Guinet that he can thank the Czecho-Slovaks for their action, this in the name of all the Allies who have decided to intervene the end of June, and the Czech army and the French Mission, form the advance-guard of the Allied army. Recommendations will follow concerning political and military points with respect to occupation and organization.

One month later the acting consul of the United States in Omsk received a cipher message forwarded from the United States Consulate in Samara. This telegram, dated July 22, 1918, read:

> Cipher despatch from consul-general assumed, Moscow, to this office (Samara) dated June 18: The last official news. Quote: You may inform the Czechoslovak leaders, confidentially, that pending further notice the Allies will be glad from a political point of view to have them hold their present position. On the other hand, they should not be hampered in meeting the military exigency of the situation. It is desirable first of all that they should secure the control of the Trans-Siberian Railway and second, if this is assumed, at the same time possible retain control over the territory which they now dominate. Inform the French representative that the French consul-general joins in these instructions, end quote.

Two days later the United States consul-general at Irkutsk telegraphed the American vice-consul in Omsk the following:

> Gray, Amconsul, Omsk:
>
> I consider this wise in view of the fact that the Allies wish the Czechs to be the main backbone and support of Allied action in Siberia and Russia against Germany.
>
> Harris.[21]

The Czecho-Slovak organization was as hopeful as it was enthusiastic when these messages were received. Despite the plans which had been made for the journey to France, they were willing to remain in Russia to fight the Bolsheviki, not alone

---

[21] Ernest L. Harris was a US consul general in Irkutsk. L. S. Gray was a US vice consul in Omsk, whose appointment was part of the State Department's plan to send Americans already in Russia to serve as consuls in eight Siberian towns.

## AT CZECHO-SLOVAK HEADQUARTERS

because the Red army had attacked their echelons, not alone because, in this manner, they could fight Germany and Austria-Hungary, but because they believed that the Allies would be indebted to them and support their aspirations for the establishment of Czecho-Slovakia as an independent republic.

But they were doomed to disappointment because the messages which had been transmitted to the National Council by the American representatives were not authorized by the Department of State in Washington. President Wilson had written a confidential memorandum for the department, outlining the American attitude toward Russia and, in this document, which has never been published, the President states definitely the opposition of the United States to military intervention. Both Consul-Generals Poole and Harris, however, received these instructions from Ambassador Francis, who sent them by courier from Vologda to Moscow during the early summer of 1918, but the United States envoy was not authorized by Washington to do this.

Through this diplomatic confusion the Czecho-Slovaks were promised assistance which the United States Government never intended and was never ready to give.

## Chapter VII
## THE BIRTH OF A GOVERNMENT IN RUSSIA

Throughout the summer, from June to September, the armies of the Czecho-Slovaks fought their way back and forth over Siberia, and by fall all of the local Soviets in Siberia had been overthrown: the Bolshevik power had been destroyed, and from Samara and Perm to Vladivostok the ghost of Bolshevism had disappeared. This the brave armies of the Czecho-Slovaks had accomplished, depending entirely upon their own physical strength and upon the supplies which they found in Russia and which they captured from the Red army. There is no territorial advance in the annals of the war as dramatic and rapid as was that of the Czecho-Slovak revolutionary army in that vast ex-empire of Siberia. These 50,000 Czecho-Slovak soldiers had established an organization in every important city along the great Trans-Siberian Railway. They maintained order; assumed direction of the railroads without interfering with any local government except those avowedly Bolshevists.

Thus, at the beginning of September, Siberia was free from the Red rule, and we find the people of that country getting together with the object of electing an All-Russian Government. Various governments had been in process of formation in the neighborhood of Samara and the Ural Mountains, Tomsk and Vladivostok, but these obviously did not trust each other, and the demand for a central representative government was so great that delegates from all of the governments in Siberia, including the Siberian Government itself, met in the city of Ufa and elected an All-Russian directorate with five ministers and five assistants. The prime minister was Afkzentieff and his assistants were Bolderoff, Astroff, Chaikovski, and Vologodsky.[1] The direc-

---

[1] This is the full list of the five members of the Provisional All-Russian Government, or Directoria:
  Nikolai D. Avksentiev (1878–1943) was a leading member of the Russian Socialist-Revolutionary Party (PSR). He was an émigré from 1907 to 1917, and in 1917, he was minister of the interior in the second coalitional Provisional Government, chairman of the Council of Russian Republic ("Pre-parliament"), and deputy of the Constituent Assembly. After the Bolshevist Revolution of October 1917, he became the leader of the Constituent Assembly Defense Committee and later, the head of the Provisional All-Russian Government organized in Omsk by former members of the Constituent Assembly in September 1918. On November 18, 1918, Avksentiev was arrested by Admiral Kolchak and forced to emigrate. Beginning in 1918, he was an active member of the Russian emigration; in 1940, he moved to the US.

torate took over full power of the various governments and decided to make Omsk the new capital of Russia until they could move to either Moscow or Petrograd, because the object of the conference at Ufa was to found a new Russian Government, which, with the support of the Czecho-Slovaks and the Allies, might ultimately succeed the Bolsheviki government which was at that time co-operating with the German organization in the East. The backbone of this new government was the Siberian Government which had been organized the latter part of June and which had selected July 4, the American Independence Day, as the date for their declaration of the temporary independence of Siberia. This document is important because of its historical interest, because the formation of this All-Russian Government was the only one in Russia since the March 1917 revolution, which could have been considered as having a mandate direct from the people. It is also important because it shows the beginning of a new government, the development of which was prevented entirely through the lack of interest and support from the Allied governments. A translation of the declaration follows:

Translation of the Declaration of the Temporary Independence of Siberia

The Siberian Provisional Government, assuming plenary power in the land after the expulsion of the Bolshevik usurpers, in line with other important tasks, considers it imperative to bring Siberia out of that undefined situation in which it was in consequence of the dispersal by the Bolsheviks of the Sibe-

---

Vasily Boldyrev (1875–1933) was a Russian military commander, politician, and general; he was a member of the Provisional All-Russian Government and military commander of its forces. After the Kolchak coup, he renounced his position as commander and traveled to Japan and the Russian Far East. He took part in the government of the Far Eastern Republic in 1920–21. After the capture of Vladivostok by the Red Army on November 5, 1922, he was arrested. In prison, he declared his willingness to serve the Soviet government and was released. He stayed in Soviet Russia and was executed in 1933.

Nikolai I. Astrov (1868–1934) was a Russian politician, Constitutional Democrat, Moscow city head (March–June 1917), leader of the All-Russian Union of Cities, and deputy of the Constituent Assembly. He was a member of the Provisional All-Russian Government (while, in fact, absent from Siberia, having been in southern Russia as a political advisor for General Denikin). He emigrated in 1920 to Czecho-Slovakia and founded Russian historical archives abroad (Prague Archives).

Nikolai Chaikovsky (1851–1926) was a Russian revolutionary and member of the Narodnik movement in the second half of the nineteenth century. From 1874 to 1907, he was in emigration in the United States and Great Britain, then returned to Russia. In 1917, he was elected a member of Constituent Assembly, and in 1918, he became a member of the Provisional All-Russian Government; he was the head of the anti-Bolshevist Provisional Government of the Northern Region under Anglo-American expeditionary forces. He participated in the Versailles Peace Conference, and died in England.

rian Provincial Duma and the continuation of the Bolshevik domination of European Russia.

The Siberian Provisional Government is clearly conscious that every delay in deciding the question of defining the state nature of Siberia is very pernicious in its consequences in connection with the present international situation; but, notwithstanding this, it would not take upon itself the responsibility of defining the future fate of its fatherland, if it did not have in this respect an authoritative indication on the part of the Siberian Provincial Duma, as expressed in the latter's declaration of January 27, 1918.

Supported solely by this declaration, in which the Siberian Provincial Duma definitely shows itself in favor of granting Siberia the full attributes of a state, the Provincial Government now holds it possible, in view of the acuteness of the moment, to take upon itself the task of settling this question without waiting for a new convocation of the Duma.

Upon this basis, and in view of the fact that the attributes of the Russian state do not exist as such, a considerable portion of the Russian territory being in the actual possession of the Central Powers, and another portion seized by the Bolshevik usurpers of the people's rule, the Siberian Provisional Government solemnly declares to all the world that henceforth it alone, together with the Siberian Provincial Duma, is responsible for the destiny of Siberia, and announces full freedom of independent relations with foreign Powers, and also declares that henceforth no other authority than the Siberian Provincial Government can act on the territory of Siberia or undertake obligations in the name of same.

At the same time the Siberian Provincial Government considers it is its sacred duty to state that the convocation of the All-Siberian Constituent Assembly, to which it will hand over its authority as is its unswerving intention, and to the earliest accomplishment of this will devote all its strength.

Nevertheless, the Siberian Provincial Government holds it absolutely necessary to declare not less solemnly, that it does not consider Siberia to be forever torn from those territories which as a whole composed the state of Russia, and believes that all efforts must be directed to the reconstruction of Russia as a state. The Provisional Government considers that, when this high aim is happily achieved, the character of the future relations between Siberia and European Russia will be determined by the All-Siberian and All-Russian Constituent Assemblies. Bearing this in mind the Siberian Provisional Government enters upon its responsible work with the firm assurance that it will be supported therein by all the patriotic and thinking elements of the country.

The President of the Council of Ministers and Minister for Foreign Affairs,

VOLOGODSKY;

Minister of Interior, KROUTOFSKY;[2]
Minister of Justice, PATOUSHINSKY;[3]
Minister of Finance, MICHAILOFF;[4]
Minister of Native Affairs, SHATILOFF.[5]
July 4, 1918.

From the report of an official who was in Siberia throughout the first and second revolutions, I obtained the following account of the events preceding my arrival in Omsk:

The Provisional Duma at Tomsk was a body which had been selected by the different political parties in January, 1918, and had not been elected by popular vote. It consisted of about ninety members, the larger portion of the extreme Social Revolutionary party. This Duma had given instructions to Vologodsky to make a government consisting of Social Revolutionists, but Vologodsky had not carried out instructions and had formed a government consisting of the various political parties, which action had met with the approval of all classes, but, of course, had displeased the Duma. At a secret meeting of some forty of the Duma, they selected ministers and an organization for a government of their own, and awaited an opportunity to get control of affairs.

---

[2] Vladimir M. Krutovsky (1856–1945), surgeon, public intellectual, and one of the leaders of the Siberian regionalism movement. In 1917, he was a representative of the Provisional Government in Siberia with gubernatorial powers and minister of interior in the Siberian Provisional All-Russian Government. He stayed in Soviet Russia for life.

[3] Grigory B. Patushinsky (1873–1931), member of the Socialist Revolutionary Party and Siberian regionalism movement; minister of justice in the Siberian Provisional All-Russian Government; opposed to the Kolchak regime. He stayed in Soviet Russia.

[4] Ivan A. Mikhailov (1891–1946), Russian politician. In 1917, he worked as an economics expert in the Provisional Government. He moved to Omsk in early 1918 and was elected minister of finance of the Siberian Provisional All-Russian Government, retaining that position after series of coups, including Kolchak's seizure of power. After the Civil War, he emigrated to China, was arrested there by the Red Army in 1945, and was executed in Moscow in 1946.

[5] Mikhail B. Shatilov (1882–1937), Russian ethnologist, public intellectual, and politician; member of the Socialist Revolutionary Party and the Siberian regionalism movement; minister of native affairs in the Siberian Provisional All-Russian Government through September 1918. After the Civil War, he worked as director of the Tomsk Regional Museum. He was arrested in 1933 and executed in 1937.

This opportunity occurred when Ivanov-Rinov[6] and Serebrenikov[7] were at the Ufa meeting at the beginning of September while Vologodsky was in Vladivostok conferring with the Allies. Ministers Krutovsky and Shatilov, who were at that time in Tomsk, and who were of the Duma party, arrived in Omsk with the president of the Duma, Jakushev,[8] and another member, Novosilov.[9] The latter was a Cossack and had worked with the Bolsheviks. A meeting was called of the ministers, consisting of Michailov (the only other minister in town), Krutovsky, and Shatilov, and the latter two named insisted upon giving Novosilov a portfolio. Michailov would not agree to this and left the meeting. Nevertheless, Krutovsky and Shatilov attempted to carry through their programme in order to secure the balance of power in the government for the extreme Social Revolutionary party, in which event it would be an easy matter to exclude all other political parties from the government. This plot was discovered by the commander of the city, Volkov,[10] and without instructions from higher authorities, during the night of the 20th–21st September, with armed officers he arrested Krutovsky, Shatilov, Novosilov, and Jakushev, who were living at the railroad-station in cars. They were taken to Volkov's private house, put in separate rooms, and each, under penalty of death, were given three minutes to sign resignation papers which had been prepared for them. Krutovsky, Shatilov, and Jakushev were released in the morning, but Novosilov was retained. It was reported that orders were given to transfer him to the prison, and two Cossack officers were detailed as

---

[6] Pavel P. Ivanov-Rinov (1869–?), Russian military commander and general of the White forces. From October 1 to November 4, 1918, he was war minister of the Siberian Provisional All-Russian Government and commander of the Siberian Army. He served at several positions in Kolchak's army, and then emigrated to China after the Civil War. In 1925, he was exposed as a Bolshevik agent among émigré circles and escaped to the USSR.

[7] Ivan I. Serebrennikov (1882–?), Russian ethnologist, member of the Siberian regionalism movement, author, and journalist; minister of food supply in the Siberian Provisional All-Russian Government and Kolchak's government. He emigrated to the US after the Civil War.

[8] Ivan A. Yakushev (1884–1935), Russian politician, member of the Socialist Revolutionary Party and the Siberian regionalism movement. In 1918, he was chairman of the Siberian Regional Duma. After the Civil War, he emigrated to Czecho-Slovakia.

[9] Alexander E. Novoselov (1884–1918), Russian ethnologist, author, and politician. By the end of 1917, he was the leader of the Omsk branch of the Socialist Revolutionary Party and minister of the Siberian Regional Duma. He was arrested on the order of the Omsk garrison head on the pretext of preventing the Socialist Revolutionary coup on September 21, and was murdered on September 23, 1918.

[10] Vyacheslav I. Volkov (1877–1920), Russian military commander, general of the White forces, and an organizer of the anti-Bolshevik movement in Siberia. Since September 8, 1918, he was the commander of the Omsk garrison and an organizer of Admiral Kolchak's coup.

guards. En route, in conversation he told the guards he had worked for the Bolsheviks, but with the intention of helping to eventually overthrow them, and that he knew where a considerable quantity of arms were buried on the outskirts of the town. The officers agreed to let him show them the place, but after he had walked them around for three hours they came to the conclusion he was endeavoring to escape and therefore shot him. The testimony of a forester says that two officers and a civilian were seen at the place where the body was found in heated conversation, and that one of the officers stepped behind the civilian and fired one shot from a revolver. The body was then thrown into the bushes and several more shots fired in that direction. This murder was undoubtedly an act of revenge on the part of Cossacks upon one they considered had tried to betray the Cossacks to the Bolsheviks.

The first information the Czechs received regarding these happenings was from agents of the Territorial Duma and, being Social Revolutionists themselves, they naturally sympathized with that party. In reporting the matter to Cheliabinsk the Czechs had evidently jumped to the conclusion that Michailov had ordered the arrests. The Czechs immediately received instructions from General Syrovy to arrest Michailov, as any disturbances in the rear of their army could not be tolerated. Michailov had received warning and could not be found. However, Assistant Minister of Interior Gratzianov[11] was arrested by the Czechs. All classes were very much upset and energetically protested against the arrest and against the interference of the Czechs in Russian internal affairs. The Cossacks were also angered, and the slightest provocation would have started a battle between them and the Czechs in Omsk. The pressure was so great that the Czechs cancelled their order for the arrest of Michailov and released Gratzianov.

In the meantime, General Ivanov hurried back from Ufa, and upon his arrival took control of Omsk, and arrested Volkov, and started an investigation into the whole affair. Orders were given for the Provincial Duma to dissolve. However, the relations between the Siberians and Czechs were so strained that Ivanov was about to resign when an Allied consul pointed out the serious results which would occur from any such action on his part, and convinced him that he must use his influence to smooth matters over while the Allied representatives promised to mediate with the Czechs and point out to them the necessity of not mixing into Russian internal politics and preventing such incidents in the future. The ceaseless efforts of the Allies were successful in preventing any drastic actions and matters were smoothed over somewhat, but the Siberians did not forget the incident.

---

[11] Alexander A. Gratsianov (1865–1931), Russian politician and surgeon. Assistant minister of the interior in the Siberian Provisional All-Russian Government and Kolchak's government. He stayed in Russia after the Civil War.

Whether the All-Russian Directorate would make Omsk or Ekaterinburg their headquarters was the next worry of the political parties. It was felt that should they decide on Ekaterinburg they would be put under the influence of the working class in that territory, and would not be able to carry out their intended programme. However, the directorate decided on Omsk and arrived there on September 9. Negotiations were immediately started between the directorate and the Siberian Government as to the formation of an All-Russian Government and the giving over of power of the Siberian Government. The Siberian Government was loath to compromise without certain guarantees.

The wages of workmen had increased very considerably since June, but their individual output decreased. It was therefore necessary to do something to bring up the standard, especially on the railway. The Siberian Government therefore passed a resolution that workmen on the railway should be paid, wherever practicable and possible, by piece-work—in other words, the workmen would have to earn their wages. Trouble started on the Tomsk railway but was quickly put down. On September 18 a general strike was declared by railway workmen here in Omsk. The Czechs, Cossacks and military organizations undertook to guard the railway yards but not before the strikers had managed to damage twelve out of the eighteen engines in the local yards. Several of the leaders were caught and immediately shot. The government and military people issued strict orders and took the necessary measures to prevent trouble, and the workmen were forced to go back to work. However, with so many locomotives out of service, train traffic was seriously interfered with.

The railway strike seemed to have been suppressed, but on the 19th a sympathetic strike of all workmen, factory employees, teamsters, barbers, bakers, etc., was declared. The situation was serious but the authorities took the matter in hand and gave no quarter. On Monday, the 23rd of September, most of the workmen had returned to their work. General Dietrichs,[12] a Russian chief of staff of the Czechs, sent a telegram to Omsk in the name of the Czech staff stating strikes in their rear would not be tolerated and "that it was no time to enforce piece-work." This statement, coming just at the time the strike had successfully been put down, caused very hard feeling amongst the authorities toward the Czechs. It gave the impression that the Czechs were taking the side of the workmen against the government. Captain Kozek, the Czech diplomatic representative in Omsk, sent a telegram to the Czech staff to the

---

[12] Mikhail K. Diterikhs (1874–1937), Russian military commander. Since March 1918, he was chief of staff of the Czecho-Slovak corps. In January 1919, he was appointed by Kolchak to be the head of the investigation of the murder of the tsar's family. Later, he was commander of the Siberian army and chief of staff of Kolchak's army. After the Civil War, he emigrated to China.

# THE BIRTH OF A GOVERNMENT IN RUSSIA

effect that they should not mix into internal affairs and that the matter had been liquidated.

The formation of the All-Russian Government was meeting with considerable opposition. It was proposed to have the directory composed of the five elected at Ufa, and under them would be a working cabinet composed of the various ministers. However, there were several contestable points between the directorate and the Siberian Government which were necessary to settle before the Siberian Government would agree to give over their power. About the 24th of October an agreement was reached between the directorate and Siberian Government on ten out of eleven points as follows:

1. Formation of an All-Russian Government was agreed upon, therefore the Provincial Government (Siberian Temporary Government) no longer exists.
2. The principle of Provincial Governments was agreed to, but districts would be agreed upon at some future date.
3. All-Russian Government takes over and uses the organization of the Siberian Government.
4. Composition of the Working Cabinet to be made by the Siberian and Directorate, but in the future the Directorate would only have the power to make appointments to vacancies in the Cabinet.
5. Members of the Cabinet will only be answerable to the Directorate.
6. President of the Cabinet must be a member of the Directorate.
7. New laws regarding the election of the Constituent Assembly will be drawn up by a special committee, one of whom must be the President of the Provincial Duma, and the laws must be ratified by the Directorate before becoming effective.
8. After European Russia is freed, the various Provinces will have the right to have their own local governments.
9. Directorate accept all laws made by Provincial Governments to date, but will look them over and make changes where necessary.
10. Army will be All-Russian and wear Russian cockade, but Provinces may wear their colors across the cockade.
11. Directorate wishes the Provincial Duma at Tomsk to assemble, with the understanding that it will pass a vote of confidence in the All-Russian Government and dissolve immediately, and this to be their only reason for assembling. Siberians, however, consider the Duma as dissolved and therefore have no right to assemble.

This last point was finally settled by the Siberians giving in. However, in choosing candidates for the Working Cabinet very serious differences arose as to the Minister of Finance. The Siberians insisted on having Michailov, while the Directorate refused his nomination. Both sides remained firm and the Directorate gave the Siberian Government until a specified time to decide the matter definitely. The Czechs were backing the Directorate as they also did not wish to have Michailov as Minister of Finance. The Directorate offered the post as Minister of Commerce to Michailov but neither he nor the Siberian Government agreed to this. The controversy became so acute that Afkzentieff and two others of the Directorate threatened to resign. In order to avoid such a catastrophe the French Consul, British Vice-Consul, and United States Vice-Consul appealed to both sides to compromise. Upon these representations the crisis was overcome without any drastic actions on either side. A final agreement was signed the evening of November 1, and this Working Cabinet was named:

| Vologodski, | Chairman. |
| KOLCHAK, | Minister of War. |
| Shekin, | " Foreign Affairs.[13] |
| Gattenberger, | " Interior.[14] |
| Michailov, | " Finance. |
| Ustrugov, | " Communications.[15] |
| Petrov, | " Agriculture.[16] |
| Serebrenikov, | " Supplies. |
| ORLOV, | " Commerce (temporary). |
| Zapozhnikov, | " Education.[17] |

---

[13] Ivan I. Sukin (1890–1958), Russian diplomat and minister of foreign affairs in Kolchak's government from December 1918 to December 1919. From 1917 to 1918, he was secretary of the Russian embassy in Washington, DC. He resigned and emigrated; lived in the US, England, and France.

[14] Alexander N. Gattenberger (1861–1939), Russian politician and minister of the interior in Kolchak's government from November 1918 to April 1919. He emigrated to China and later to the US.

[15] Leonid A. Ustrugov (1877–1938), Russian engineer and minister of communications in Kolchak's government, November 1918–1920. After the Civil War, he emigrated to China, returned to the USSR in 1935, was arrested in 1937, and executed in 1938.

[16] Nikolai I. Petrov (1884–1921), Russian economist and minister of agriculture in Kolchak's government from November 1918 to December 1919. He emigrated to China.

[17] Vasily V. Sapozhnikov (1861–1924), Russian botanist and geographer, rector of Tomsk University, minister of education in the Siberian Provisional All-Russian Government and Kolchak's government. After the Civil War, he continued to research and teach at Tomsk University.

Starenkevitch, " Justice.[18]
Krasnov, " Control.[19]

Considerable opposition to the All-Russian Government, especially from the Monarchist party, developed. The peasant class as a whole were indifferent and knew little about political affairs. They could be swung by the party offering the best promises to their personal welfare, and there was the additional danger that the church, which sympathized with the extreme Monarchist group, could swing the peasants their way, for the peasants were superstitious and could be influenced by the church, as has been the case for centuries in the past. The Monarchist party believed the future of Russia lay with General Denekin and the army fighting in Southern Russia. It believed that, when those forces and the Siberian forces joined, Denekin would become dictator or a monarchy would be declared.

The All-Russian Government struggled along through the summer and fall. Envoys were sent to the Allied countries in an effort to obtain their sympathy and support. Prince Lvoff, who had been premier in the provisional government in 1917, was sent to the United States as a special representative of the All-Russian Government. Russians throughout the Allied countries gave this government their moral support. Alexander Kerensky, who had been minister of justice and premier of the provisional government, telegraphed his support to Omsk, and it looked as if Siberia was to witness the birth of a real Russian representative democracy. The new government, however, was confronted at home by the following conditions:

1. While it had the support of the Czecho-Slovak National Council and the military backing of that revolutionary army, it could not obtain the wholehearted support of the Allied representatives in Siberia, and
2. The government had to struggle immediately with the problem of reconstruction in the industry and social life of the nation.

Although the Allies, the French, British, and American representatives, had promised to support the Czecho-Slovaks, several months had passed before troops were landed at Vladivostok and Archangel, and after they were landed, instead of

---

[18] Sergei S. Starynkevich (1874–1933), Russian lawyer and politician, minister of justice in the Siberian Provisional All-Russian Government and Kolchak's government. In 1919, he took part in the anti-Kolchak conspiracy in Vladivostok, and after its failure, he emigrated.

[19] Grigory A. Krasnov (1883–1933), Russian economist and state controller in Kolchak's government. He stayed in Russia after the Civil War, was arrested, sentenced to life in prison (1920), amnestied in 1922, worked in Soviet economic organizations, and in March 1933, he was arrested and executed.

their co-operating with the Czecho-Slovak forces, they remained in eastern Siberia as an army of occupation in fact, if not in principle. After the Czechs had been fighting four months they began to ask why the Allies did not hurry their armies across Siberia, and they began to doubt whether they could rely upon Allied assistance.

Meanwhile the living conditions of the people grew worse. Millions of refugees rushed to Siberia from central Europe and from Asia and other parts of the world. Siberia became densely overcrowded, food increased in price as it became more and more impossible for Siberia to feed the influx of citizens. The factories had been closed because of a lack of raw materials and capital to operate them. The railroads were badly demoralized. The Allies could not agree upon a method of operation or control and the new government, with hundreds of questions of administration to decide every day, soon found it could not keep up with the public demands. It was faced by a certain collapse unless the Allies assisted wholeheartedly in the reorganization and reconstruction of Russia. How this was to be accomplished was the issue which again divided the Allies. England, France, and Japan maintained that the only hope for the re-organization of Russia lay in a strong military organization, and urged the creation and development of an All-Russian army. Admiral Koltshak had been brought to Siberia by representatives of Great Britain because of his great ability as an organizer and executive, which he had displayed as commander of the Russian Black Sea fleet, and because of his loyalty to the Allies, which had been tested both before and during the revolution. Admiral Koltshak had been made the minister of war of the All-Russian Government, and had begun the reorganization of a Russian army with the cooperation and assistance of General Knox, the British commander, who had been for seven years military attaché of the British embassy in Petrograd.

Representatives of the United States, under instructions from their government and also because of their own ideas, had been contending that Russia could never be assisted in her reconstruction period unless the economic organization was first given new life. This is where the policies differed. One group of Allies maintained that Russia's hope lay in military intervention. Another group of Powers insisted that economic rehabilitation should be the beginning, and that the question of a large army should be left entirely to the Russian people and the Russian Government.

The All-Russian Government was in a quandary. With the Allies apparently hopelessly divided and with conditions growing worse and the public demands for order and bread multiplying every hour there developed a struggle among the Russians themselves as to the best means of bringing about the rebirth of Russia.

In Omsk I met Afkzentieff, who had been elected the president of the directorate, and who was looked upon as the dominant figure in the new All-Russian Government. During a long interview he explained these difficulties which confronted the directorate and said that the question would come to a head in a very short time, and that the government in Omsk would either become a military dictatorship to co-operate with General Denekin, who was commanding an army of Cossacks in southern Russia, or the All-Russian Government would continue with the economic and financial assistance of the Allies.

The fight between these two factions was directly accentuated by the Allied representatives in Siberia who, despite the instructions from their governments, took part in Russian internal affairs. The issue reached a climax during a dinner given in honor of the Allies in Omsk early in November, 1918, by the All-Russian Government. Official representatives of the United States, France, and England were present at the dinner. After speeches by representatives of the government the band began to play "God Save the Tzar." Captain Kozek, who represented the Czech National Council in Omsk and who had attended the dinner on behalf of this council, arose from the dinner and warned the chairman of the meeting that the Czechs would withdraw from the hall if the band played this old Russian national anthem again. Similar warnings were expressed by the other Allies, but within a few moments the band played again, "God Save the Tzar." The Allied representatives left the hall in a body.

The following morning the British and American vice-consuls called at the Foreign Office, demanding an explanation. By noon they had addressed an official note to the All-Russian Government stating that unless the government immediately apologized for the events of the previous evening and punished the Cossack colonel who at the point of a revolver had forced the band to play the former national hymn, the Allied representatives would inform their governments. This the All-Russian directorate knew would injure the chances of recognition, and the members also felt, that while they would eventually have to take drastic steps against the militarists in Omsk, they were not prepared at the moment to do so.

These were critical days in Siberia, and decisive days for Russia, too. Before a week had passed, the militarists had succeeded in overthrowing the All-Russian Government. President Afkzentieff and two other members of the directorate were arrested, compelled to sign statements of their resignations, which had been prepared for them, and ordered to leave the country. Admiral Koltshak was made the dictator, or supreme commander, of the government of Omsk, and the old directors were taken to Harbin, Manchuria, under guard of Russian and British soldiers.

The constituent assembly which had been organized in Ekaterinburg was immediately abolished; an attempt was made to assassinate the chairman of the assembly and some sixty members were taken to Ufa under the protection of the Czechs.

These developments did more than destroy the great hopes of Russia's friends. They also brought about the disintegration of all of the governments of Siberia and Russia outside of the Bolshevist area. They divided the Czech army and Czech National Council. General Gaida supported Koltshak, while the National Council condemned the November coup d'état. Until this time the All-Russian Government had not only the official support but the co-operation of all of the political parties of Russia excepting the extreme left of the Social Democrats, which was supporting the Bolsheviki. After the organization of the dictatorship a new civil war broke out in Siberia. General Semenov, who controlled an army of Cossacks in the neighborhood of Tchita and General Kalmykoff,[20] the ataman of the Usuri Cossacks, refused to support the new government. General Horvath,[21] vice-president of the Chinese Eastern Railway and the chief political factor in Manchuria, and the Amur, withheld his support. The Japanese had been openly hostile to Admiral Koltshak who was commander of Port Arthur at one period of the Russo-Japanese War. The British were enthusiastic in their support. The French representatives did not approve of the turn of events but were ready to co-operate with any Russian government which had for its object the beginning of a new order in Russia. The American representatives were disappointed but powerless, and looked upon the change as the beginning of a new Monarchist movement because of the support which the followers of the Tzar's Government gave the new cabinet of Admiral Koltshak.

There were many indications in Russia at the time that the Allies were on the verge of recognizing the All-Russian Government, but the possibility of this action disappeared when it became known in official circles in Vladivostok that the American Government had turned down the recommendations of its officials that a small force of Americans be sent to the Ural Mountains. (The details are given in Chapter IX.)

After the birth of the All-Russian Government it was not doomed to death, but done to death by the failure of the Allies in uniting upon a Russian policy. The history of Russia to-day might be totally different if this mistake had not been made, because at this time the strength of the Bolsheviki government was constantly decreasing, and Russians of all political faiths were looking forward to the new government in Omsk as being the beginning of a Russian democracy. But immediately after the appointment of Admiral Koltshak not only the influence of the Allies in Siberia and Russia decreased, but the sympathy of the Czecho-Slovaks disappeared, the civil war recommenced, and the Bolsheviki agitators again came from their hiding places.

And thus we find Bolshevism appearing again upon the scenes of Siberia as a direct result of the chaotic conditions. It was another proof of the contention that Bolshevism develops where governments fail, and the reason the Bolsheviki are considered the strongest force in Siberia and in Russia, is because all other Russian gov-

---

[20] Ivan P. Kalmykov (1890–1920), Russian military commander (White) during the Civil War and ataman of the Ussuri Cossacks who was notorious for his cruelty. After the Civil War, he emigrated to China, was arrested by Chinese authorities, and killed during an attempt to escape.

[21] Dmitry L. Horvat (1858–1937), Russian engineer and military commander, one of the leaders of the White movement in the Far East during the Russian Civil War; chief manager of the Chinese Eastern Railway from the period of its construction in 1903 to 1918. On July 1918, he proclaimed himself the provisional ruler of Russia, and in September 1918, he agreed to the supremacy of the Siberian Provisional Government. After the Civil War, he moved to Peking, and was the leading person in the Russian emigration in the Far East.

ernments have not succeeded and because the Allies themselves have not been able to get together upon a policy of assistance.

Everything was changed, too, by the armistice. The hope of the Czecho-Slovaks and of the Allies, as well as of the Russians, was that with the collapse of Germany would follow the downfall of the Red army reign in European Russia. But Bolshevism was not weakened by the armistice but rather strengthened. Before the armistice military intervention in Russia might have succeeded. Before the armistice economic rehabilitation could have been successful. But after the cessation of hostilities in Europe military intervention in Siberia became not only impracticable but impossible. For the Allied soldiers the war was over and they desired to leave. For the Russians, they wished no more fighting and desired only order and an opportunity to live and work. All of the things which might have been done before the 11th of November in the interest of Russia and on behalf of the Russian people became impossible after that date.

So the world is to-day confronted with a new set of conditions in Russia. The Bolsheviki have gained strength, not alone because of the failure of those opposed to Bolshevism to unite, but because authority has also tempered the policies of the Bolshevist government, and the leaders find that they cannot be as radical in office as they can on the platform. Between the statement of an ideal and its realization is a gulf which can only be bridged by co-operative effort of those who direct and those who execute. Thus far the Bolsheviki have not been able to succeed with their industrial programme as Lenin himself admits.

But Russia remains what it has always been, a world problem of reconstruction, and the solutions are the same as those to be used the world over. There is the local Soviet of working men and there is the national and international organization of governments. The nations of the world will either co-operate in an effort to rebuild Russia, not by military means, but by economic assistance, or Russia will be left temporarily in the hands of the Bolsheviki and Russia will go through a long period of regeneration as a sort of international exile. And out of this condition almost anything may develop. Russia may be the bridge to connect Germany and Japan, for there are military parties still existing in these two nations and a military dictatorship may follow the Bolshevist dictatorship in Russia. From the Atlantic to the Pacific such a strong military government may develop to threaten not only a league of nations or any union of world governments, but also to threaten individual nations if these nations do not now unite in an international organization and follow a definite plan of constructive action in Russia.

The advantages of a world organization of representative governments are not only the advantages of an international organization for the reconstruction of the world, but also advantages of national protection against the formation of any future union of military governments. A league of nations can only exist where its authority is supreme and where its support is international.

The failure of the Allies in Russia cannot be held against the Allies as an organization but only against these nations as individuals, because the Allies did not work in Russia as a unit. The collapse of Bolshevism in the summer of 1918 in Siberia was due not alone to the military assistance of the Czecho-Slovaks, but to the fact that a government was organized which represented the different political parties and had the confidence of the people. Bolshevism redeveloped when these factors disappeared. This is true of Bolshevism everywhere. The Bolsheviki obtained control of Hungary because of the failure of the Karolyi and the Allies. When Bolshevism has appeared upon the horizon of Germany it has been always where the government or the industries had failed.

This is where the arguments of the Bolsheviki gained ground. Their officials maintain that all of the governments which the world has had during the past five or six centuries have failed to develop with conditions, and that Bolshevism represents the new era. But the fallacy of this argument is that wherever Bolshevism has developed so far it has only been in countries where there was previously a strong autocracy or a military government. Europe has never really seen democratic or representative governments on a great scale excepting in England and France, and the Bolshevist J agitation in these countries is not against the democratic form of government but against the influences which are back of the present government. In Germany, Austria-Hungary, and Russia, where Bolshevism has gained its greatest strength, there were previously monarchies where there was no representative government.

Those who are working for a league of nations in Europe are mostly the representatives of governments where the people have an opportunity at regular intervals of expressing themselves by ballot upon government policies. Their object is to apply this democratic national principle to world politics, and if they succeed we shall see a union of world governments organized with public opinion as its chief support. But the contest between this new force of reaction, which is Bolshevism, and of progress, represented by a league of nations, is only beginning and is certain to continue during the next decade.

## Chapter VIII
## AMERICAN AND ALLIED EXILES IN RUSSIA

Into this whirlpool of Russia the American and Allied soldiers came in August and September, 1918, on the dual and confused mission of aiding the Czecho-Slovaks and assisting the Russian people. The war with Germany was approaching a crisis. The Bolsheviki were declared to be agents of the Central Empires, and the break between the Red army and the Czechs seemed to confirm this. There was talk among military men of a new Eastern front. Transportation, commerce, and industry had collapsed. The revolution had reached the summit of destruction. Chaos was king and misery the vassal in the new order of life.

The Doughboys,[1] Canadians, Frenchmen, Japanese, and Britishers were eager and excited over the possibilities of fighting in Russia for a speedy termination of the war. Russia was a part of the war theatre. The Bolsheviki were considered enemies. The Czechs and Slovaks had been combating Bolshevism in Siberia and Russia for four months and were weary and exhausted. Apparently the Allied governments were united upon a Russia policy. Apparently there was to be action after more than a year of hesitation and indecision. There was, at least, hope; and Russians and Allies were one in their optimistic forecasts. But, in less than two months the situation again was practically hopeless. Troops which went to fight remained idle. High commissioners and "experts" who were sent to advise and direct became entangled in the red tape of official instructions from Washington, Paris, London, and Tokyo. Instead of action there was delay; in place of decision there was diplomatic discussion, and the American and Allied soldiers became exiles in Siberia and Murmansk.

"If there ever was such a thing as an abandoned ship of state," I wrote in *The Independent*, "it is Russia. While the Bolshevist crew has been attempting to run the ship itself, thousands of friends of Russia, including Russians and Allies, have been attempting to direct the course of the ship from the outside, by giving constant advice and criticism in a sort of ceaseless wireless communication. Experiments directing the course of a craft at sea from some firm point on land have not been limited only to ships, but have been extended to ships of state as well.

---

[1] Doughboy was an informal term for a member of the United States Army or Marine Corps, especially used to refer to members of the American Expeditionary Forces in World War I.

"For considerably over a year attempts have been made to run Russia by wireless but Russia is still on the rocks, and all the efforts of the crew in one direction, and the friends of the ship and passengers from another, have been unable to rescue it, and it seems high time for those who are really interested in salvaging Russia to stop experimenting and to begin considering, first, the facts regarding the present situation, and second, practical means of launching Russia again on the sea of politics and commerce.

"In Vladivostok I saw a number of Russian warships and merchantmen lying at anchor in the bay. Since the counter-revolution of the Bolsheviki these ships have belonged to the crews and their families. Stokers and sailors alike have converted these former vessels into floating residences, but they never put out to sea. These ships rise and fall with the tide. Barnacles cover the hulls, the gray coats of paint are scaling off, and the rusting craft is at the mercy of rigorous winters and sultry summers.

"How typical of Russia to-day. That nation is simply a huge ship of state taken over by the crew; tossing in the sea of international political and industrial turmoil. All of the old officers, all of the former leaders, most of the sane elements have left the country for the safety of foreign shores. The friends of Russia no longer go near the ship, but stand on the shore and try to tell the Russian people how it should be run. The crew has not been successful either in managing the ship itself, or in steering it; and certainly those who have been experimenting from the outside and attempting to run Russia by wireless have not had much success."

Why? One reason is that the Allies in Russia are exiles exiled by the politics of their own governments and by the Russians, too.

To comprehend the causes which brought about American co-operation in limited military intervention in Russia, the chronicler must go back to the events of March, 1918, when the German armies broke through the British front in France and swarmed back of the line. On the night of the 20th of March I left Switzerland for Paris, arriving in the capital on the morning of the first day's bombardment by the long-range gun, and remaining until the crisis of the first great attack had been passed. It was so obvious that the Allies were worried over the military situation that the leaders were grasping for final straws to avert a catastrophe, and suggestions of statesmen and generals ranged from a united general staff under one Allied commander to the recreation of the Russian front and a new Allied offensive in 1919 and 1920. There was serious talk of five years more of war! Criticism of all nations was so universal, gossip so wide-spread, that the days of March seemed to be the forecast of another Waterloo with the victory on the other side.

The German high command, calculating upon an easy victory, delayed the second blow long enough for the Allies to form a single general staff, and for the relaunching of a campaign to permit the Japanese to invade Russia via Siberia for the purpose of attacking the Germans from the rear.

When the military staffs were united under Marshal Foch,[2] the diplomatic centre of controversy shifted from Paris to Tokyo and Washington, and, led by France and England, ceaseless pressure was brought to bear upon the United States Government to take part in military intervention in Russia or consent to a military campaign by the Japanese. The obvious intention of those who were placing their plans before the United States was the establishment of an Eastern front, an object which the United States General Staff did not approve because it was believed to be impossible and impracticable. At this juncture in the negotiations there developed again the fundamental difference between the policies of the Allied governments and that of this country. The United States looked upon the Russian problem as one of reconstruction, while the European Powers and Japan were insistent in considering it a belligerent question until the war was over everywhere. Judging from the attitude of President Wilson and the Department of State, it is obvious that there were grave fears surrounding the plan of exclusive Japanese intervention because of the more or less confirmed reports that the German military party and the Japanese military party were, at least, unofficially and strictly confidentially, in communication with each other, and there was a danger of Russia being made a bridge between the militarism of Japan and Germany.

The first intimation I had of any such an arrangement was during December, 1917, and January, 1918, when I was in Switzerland making a study of internal conditions in Germany. At that time I learned through trustworthy sources that Germany was making every effort to come to an understanding with Japan, and when I noticed in the German press, early in 1918, the names of the diplomatic, consular, and military officials Germany was sending to Russia, I observed that such men as Baron Murom von Schwarzenstein, former imperial ambassador to Tokyo and chief of the Far-Eastern propaganda department in the Berlin Foreign Office, were being sent to Russia.[3] Associated with him were Germans who had had experience in Japan and China. All of them were what the Germans called "experts" on the Far East, and only one or two had ever been in Russia before. This was the type of men Germany sent to revolutionized Russia.

The intention was obvious. Germany, which was always careful to select men for foreign posts who had had experience in the country to which they were accredited, was not sending German "experts" on Japan to Russia for Russia alone. Later there

---

[2] Marshal Ferdinand Jean Marie Foch (1851–1929) was a French general and marshal of France, Great Britain, and Poland, and the supreme allied commander during the First World War.

[3] Philipp Alfons Freiherr Mumm von Schwarzenstein (1859–1924) was a diplomat of the German Empire. From 1909–11, he was ambassador of the German Reich in Japan. He retired in 1911, but was reactivated 1914 in Berlin. From March to November 1918, he represented the German Reich in Kiev (Ukraine).

came the famous Terauchi[4] interview in *The Outlook*, in which the prime minister of Japan showed decided leanings toward the Central Powers. Still later came the interview with Leon Trotsky in which he claimed that he had seen documents in Russia to show that there was a secret treaty between Japan and Germany regarding Russia, to the effect that Germany was to have European Russia and Japan the trans-Baikal district after the war. In the Far East one of my colleagues had an interview with the Japanese minister of foreign affairs in which he asked whether there was an agreement between Japan and Germany, and the minister replied that if Trotsky had made such a statement the only answer he (the minister) cared to make was that Trotsky had given Germany part of Russia, but had not given Japan anything!

In both Japan and Siberia I made every effort to learn the basis for the charges which were being made so freely against Japan. The most reliable information I received was to the effect that the German military party, during the winter of 1917–1918, did make proposals of separate peace to certain military circles in Tokyo, but that when the "Peace party" and business interests learned of this they quickly destroyed any possibility of either an agreement or an exchange of definite communications.

I do not doubt but that one of the chief reasons the United States vetoed the Allied proposal of an independent Japanese campaign in Russia was because of the possibilities of a Japanese-Russian-German Alliance.

But the European Powers were so insistent and public opinion was so determined in demanding that something be done in Russia, that the United States finally agreed to the landing of Allied troops in Russia, at Vladivostok and Archangel, although the American Government never changed its policy of non-interference in Russian affairs, and adhered to the plan of economic rehabilitation. Accordingly, under the agreement between the Allies, a limited number of troops were landed.

In this way Allied intervention in Siberia began under the direction of the Japanese General Kitsuzu Otani, Commander of the Fourth Army division in Manchuria during the Russo-Japanese War, and later commander of the Garrison of Tsing Tau after the Japanese seized this German stronghold in China.[5] At this time there were three American officials in Vladivostok under strict orders from Washington to execute the American programme in the Allied plan of limited co-operative inter-

---

[4] Terauchi Masatake (1852–1919) was a Japanese military officer, proconsul, and politician. He was a gensui (or marshal) in the Imperial Japanese Army and the ninth prime minister of Japan from October 9, 1916, to September 29, 1918.

[5] General Baron Kikuzuo Otani (1856–1923), commander in chief of Japanese forces in the Russian Far East from 1918–19 and former commander of the Allied troops there.

vention. Admiral Knight,[6] commander of the U.S. *Asiatic Squadron*, had been living aboard the *Brooklyn* in Golden Horn Bay throughout the summer, reporting on conditions in Russia and interviewing all classes and representative Russians who visited or lived in this city. The United States Expeditionary Force was commanded by Major General William S. Graves, a former General Staff officer in whom both the President and the War Department had absolute confidence, and upon whose judgment they could depend in handling a delicate diplomatic situation. General Graves had received his instructions verbally from Secretary of War Baker.[7] He knew this government's Far-Eastern policy, and he was a general whose ability would be an asset to the Allied staff if extensive military operations were decided upon later. Through his chief of staff, Lieutenant-Colonel O. P. Robinson,[8] the American commander had a staff officer with years of experience and judgment in transporting and supplying troops; a man whose ability as an organizer was demonstrated when, in one week before the Americans sailed from San Francisco, he purchased and placed on transports sufficient food, clothing, and supplies to last the expeditionary force more than two months, an accomplishment the significance of which can be realized when one considers the importance of the question of tonnage at that state of the war. Associated with these two army men were officers from the Military Intelligence division, led by Lieutenant-Colonel Barrows, who had spent years in the diplomatic and army service in Russia and the Far East.[9]

---

[6] Austin Melvin Knight (1854–1927) was an admiral in the United States Navy and commander in chief of the US Asiatic Fleet from 1917 to 1918. His 1901 textbook, *Modern Seamanship*, was a standard reference for over eight decades.

[7] Newton Diehl Baker, Jr. (1871–1937), was an American lawyer, politician, and government official. He served as the thiry-seventh mayor of Cleveland, Ohio, from 1912 to 1915, and as the US secretary of war from 1916 to 1921.

[8] Oliver Prescott Robinson (1879–1941), US Army officer and military theorist. He served during the Spanish-American War and in Cuba and the Philippines; he was an instructor for the Infantry School of Arms, 1915–17. He served in the general staff of the War Department, chief of staff in the Eighth Division, and chief of staff in the American Expeditionary Forces in Siberia during World War I. He is the author of *The Fundamentals of Military Strategy* (Washington, DC, 1928).

[9] David Prescott Barrows (1873–1954) was an American anthropologist, explorer, and educator especially praised for his books on Morocco and the Philippines. During the First World War, he served in various capacities as a member of the American Commission for Relief in Belgium, as a major of cavalry unit serving in the Philippines, and as an intelligence officer in the Philippines and Siberia with the American Expeditionary Forces. From December 1919 to June 1923, he was the elected president of the University of California. In 1939, Barrows admitted that he had been friendly with Ataman Semenov during his time in Russia. While claiming to have no bias against communists, Barrows asserted that they were, by nature, violent. Barrows defended General Semenov's cruel policies on the Far East, stating that he was "just a soldier ... who did what any other would do under such circumstances."

In Tokyo, for more than a year previous to the landing of American forces, Ambassador Roland S. Morris[10] had been making a study of the Russian situation, and during the Allied campaign for intervention during the summer of 1918 he was the centre of all negotiations in Japan. Because of the reliability of his reports and the confidence which the administration had in his judgment he was made in fact, although not in name, the United States high commissioner to Siberia, and from the time of his arrival in Vladivostok to co-operate with Admiral Knight and Major-General Graves our activities in Russia, with one exception, which I shall discuss in the chapter "Decisive Days in Siberia," the United States Government relied explicitly upon his suggestions and recommendations.

Another American official of importance was Brigadier-General John F. Stevens of the United States Railway Service Corps, who was sent to Russia with a staff of experienced railroaders from the Northwestern States under an agreement with the Kerensky government, to take over and operate the Russian railroads, especially the Trans-Siberian line. Stevens and his chief assistant, Colonel George Emerson, were, however, without a railroad by the time they landed in Vladivostok, because the provisional government had been overthrown in Petrograd, and the Bolshevist regime did not recognize agreements made by that government.

England and France, at this time, were represented by high commissioners. Sir Charles Eliot,[11] who represented Great Britain, had been in Russia some time, and was ably assisted by General Knox, former attaché to the British Embassy in Petrograd, and a staff of British officers who had been attached to the Russian army during the war. Ambassador Eugene Regnault, the French representative,[12] had been for five years ambassador of the Republic of France to Japan, and was to the French Government what Ambassador Morris was to the United States. Later the military tasks of the Allied intervention programme, as far as France was concerned, were delegated to General Janin,[13] who had been sent from Paris in August to succeed General Paris, of the French staff, who was attached to the Czecho-Slovak army as the chief military

---

[10] Roland Sletor Morris (1874–1945) was a US diplomat and politician. He was the American ambassador to Japan from 1917 to 1920.

[11] Sir Charles Norton Edgecumbe Eliot (1862–1931) was a British diplomat, colonial administrator, and botanist. He served as commissioner of British East Africa from 1900 to 1904. In 1905, Eliot was the first vice chancellor of the newly created University of Sheffield— until 1912, when he was appointed the first vice chancellor of the University of Hong Kong. He served there until 1918, when he was recalled to the diplomatic service to become high commissioner and consul general in Siberia. He was British ambassador to Japan from 1919 to 1925.

[12] Eugène Louis Georges Regnault (1857–1933), French diplomat, ambassador to Japan from 1914 to 1918.

[13] Pierre-Thiébaut-Charles-Maurice Janin (1862–1946) was a French general and military commander who was the chief of the French military mission in Siberia during the Russian

adviser and foreign director of the new army. Janin and Paris co-operated thoroughly until the spring of 1919, when General Paris returned to France to report on the situation in Siberia to the Peace Conference.[14]

Upon these men, all of whom, with the exception of the British high commissioner, I met on numerous occasions in Russia, rested the responsibility of doing something with the restricted Allied programme. Upon these officials the Allied governments depended for their information and recommendations. These men would seem to be the ones to bear the responsibility for what the Allies did and failed to accomplish in Siberia, but what actually happened, was what so often develops under similar circumstances, the governments listened and read the reports but seldom approved them. And the natural outcome was that these men, all reporting to their governments their view-points and information, received conflicting instructions from Tokyo, Washington, Paris, and London, and their plans clashed.

After the landing of Allied troops Vladivostok became the political centre of the Far East. It was a dual city. Diplomatically Japan and the Allies met for the first time, attempting to solve by co-operative action one Far-Eastern question. Militarily the Allies met in Vladivostok to help Russia. Thus the city became not only the base for Allied operations and programmes in Russia, but the political centre in which many of the serious differences between the policies of the Allies in China and the Amur were to conflict in actual practice.

At the beginning of Allied operations it was a wonderful experience to witness the nucleus of a league of nations already at work in harmony in Russia. It made optimists of confirmed pessimists, and of the Allies at this time it may justly be said: "They came, they saw, and they conquered"—until they reached the inevitable stumbling-block, the restrictions placed upon the Allied commanders and officials by their governments, both as regards military operations and political and economic policies.

In Vladivostok, early in October, I had conversations with numerous representatives of the Allies, and learned from them that the original plan of establishing a new Eastern front had been abandoned. Even General Knox, who had been one of the original advocates of such a plan, declared in an interview that the reconstruction of a Russian front similar to the one which collapsed with the second revolution was an impossible task. General Otani voiced the same opinion, but both officers contended that the Allied task was to train and equip a new Russian army to fight the Bolshevists and thus, indirectly, take part in the World War against Germany. While the French, British, and Japanese representatives were united upon this plan the American officials were united in their belief that the Russians were war-weary, and that

---

Civil War. As such, he commanded the Czecho-Slovak Legion. It is believed that he betrayed Admiral Kolchak by handing him over to the Bolsheviks in Irkutsk in December 1919.

[14] Other sources mention Captain (later Major) Paris.

a new army could not be built in time to make itself felt in the campaign against the Central Powers.

Within a few weeks after their landing the Allied plans had so materially changed, and the situation in Siberia had been so altered, that the Allied governments were faced by the necessity of making new plans in Russia. It was at this time that all of the American representatives united in recommending to Washington that the United States join the Allies in sending a small detachment of troops to Omsk for its moral effect upon the Czecho-Slovaks, who were discouraged and who had been waiting four months for Allied assistance, and because the strengthening of the All-Russian Government in Russia itself would develop from such action. (For the details of this I shall again refer the reader to the following chapter: "Decisive Days in Siberia.")

While the American representatives had recommended to the United States Government the sending of a small force to the Ural Mountains, their previous recommendation that the Trans-Siberian Railway be placed under the full control and jurisdiction of the American Railroad Service Corps had been approved and the consent of nearly all of the Allies had been obtained. England, France, and Italy had given the United States power of attorney to reorganize the railroad and run the trains. To those who were watching developments in Russia it was obvious that the backbone of the nation was the railroad, and that unless it was reorganized there was no opportunity either for military intervention or economic rehabilitation. Everything depended upon the railroad, so when England, France, Italy, and the United States came to an agreement the matter was placed before the Japanese and Chinese Governments because one of the main lines of the road crossed Chinese territory and another line, while in Siberia itself, was looked upon by Japan as being within her sphere of influence. Allied unity was necessary in any case, and the permission of China and Japan was as essential to the operation of the railroad as the consent of any other Power. How difficult it is for any group of nations to act together was indicated in the diplomatic discussions which followed the American proposal that the railroad be operated by the Allies through the American commission. But Japan could not bring herself to the point of approving the policy and made various counter suggestions and, in the meantime, brought pressure to bear upon Peking, inducing the Chinese Government to withhold its consent. The long argument which followed these developments is discussed in another chapter on the Japanese activities in Siberia. The incident is mentioned here only because of its effect upon the American plans and policies and upon the attitude of the American engineers. These men had left important positions in the United States. All were practical railroad workers from general managers to engineers and section hands. They knew every angle of the railroad business. They had learned it by experience in the northwest, and they had joined the American Railway Service Corps at the sacrifice of permanent, responsible positions in the United States and good incomes, with the idea of helping their country during the war. When they reached Siberia they found they were handicapped every place. The railroads were not turned over to them to be operated. They were given no authority. Their recommendations were unheeded. The only thing they were permitted to do was to ride the trains or sit in the telegraph or tram despatched offices at the various depots. They were active men on a lazy job. They saw the intrigue and opposition of the Japanese everywhere, but they lived in the hope that ultimately they might be given permission to take over the job which had been promised them.

These engineers I met in Siberia and Manchuria. They rode some of the trains that I travelled on. I rode with Stevens and Emerson on one of their trips from Harbin to Vladivostok. I heard their comments upon the operation of the railroad and understood their feelings of distress because the railroad, which was like a toy to them because it was so easily mastered, was going to pieces under their very eyes and they were powerless. Instead of a hundred trains going in and out of Vladivostok every day the number had dwindled to six or eight. Instead of regular fast passenger service across Siberia in five days there was now only an intermittent service in nineteen and twenty-one days. Instead of sleeping-cars and comfortable coaches there were now dilapidated box-cars and filthy old passenger-wagons to accommodate the public.

In the factories of Vladivostok and Harbin, where the American-made locomotives were assembled and the freight-cars built upon the trucks shipped from the United States, the capacity had dropped from thirty locomotives a month to three and from over a hundred freight-cars to less than twenty, depending upon the feeling of the Russian workmen as to the number of hours a week they should work.

The railroad was disintegrating because no one had the authority to do any repair work, and everything depended upon the attitude of the Japanese. Almost every one realized after the fatal days of October that nothing would be done in either Russia or Siberia without the railroad, but while this question was being discussed and considered by the Foreign Office and business interests of Japan there were other grave problems confronting the Americans.

As soon as the armistice was signed the troops became restive and wanted to go home. The morale had been weakened, not by lack of action, because the men were constantly drilled and disciplined, but because of the lack of a definite policy which made not only Americans but all Allies in Siberia feel that they were there on a futile mission; that they were wasting their own time and that of Russia as well. Ambassador Morris, General Graves, and Admiral Knight had accepted the final decision of the President with good grace and had notified both the Allies and the Czecho-Slovaks that the United States under no circumstances could be expected to take part in any military activities in Siberia. Aid was promised the Czecho-Slovaks through the Red Cross and the Y.M.C.A., and the Russians were informed that the War Trade Bureau would be in a position to license imports and exports, and that special ships had been set aside by the United States Shipping Board for the explicit purpose of bringing supplies to Siberia and taking raw products from Russia to the United States. This information came as such a surprise to the Czecho-Slovaks that when they were informed in Vladivostok by Colonel O.P. Robinson that the United States would not send an army to the Ural Mountains and by Major Slaughter in Ekaterinburg, they were afraid of the moral effect upon their own army and withheld the information. The result was that when I reached the interior of Russia I found every one expecting American troops to come and no one telling either the public or the Czechs the truth as to America's attitude.

Then came the armistice and the whole situation changed in Russia. It was so clear to every one in Siberia that the Allied governments were making such great mistakes in handling the Russian problem that nothing constructive could be expected, and the whole attention of Allies and Russians was centred upon the Peace Conference at Paris. In the meantime affairs developed from bad to worse. The Bolshevist government gained strength in European Russia by modifying its policies and the Bolshevist agitation in Siberia increased as the funds for propaganda were advanced.

The English and French representatives, however, had not given up their hope of a strong Russian army. France had sent General Janin with a staff of officers from Paris to Siberia to organize a Russian army. His instructions from his government were the same as the instructions given to General Knox by England. Apparently England and France had sent representatives to Russia to do the same thing without either government consulting the other. General Knox had been at work in Siberia for several months. He had established officers training-camps and had succeeded in getting the support of the Omsk government for his plan of mobilizing a Russian army. As General Janin arrived it was obvious that there might be two generals working in different ways for the same thing, which would eventually lead to a conflict unless there was some understanding between the two military men. In December they met in Vladivostok for a conference and divided Siberia, as far as their work was concerned, into two spheres, one from Vladivostok to Lake Baikal and the other one from the lake to the Ural Mountains. By agreement between the two officers General Knox was to have command of the Russian army in eastern Siberia while General Janin was to be the commander in western Siberia. This step by the two Allied generals was taken without consultation with representatives of the other Allied armies, with the possible exception of the Japanese, and the others were apprised of this move only after it had become an accomplished fact, and, after the "treaty" had been signed by the two generals. By this time there was not the slightest evidence or indication of Allied unity in Siberia. The only nations to live up to the terms of the original agreement were the United States, Italy, and China. England, France, and Japan had long since adopted their own policies in Siberia, and Russia continued to crumble.

It is not my object to fix the blame for any of the steps which were taken, but only to point to the facts and the consequences. There were capable officials of the Allies in Siberia who might have been in a position to help Russia get together if their own governments had supported them, and if they had not been handicapped by the individual activities of the military officials. I doubt whether the Allies or the League of

Nations will ever select more capable men to study an international problem and to carry out instructions of organized governments than the men like the following, who were sent to Siberia: Ambassador Morris, General Graves, Colonel Robinson, Ambassador Eugene Regnault, Sir Charles Eliot, John F. Stevens, Vice-Consul Palmer,[15] and Mr. Matsudaira, chief of the political division of the Japanese General Staff,[16] and a representative of the Japanese Foreign Office in Vladivostok. But the colossal task which faced these men was made impossible of execution because of the lack of the very thing which will make a league of nations successful, namely, unity of purpose and of action. The Allies failed in Siberia because they were not united. They were not even agreed upon fundamental principles. Men who represented the Powers in this country needed authority to accomplish anything, and this was withheld.

That the Allies will eventually be compelled to withdraw their armies from Siberia and Russia as belligerent forces is the only outcome of a situation created by limitless mistakes. It may be necessary for them to make an agreement with the Bolsheviki, or any other de facto government of Russia, in order to begin the actual work of reconstruction. They may send food in the beginning and end by recognizing a Soviet Government in Russia, but neither the Allies nor a League of Nations will remain or endure if they recognize the principles of Bolshevism. But they are faced by this predicament because of past indecision. This is the reason the goblins of Bolshevism hovered over the Paris conference and the statesmen warned the world that "the Bolsheviki will get you if you don't watch out." Bolshevism is a world force which has grown in Russia under the very eyes of the Allies and former Central Powers.

Departing from Vladivostok for Harbin my last view of the foreigners in the city was of the Allied sentries at the railroad-station. Three of them, one Czech, one American, and one Japanese, were standing in the entrance to the depot, bored, idle, and silent. Symbolical of the Allies they were helpless spectators of the tragedy of Russia; military exiles in Siberia.

---

[15] Henry L. Palmer, formerly an International Harvester agent. In 1918, he was appointed US vice consul in Ekaterinburg.

[16] Tsuneo Matsudaira (1877–1949) was a Japanese diplomat. From 1920 till the 1930s, he was Japanese ambassador to England and the United States. After World War II, he served as the first head of the House of Councillors from when the Japanese constitution was first effective until his death in 1949.

# Chapter IX
# DECISIVE DAYS IN SIBERIA

The days of October, 1918, were critical days for Siberia and decisive days for Russia. The Allies had landed small forces at Vladivostok in August, but after two months practically nothing had been done either for or against Russia. The demands for more extensive military operations, which in its final analysis meant action, reached a climax during the first days of the tenth month.

That the United States had not been at war with the Bolsheviki was obvious; that the Allies were not planning to attack the Red army along the Ural Mountain "front" was equally evident. The opaqueness of the Allied policy was causing so much criticism that the American leaders in Siberia held a conference and made recommendations to Washington, which, when acted upon, had the effect of changing the whole course of Russian events.

The story of the Americans in Siberia is the narrative of one contest after another, one conflict of opinion upon another, and differences in the attitude of our own officials and the Allied governments. Instead of landing a belligerent force in Siberia, with definite objects and clear instructions to cover a longer period of time than the first days or weeks after lading; instead of giving the army and officials something to do, the Americans who landed there became, after a very short period, our first political exiles. That all of these Americans should wish to leave; that the Russians should be anxious to have them go, are the two only outcomes of the developments in Siberia. Not only the men but the officers wished to leave. Why? That is the story of the decisive days in Siberia.

Shortly after the first American troops were landed in Siberia I arrived in Vladivostok as a correspondent with the Allied armies. As the ship pulled into the harbor, I saw on the shore American sentries guarding warehouses and war materials scattered along the banks of the bay. Five thousand miles away from the Pacific coast, these men were in Russia, so they thought, to fight the Bolsheviki, but instead they found themselves there as spectators. Not far from where the Japanese passengers-ship docked were the war-ships of the Allied nations swimming at anchor. In the middle of the bay was a Japanese war-ship. Closer to the shore was the U.S.S. *Brooklyn*, with Admiral Knight aboard, the British Cruiser, H.M.S. *Sussex*, a French cruiser, and a Chinese gunboat.

Vladivostok, being situated on the hills, appeared to be a great amphitheatre as one entered the harbor. From the tops of the tallest buildings could be seen the flags of the Allies. Along the docks were Chinese "coolies," a few Russian merchants, some of whom spoke German, a few American and French marines, and a half-dozen or so of lazy Russian workmen.

I sauntered up the hill to one of the tallest buildings in the city from which the American flag was flying and in front of which stood a Yankee sentry. This was the headquarters of Major-General William S. Graves, Commander of the A.E.F. in Siberia. Four miles up Golden Horn Bay in huge frame storehouses, built by the Czar's officials, were housed the American troops. This was the base and the whole works of the American army in Siberia. German prisoners were busy along the dock stacking hay which had been unloaded from the United States Transport *Dixie*. Along the temporary tracks which the engineers had built ran small locomotives our army had found idle and out of repair in the yards of the city.

Svetlanskaya is the name of the main street of this city which was once "The Czar of the East." Not only the business but the military and political affairs of Vladivostok and of Siberia were centred here. Motoring into the city from the American Base I passed the barracks where 600 Chinese soldiers were encamped; farther on were Japanese barracks, an American Red Cross hospital, barracks which the United States Railroad Service Corps had taken over, and a large, white cement apartment-house, on the first floor of which the American Red Cross had its headquarters.

On the other side of the street stood the five-story red-brick building which was used as the French headquarters and from the top of which could be seen French marines, wigwagging their signals to another station across the bay. Not far from the French headquarters, and practically across the street from the Vladivostok offices of the Czecho-Slovak army, was the headquarters of the Japanese army, a two-story stone structure which had been a German department store. Near the railway depot was the British headquarters and the offices of the Siberian Government. The Allied consulates were scattered about the city, as their interests were scattered. There were Japanese, Americans, Chinese, and Russian shops. Two German department stores were still in operation. British interests had opened a branch bank and everywhere the money lenders and money changers were to be seen, because, with the arrival of the Allied forces, Vladivostok became a sort of money stock exchange where there was continuous speculation in roubles, dollars, and pounds.

When the Americans arrived there was what was called a Bolshevist nest in the neighborhood of Khabarovsk and Blagovestchensk, and, under the command of General Oii, Japanese, American, French, and British Forces were sent down the Usuri and Amur River valleys. Khabarovsk had been a prison-camp for German and Austrian prisoners. Before the war it was the headquarters for the Third Siberian Army Corps, and after the European War broke out some of these barracks were fenced off by fourteen-feet barbed-wire fences. Into these stockades went the prisoners of war, whose suffering can only be compared to that of the Russians under the most unfavorable conditions in Germany. After the revolution the barbed wires were cut (the ends dangle in curious fashion in the air to-day), and from the camp fled several thousand former soldiers of the Central Empire. Under orders from Berlin and Vienna these men joined the forces of the Bolshevist army operating in the Amur, and they put up a strong fight against the combined forces of the Allies marching from Vladivostok.

Some days after the first and only engagements between the Americans and the armed forces of the Red Guard, I journeyed 800 versts with General Graves and his staff.

These were the early days of October and Siberia, famed for its cold, was warmer than San Francisco a month before, when I sailed for the Far East, although not as comfortable as it is during the summer months—that period of the year which had made Vladivostok a favorite summer resort in the Far East.

After I had been in the city a few days I was invited by General Graves to accompany him on his first journey into Siberia. Upon the appointed day I drove to the railroad-station, walked out through the yard looking for the general's train. There were scores of other cars and special trains standing along the siding, but no one could tell me where the train was which had been selected to take the American commander. After searching around the yard for some time I encountered Major Eichelberger,[1] the assistant chief of staff, accompanied by several staff officers, inquiring for the same train that I was.

Searching for trains is one of the chief pastimes of any one who stays in Siberia and travels; so I learned by experience. It is not an unusual thing to lose your home on wheels, and later, on another occasion, I spent every hour and every moment from ten o'clock in the morning until ten at night searching for the car which I had left standing at a certain spot in one of the railroad yards.

The night before General Graves was to depart, Major Eichelberger had, after two days' work, succeeded in obtaining one sleeping-car and one dining-car, which he had had connected up and cleaned in preparation for the journey. But when he arrived in the yard the following morning the cars had disappeared, despite the orders which the Inter-Allied Railroad Commission had given, designating these two cars to General Graves for his inspection trip. It was a long hot journey up and down the track between the rows of cars, through the yard, before they were found. In the

---

[1] Robert Lawrence Eichelberger (1886–1961) was a military officer in the United States Army. A 1909 graduate of the United States Military Academy at West Point, he served in several missions. In June 1918, he became an assistant to Brigadier General William S. Graves, the commander of the US Army's 8th Division bound for Siberia. The American Expeditionary Force, Siberia departed San Francisco on August 15, with Eichelberger as its assistant chief of staff, G-2 (Intelligence). Soon after arriving, he was appointed to the ten-nation Inter-Allied Military Council, which was responsible for Allied strategy. He was awarded the Distinguished Service Cross for his service in Siberia. Later, he became a general and commanded the Eighth United States Army in the Southwest Pacific Area during World War II.

meanwhile a Chinese "coolie" who was lugging my sleeping-sacks and suitcase stumbled along over ties and tracks in a frantic effort to keep up.

After the major succeeded in corralling a switch engine the two cars, when located, were hitched together again and American sentries were placed at the doors with fixed bayonets and strict orders not to permit any one to enter or move the car without written instructions from American headquarters. The cooks from headquarters came to the train with their provisions for the week's journey, and, many hours after the schedule time of departure, the special was pulled up to the depot, two large American flags were nailed on the sides of the diners, a big American locomotive was brought over from the roundhouse, and General Graves and his staff stepped aboard.

Not all of the American troops were in Vladivostok at this time. About 3,000 of them were stationed at Khabarovsk and in the towns along the Amur railroad, but outside of this section there were no American army units in any other part of Siberia, although the zone of activity as defined in the agreement between the United States and the Allied governments extended from the Pacific to Lake Baikal. Altogether, there were only a few more than 7,000 Americans in Siberia, about half this number being in Vladivostok and the other half in small units along the Amur line. Journeying with General Graves, I had an opportunity of not only following him everywhere on his inspection trip, but I was permitted to see the side-lights of the expedition, which brought out the objects and the policies of the United States clearer than they could have been in any other way. Every time the train passed a group of Americans the general would stop to speak with them. I recall my first introduction to these meetings in a little town where forty-two soldiers were stationed. The men were living in boxcars along a siding. They were commanded by a young lieutenant. The men were all regulars, while the officers had been schooled in one of the war training-camps, and had taken a sort of post-graduate course on the transport coming over. The general answered his salute, and said:

"Good morning. I have come to inspect your quarters."

(In the dialogues which follow I have reported the conversations as recorded in my note-book, kept during the journey. I believe them to be accurate, but I could not have their inclusion in this book verified by General Graves because, at this writing, he is still in Siberia.) The lieutenant saluted, turned and led the way to the cars. The general climbed into each car, inspected the beds, the floors, and the provisions, the stoves, and the men, pointed out his criticisms or comments to the young officer, and asked him whether there was anything he wanted.

This was the general's method of inspection. He saw every American who was along the railroad or in any of the towns off of the railroad. He talked to the men and to the officers. He inspected their quarters, their food-supplies, and asked them what they were doing. The invariable reply to these questions was that they were doing nothing but guarding railroad-stations or bridges, and that they wanted shotguns and extra ammunition so they could hunt bear, ducks, and pheasants, which were abundant in the neighborhood. But the general was interested in more than the mere details of their rather routine day. Frequently he would approach an officer or a "non-com" and ask the blunt question:

"What are you here for?"

That question was frequently answered by a salute and a statement:

"I am here to fight the Bolsheviki."

"Are those your orders?" the general would ask.

"Yes, sir."

"Where did you get those orders?"

At this point in the quiz the men were usually in such an uncomfortable position they were prepared to make a quick retreat, both by statement and body. But the general's questions came like bullets from a machine-gun, although at heart he was very human and not stern beyond the point of being firm and exacting.

"Who are the Bolsheviki?" the general would ask.

It was seldom that any man or officer gave the same reply. One lieutenant, looking the general square in the face, remarked boldly and confidently:

"The Bolsheviki are the men who are trying to destroy Russia by killing off the good people and burning the property."

"Have you seen any Bolsheviki around here?" the general asked.

"Yes, sir."

"Well, what do you do with them?"

"We arrest them, sir."

"Have you any in jail now?" the general asked.

There was in one town a Russian in the army prison, and I walked with the general to see my first Bolshevik; as we walked over to the basement of the building, which was being used as a guard-house and prison, I thought of some of the questions the general had asked another officer when he asked him to describe the Bolshevik.

"Does he have a long black beard, long hair, dark eyes, torn clothing, and big hands?"

The customary answer was in the affirmative, so, as I entered the prison, following the staff of the general, I found two American soldiers standing in front of a heavy wooden door; about four feet from the floor was a hole, about six inches square, through which one could see into the cell.

All of us took a good look at the prisoner. He was nothing more than a replica of the type of Russian peasant which one sees by the hundred thousand in all parts of Siberia. He was seated on a bench against the wall and looked resignedly at the faces which peered at him through the opening.

After we had all seen our first Bolshevik, and saw no difference between him and thousands of Russians we had already seen in Vladivostok and along the railroad line, we stood in a circle while the general began to requestion the young American officer.

"What did that man do?" General Graves asked.

"Why, nothing, sir," the officer said hesitatingly.

"Why do you have him under arrest then?"

"Why, he said he was a Bolshevik."

"Do you have orders to arrest the Bolsheviki?"

"Yes, sir."

"Where did you get those orders?"

This left the officer in the quandary the general expected to place him. To this young warden the general made the following statement:

"Whoever gave you those orders must have made them up himself. The United States is not at war with the Bolsheviki or any other faction of Russia. You have no orders to arrest Bolsheviks or anybody else unless they disturb the peace of the community, attack the people or the Allied soldiers. The United States army is not here to fight Russia or any group or faction in Russia. Because a man is a Bolshevik is no reason for his arrest. You are to arrest only those who attack you. The United States is only fighting the Bolsheviki when the American troops are attacked by an armed force."

This was my first intimation that the United States did not consider the Bolsheviki everywhere as enemies of the Allies. But as I travelled into the interior I found that while General Graves had very definite ideas, and very exacting orders, that not all of the Americans representing our government in different capacities were acting as he was. The outcome of this visit to the army prison was that the Bolshevist prisoner was turned loose, as were all others along the line wherever the general encountered them, unless they were soldiers of the Red army who had engaged in a conflict with either the United States or Allied troops.

The world has seen experiments throughout the war between Great Powers in an endeavor to act together both in military, political, and commercial affairs. To obtain united action is a far more difficult task than to plan an attack on an organized enemy. The interests of all the countries are totally different because each has a different history, different obligations, and different financial interests. We have a league of nations at work in the United States. All nationalities are represented here, but our government is successful because there are well-defined functions for the different departments of the government and because every one can have a voice in affairs at the regular elections. But imagine the United States as a nation without a government and without a fundamental law and all of the races of peoples coming from all parts of the world getting together in an effort to unite upon a government policy and a plan of action, and you will have in a small way an example of the difficulties which confronted the Allies, acting as a society of nations, in Siberia and Russia. Not only were the interests of the governments greatly at variance with each other, but the individual representatives of the Great Powers interpreted their instructions differently, and there were personal as well as national differences of opinion.

The fundamental principles which formed the basis for action in Siberia were, briefly, the following:

1. Each Ally should land about 7,000 soldiers;
2. Until further discussion between the Allied governments the sphere of activity for the belligerent armies should be east of Lake Baikal, and,
3. These limitations were placed upon the movements of the Allied forces because of the gulf which separated the policy of the United States toward Russia and that of the other Allies. The United States was reluctantly brought around to the plan for military intervention. Our government considered Russia essentially a reconstruction problem and not a war question, while England, Japan, France, and Italy hoped to see Russia as a belligerent fighting Germany along an eastern front. The United States believed that Russia's salvation lay in her ability to recommence work. The Allies contended that Russia could never become a Great Power without a strong army, and that an army must be built immediately by the Allies for the Russians.

These differences were not eliminated nor even bridged by the landing of troops at Vladivostok and Archangel. They were rather accentuated, because there was a general feeling among our Allies that if American troops could be landed in Russia there would be no end to the number who might be sent later. The result was that as soon as the high commissioners, ambassadors, and generals of the Allies met in Vladivostok each had a different idea of what should be done. General Knox, of the British staff, had been sent to Siberia by his government to raise a volunteer army of Russians to fight with the Czecho-Slovaks against the Red army along the Ural Mountains. Although he was attached to the Japanese General Staff as a military observer, he was not to be under the authority of the Japanese army in this work. General Otani, who had been named as commander-in-chief of the Allied forces in Siberia, was commander only as far as Lake Baikal, and as the Russian army was not under his jurisdiction he had nothing to say as to the plans of General Knox.

But one day at a meeting of the generals commanding the Allied armies at Japanese headquarters, General Knox proposed that all of the war materials, with an estimated value of nearly $1,000,000,000, should be turned over to the new Russian army which was being formed. This met with the immediate objection of General Graves, who had been instructed by our government under no circumstances to give his consent for the use of these war materials on the ground that they were not the property of the Allies but of the Russian people; that no government had a right to them except the Russian Government, and that inasmuch as there was no recognized Russian Government, and the primary object of the Allied landing was to help Russia, the only thing the Allies could do was to protect these materials. Before this meeting the city of Vladivostok had been divided into inter-Allied zones, and each Ally undertook the responsibility of guarding the supplies in its zone.

The outcome of this conference was that the Allies did not vote upon the Knox proposal, and after that the question was never brought up again, although the Czecho-Slovaks, on the ground that they were fighting for Russia, commandeered automobiles and other supplies which they needed for their poorly equipped army.

The French and British campaigned incessantly for military intervention. They are carrying out the instructions of their governments and the recommendations of their military leaders, whose object was the recreation of an Eastern front. They were panicky after the March and May offensives of Germany in France, and forecasted a military disaster for the Allies unless a two-front war was re-begun via Russia.

American representatives were sceptical of the practicability of extensive military intervention, but they were reporting all the facts and their observations directly to Washington and following only the instructions which they received from their department chiefs. Although they were in as close contact with Russian affairs as any of the Allied representatives, they weighed more carefully than the others the objections and points in favor of intervention, because they realized, and the Allies knew, that if there was to be an extensive military campaign in Russia the burden would fall upon the United States and Japan, because neither England nor France had the troops to spare for a Russian campaign. Great Britain was so short of effectives, for instance, that when General Knox arrived in Siberia and inspected the British soldiers who had been sent there he called them his "hernia battalion," because every man had been previously discharged from active military service because he had been "gassed." While well-equipped, the French soldiers were from tropical countries and unaccustomed to European warfare, and the Italian troops, upon their arrival in Harbin from South China in late October, nearly froze to death because they had no winter equipment of any kind.

But Ambassador Morris, General Graves, and Admiral Knight were making a special study of the situation. The American Government had already tested, in difficult positions in the past, the opinion of each man and each was known to be vitally interested in helping his country help Russia through the difficult period of reconstruction. The pressure which was brought to bear upon these three men in favor of military intervention and against the policy of the United States Government was as tremendous as was the influence from Washington and the government in favor of a "sit-tight policy." Each official had been in Russia several months, had read all of the reports from American representatives in all parts of Russia, and had conferred with thousands of Russians and Allies. Each had held the individual opinion that the United States should not take part in military intervention, on a great scale, for various reasons. With the exception of Admiral Knight they held that the United States needed to concentrate all of her attention and strength in France in order to win the war; they believed Bolshevism could not be defeated by an army, and they believed the Russian people would consider an Allied army an enemy and not a friendly force.

In October events were moving rapidly in France and Belgium and no less rapidly in Russia. It was quite evident that the All-Russian Government which was in power in Omsk had the support of the people. It was equally clear that the Bolsheviki authorities had practically reached the limit of their strength and public support. At any moment the Czecho-Slovaks expected to see developments in European Russia follow the same line as those in Austria and Germany when there were demands from the Central Powers for an armistice.

In order to understand the military situation it should be made clear that the Czecho-Slovak forces had been fighting in Siberia since May; that they had had nothing but the moral support of the Allied representatives; that they had been promised definite military assistance, but that after six months of fighting they were so exhausted as to be incapable of further aggressive action. The Allies had landed at Vladivostok ostensibly to help the Czechs but so far nothing had been done. The Czech soldiers and members of the Czecho-Slovak National Council in Russia were not only disappointed but discouraged, and they realized that unless the Allies assisted them they would be forced to withdraw from Russia, and that if they withdrew the All-Russian Government would fall and the Bolsheviki would succeed to authority in Siberia.

All of these elements entered into the consideration of the Russian problem by the American representatives. They had also the instructions of their government. They knew the attitude of the Allies. They knew the stupendous and almost unmeasurable difficulties confronting the problem of transporting and supplying an army in Siberia. They knew, for instance, that the United States could land a hundred thousand soldiers in France to a thousand in Siberia because of the lack of ships on the Pacific.

Despite all of these objections, and after considering the situation as it existed in Siberia, these three representatives cabled a joint report to the State, War, and Navy Departments for the President, going into great detail and recommending, not that the United States send a large army to Siberia but that a small detachment of men be sent from Vladivostok, together with detachments, representing the other nations, to the Ural front to assist the Czecho-Slovaks, for its moral effect upon Siberia and because of the encouragement which this would give to the armies fighting the Bolsheviki in case the developments of October in Germany should be such as to indicate Germany's withdrawal from the war. This document was probably the most important American report ever sent from Russia. The President himself regarded it as "the most convincing document" he had read on the Russian problem.

For a time it looked as if it might be possible for all of the Allies to unite upon this recommendation of the three American observers, but after careful consideration President Wilson replied to his representatives in Vladivostok that the chief of staff of the army had vetoed the plan of action which was proposed.

This decision was probably the gravest and most decisive as far as Russia is concerned, for the events which followed the failure of the United States to join the Allies and do what obviously should have been done, and what the American representatives themselves recommended, changed the whole course of Russia's future. The events which followed this decision, which in light of recent developments was the greatest mistake in the whole Allied programme toward Russia, brought about the downfall of the All-Russian Government, the Koltshak dictatorship in Omsk, the complete discouragement of the Czecho-Slovak forces, and their gradual withdrawing from the front. It was followed by the growth of Bolshevism in Siberia, and instead of the war ending in Russia, as dramatically and suddenly as it ended in Europe, we find the civil war continuing and the Allies still discussing what should be done in Russia.

October, 1918, was the decisive month in the history of Russian independence as expressed by the revolution. The decision of one government had the effect of the decision of a Roman Emperor when he turned down his thumb before a gladiator.

It is pathetic to describe the effect of this decision upon the Czecho-Slovak soldiers in Russia. They had great expectations. They had been promised assistance by official representatives of the United States. They had been encouraged to believe that the Czecho-Slovak army would be "the backbone of Allied action in Russia," as the United States consul-general in Irkutsk had telegraphed. As far back as July they had been hoping. On July 4, 1918, they sent the following official letter to President Wilson:

OMSK, SIBERIA, July 4, 1918.

To the President of the United States of America:

MR. PRESIDENT: On this, the American national holiday, the Czecho-Slovak army on the banks of the Volga, on the slopes of the Urals, in the forests and on the steppes of Siberia, fighting against the insatiable hydra of Austro-German imperialism, sends to you, Mr. President, and through you to all the noble people of the United States of America and their brave army, sincere congratulations.

The revolt of the North American Colonies in 1776 was a struggle not only for the political freedom of the individual citizen, but also for a condition of natural political independence, all of which has been preserved to history.

The present war is a continuation of that revolt. Therefore it is quite natural that America, together with the other Allies, and the oppressed nations of Central and Eastern Europe, should fight for the same idea for which she fought 142 years ago.

Please accept, Mr. President, from the Czecho-Slovak army in Russia, the sincere expression of its respect and thanks for your noble effort in behalf of the triumph of justice and liberty, which will be also a triumph for the Czecho-Slovak nation.

(Signed) FIRST CONGRESS OF THE CZECHO-SLOVAK ARMY AT CHELIABINSK:
K. Zmrhal,[2] Chairman.
J. Hrbek, Secretary.
Executive Committee of the Czecho-Slovak Army: Branch of the Czecho Slovak National Council for Russia:
B. Pavlu,[3] Chairman.
Fr. Richter, Secretary.

On the same day a letter was despatched to "The Commander-in-Chief of the American Army" in Washington, signed by the same officials, in which the hope was expressed that the Czecho-Slovak army would "soon meet its American brother soldiers on the same front." This letter I shall give verbatim because it was one of the numerous official communications which have never been published.

OMSK, SIBERIA, July 4, 1918.

To the Commander-in-Chief of the American Army.

SIR: In the name of the Czecho-Slovak army, which, in the wide territory of the Russian Empire, is defending itself against the intrigues of Austro-German imperialism, we beg that you notify the brave army of the United States of America on this American national holiday, the Czecho-Slovak soldiers are thinking of their American brothers in arms and send their ardent wish for continued success on all fronts.

The Czecho-Slovak army is firmly convinced that it will soon meet its American brother soldiers on the same front, and that the unity of effort and unity of aim which strengthens us will be sealed and consecrated by the blood jointly poured out for the highest ideals of humanity. Eternal memory to the American heroes who laid down their lives for liberty! Glory and success to the brave warriors who to-day are carrying their blood to the altar of humanity!

---

[2] Karel Zmrhal-Sázavský (1888–1933), Czecho-Slovak officer, later an author of books and articles about Czech experiences in Siberia.

[3] Bohdan Pavlů (1883–1938), Czecho-Slovak journalist, politician, and diplomat; a representative of the Czecho-Slovak Republic in Russia, 1918–19, and member of the Czecho-Slovak National Council. After his return to Czecho-Slovakia, he worked as an editor and then as ambassador to Bulgaria, Denmark, and the USSR.

The enthusiasm of the Czecho-Slovaks for the United States was very real and was still as unbounded in October as it was when these letters were written in July. The faith of that army alone in Russia in America's help was so extensive and vital that when Major-General Graves and Ambassador Morris communicated the fatal decision of Washington that United States forces would not be despatched to the Urals, the officials of the Czecho-Slovak National Council in Vladivostok and the army leaders in Cheliabinsk and Ekaterinburg would not communicate the message to the Czecho-Slovak soldiers for fear of the reaction it would have upon the morale of the soldiers. The Czech officials in Vladivostok did not even telegraph the announcement to the representatives of the National Council in Ekaterinburg, and as late as December, two months after America had decided against further intervention, the officials of the Czecho-Slovak National Council at the headquarters in the Ural Mountains did not know it. They were still hoping and praying for help, not knowing the "thumbs were down." Having been informed of the decision before I left Vladivostok, I asked both General Syrovy, the chief-adjutant of General Gaida, and the vice-president of the National Council whether they had received such information, and they answered that all the reports they had, indicated that American military aid would be forthcoming, and they were further encouraged in this belief by several American officials at that time in Siberia who had been campaigning for American military intervention, and had ignored their instructions from Washington not to take part in politics.

Having observed something of the intrigue and having encountered a part of the propaganda of deception which was so extensive in Russia during the fall and winter, I was not surprised when I learned that the Czecho-Slovak troops had mutinied and refused to go to the Bolshevist front. This refusal of brave and trusted men to carry out the orders of their commanders was a pathetic contrast to the enthusiasm in which they entered the first battles against the Red army of European Russia, when the Soviets broke the treaties which were made in April.

I was in Ekaterinburg at the time at the headquarters of Major-General Gaida when he announced that he had ordered several regiments to the northern front in preparation for an attack on Perm, which was held by the Red army. Gaida's staff had been laboring for several weeks on a plan of campaign, which, as explained at the time, appeared to be a simple operation. Gaida's orders were for an advance on November 24. When his orders were transmitted to the troops they refused to obey and sent representatives to the National Council to protest against further fighting against the Bolsheviki. General Syrovy had already informed me in an interview that the Omsk coup d'état "had killed his soldiers," because they believed that Admiral Koltshak represented the old Russian Government and not the Social Democrats. The colonel of one of the Czech regiments committed suicide when his troops refused to obey his orders. And because some five regiments mutinied there was a decisive crisis in the Czecho-Slovak armies which demanded immediate attention.

On the night of the 24th, after his plans had been made useless by this action of the troops, Major-General Gaida left for Cheliabinsk to confer with his colleague, Major-General Syrovy, an heroic commander who had already lost an eye in his fighting with his troops against the Bolsheviki. At this conference the date of the offensive was advanced to the 27th, and the following night when Gaida returned to Ekaterinburg he had regained his confidence and plans were made for the new attack.

On this quick journey I had accompanied Gaida, together with Major Slaughter of the United States army, who had had been attached to the Czecho-Slovak army by Major-General Graves early in May, and who had accompanied them throughout all of their campaigns in Russia and Siberia. Slaughter was a young regular army officer, who, as military attaché, had seen more of the Czech fighting than any other American. As an observer he was powerless to do more than report the developments to the American headquarters in Vladivostok, because he had already been informed by Graves that the American army would not reach the Urals, but he followed with intense sympathy and interest every move of the military chessboard of Central Russia in his second-class railway coach, which was his travelling home, and which he held in readiness for the American consul in Ekaterinburg and his family in case of a break in the "front."

The reasons for the Czecho-Slovak troops' refusal to fight was more fundamental than a mere objection to the changes in the Omsk government. Ever since the armistice the Bolshevist propagandists had been active along the fighting-line, distributing leaflets and posters appealing to the Czechs to return to Bohemia via Russia. These documents, copies of which I saw in Ekaterinburg, informed the Czecho-Slovak soldiers that there was a revolution in Austria-Hungary; that all property was being divided; that the workers were seizing everything from palaces to factories, and that unless the Czecho-Slovak soldiers in Russia returned home they would not share in the "new distribution" of wealth and property! These appeals were very similar to those sent abroad to the American and British forces in Murmansk which resulted later in the mutiny of American troops on that front.

October was a decisive month for Russia, and November was the critical month for the Czecho-Slovaks. The first destroyed all possibility for an overthrow of the Bolshevist Government in Moscow and Petrograd, and the second was the beginning of the withdrawal of the Czecho-Slovak troops from the Ural front to guard the railways of Siberia for the new Russian army under Koltshak.

## Chapter X
## VAGABONDING BACK TO VLADIVOSTOK

Even at forty degrees below zero there is an unusual fascination about a vagabond journey through Siberia. One forgets the trail of the Bolsheviki and follows the route of the revolution. Often during my stay in Ekaterinburg, after driving about the city in an open sleigh, bundled in furs and breathing the sharp, invigorating air; after walking through the second-hand "lombards," and the shops of the Russian Co-operative Union, I trekked over to the headquarters of the Czecho-Slovak National Council in the "Amerikansky Nomera" to chat with the revolutionists of central Europe, of Prague, Pilsen, and Karlsbad about the armistice, the Omsk government, the future of Russia, and the glorious days of the Czecho campaign against the Bolsheviki—the days which ended so tragically for Russia, for the Czechs and Slovaks, for the Allies, and for the world.

There were reminiscences of heroic times in these conversations. Earlier in the war, as a correspondent with the German and Austrian armies, I had listened to the denunciations of the Czechs by the military leaders of the two Kaisers when I visited their headquarters in Poland and Galicia. I heard them defamed for their loyalty to Czecho-Slovakia and their hatred of the Dual Monarchy. In the minds of the Militarists of central Europe these men were "deserters," "cowards," "fanatics," "revolutionists," and "anarchists." What a contrast it was between those meetings with the leaders of the "old world" and these young men in Russia, the vanguard of the "new order" in central Europe!

To meet the Czechs face to face, after listening to their enemies' denunciation of them, was to meet the men of the future, for the Czechs and Slovaks, although revolutionists and Socialists, had a glorious past and a promising future as leaders in the reconstruction of the war-wrecked monarchy of the Hapsburgs.

Of their fighting in Russia, in a foreign land, for their own freedom and the defeat of Bolshevism because of the danger of Bolshevism in Russia to their own new nation of Bohemia, I learned at first-hand from some of the participants who were laboring ceaselessly at the headquarters in Ekaterinburg. The tale of the encounter at Penza, which one of the young men related in broken, colorful English, was typical of the new folk-songs which, for generations to come, will be handed down to the children of Czecho-Slovakia as the account of an heroic moment in the fight of these oppressed people for their national independence.

"I was sitting in the window of my coupe," said a young Czech in relating the epic of Penza. "I looked at the city of Penza, the beautiful, white town, which now contains a part of the history of our army. There was determined the fate of our echelons; also the fate of the Soviet Government.

"This view of the white, oriental Penza always awoke in me emotions," the narrator continued. (I shall give his own words, jotted down at the time in my note-book.) "Destiny sent its artists to the enormous scene of the great Siberian Railway, on a front having a length of 7,000 miles from Serdobsk to Vladivostok. Over every mile was six of our soldiers, badly armed, which the Soviet Government gave the name 'rebels' and 'counter-revolutionists.' 'Everyman has the right to shoot them like dogs,' said the Soviet. 'If they give up their arms, they are allowed to go into prison-camps and shall have time enough to think about their stupid deeds, for these people will fight against the German-Magyar reaction.'

"After the occupation of Cheliabinsk came the official, bloody telegrams of Tovarish (Comrade) Trotsky. They also came to us in Penza. And it began the first act of the tragedy.

"Yes, it is necessary to say aloud: 'The Czecho-Slovak Communists were the causers. They falsely informed their Russian comrades. They provoked against us the simple Russian workmen and soldiers!'" My Czech informer was relating what the Bolshevists said about the Czechs. "'In their army,' he continued to quote, 'they were soldiers with five roubles a month salary, when they might go to the Red army where they become colonels, etc., with 600–1,000 roubles salary, four horses and servants.'

"The time in Penza, especially the last two weeks before the fight, has been the hardest of our life. Our soldiers have been daily offended, and I myself admired the character of them, who gave no answer to the provocations, having no order to do so.

"On the 27th of May, at three o'clock in the afternoon, came Tovarish Kurajev on the station. He was willing to speak to our soldiers at a meeting. The meeting has been prepared. Our soldiers were standing around a wagon he was to speak from. At the meeting have been only our soldiers, no officers, so I gave Kurajev the occasion to speak only to them. How he thought about these soldiers he showed in his oration. This oration was the most demagogical I heard in my life. I felt 'How he offends our soldiers.' He thought to have before him a flock of sheep. Besides him was standing the Czech Communist Rausher. After Kurajev spoke Minikin, and he spoke worse than his master. He told us: 'You are fighting to hold the throne of the Czar. You are not going to France but to Africa to fight negro workmen and peasants. France only will have use of you and give nothing. You are sold to American millionaires. You are goat meat.'

"A part of our soldiers laughed and another part cried: 'Down with the swindler, the shark!'

"Between the oration of Kurajev and Minikin spoke some of our boys. They spoke shortly: 'We believe our political leaders. We shall not give one rifle. Who desires our rifles shall come and get them. We go with our officers and we win,' said our soldiers directly to Kurajev. 'We do not know the word bourgeoisie. We are one family of exiles, without home, proletarians without bread. We only have our rifles. Who touches our army touches our revolutionary movement and our existence. If it is necessary we will fight against everybody, against all the world.' These were the answers of our boys.

"Thunder, lightning, and wild rain interrupted so the meeting finished. Kurajev dropped out and I had the occasion to ask how agreeable it was for him, but he went to the telegraph and asked Moscow for help.

"Our situation was critical. Being enclosed by the influence of the hostile Soviet, a drop in the sea of the enormous Russian nation, we did not know what to do, in what direction we should expect the hostile attack.

"We resolved to make an end, to take Penza, but we did not fulfil this plan immediately. Perhaps it was the good spirit of our nation who acted for us and did not allow us to begin the fight with the disappointed Russian nation, with our brethren, although the occupation of Penza at this time would not cost us such victims as later. But we can be satisfied. We remained true to the traditions of our nation, who raises his sword only against an attack.

"But to leave Penza against the will of the Soviet was impossible. Everywhere was his influence. To leave the town was necessary, to destroy this influence in the town and surrounding country, to take the power in our hands. Against an aggression we were guarded by sending night patrols, without rifles, with only a hand-grenade in the pocket, and observe the enemy all the way from the town to the station. The Soviet endeavored to strengthen his power in the town and around us. In the barracks near the station were formed new companies of internationalists, of Magyars and Germans. It seemed to be a madness, a few men to fight against the great Russian state. Perhaps we should give up the ammunition and the Soviet, though 'we shall make them give up.' That we would have any progress, that we could occupy the town and oblige the Soviet to fulfil our will, to go to the East, they did not think, but the conflict neared with every moment.

"On the 28th of May, about nine o'clock in the morning, a new train arrived on the station, on which also were three armored automobiles. One of them was large, armed by an 8-cm. gun and some machine-guns; the other two smaller, with two or three machine-guns. The train stopped directly beside our train and the machine-guns, occasionally, were directed on our train.

"'These armored trains are for us. We must take them.' It was the presentiment, the feeling of our men who were in a dangerous position. The order was given to Lieutenant Shvetz, who designated for this work the Fifth Company of the First Regiment. Like shadows went our boys between the trains, then under the hostile train, some leap on the platform and the autos are ours without a shot.' The other part of the company deserted the enemy, who was in the wagons. No resistance was met. The order 'Hands up' was sufficient. And there were also our first prisoners, fifty men, one of them wounded. The automobiles are in our hands. We began the hostilities ourselves but we have been obliged to do so to hinder an attack. We tried to continue the conference. The automobiles will be ours as long as the situation is not cleared. And, to make the situation not worse, we gave the first wounded back to the enemy though his wound was bad. He died the same night. To the automobiles we gave our guards and hoped still the Soviet would let us go willingly.

"The station was filled with peasants with baggage, who had been waiting two days already for a train. They showed their spite against the Red army in loud abuses, and we were obliged to defend our prisoners against the crowd. In little groups stood our brothers speaking to the peasants who we are and what we desire and why the Soviet detains us.

"In the town, when the Soviet had been informed about the incident, began an alarm. We heard it. It begins to sound a siren in a factory, without an end. Then a second, third, etc. In all factories alarm. It seems the town cries for help. This horrible sound mobilizes the Bolsheviki workmen. The situation continues all morning. The Soviet concentrates his forces.

"A change began in the afternoon. From the right side, near the railroad bridge, we hear some shots. The Bolsheviki attacked some unarmed brothers and these have been our first wounded. We are momently in our positions. The second battalion captures the houses near the station. Our company of the battalion occupies the barracks on the other side. They are not Communists but prisoners, Germans and Magyars, who betrayed the Social Republic, taking their old uniforms and running into the forests.

"Again silence. We get an order to remain in good positions. Only on the right flank, direction Penza I. (there are usually two depots in Russian cities, called Penza I. and Penza II.) we hear shots. A part of the battalion of the first reserve regiment (such of them who had rifles) got an order to take the station Penza I. and occupy the locomotive depot. They made it. And all locomotives came on the station Rjazansko-Uralsk.

"We don't shoot for there is nobody we can shoot at. But in the town the shooting becomes stronger and stronger, every moment appears a new machine-gun and shows his presence by shooting. But they shoot into the air. It seems to be a fight in the town itself, in consequence of the wild shooting therein.

"An attack we could not expect being guarded very well. For the Red army to attack the town from the Rjazansko-Uralsk station was possible only for the price of great losses. Therefore he could attack only from the direction of Rtishevo, or from the northeast side, from the station Penza I. After the occupation of the station, Penza I., by our forces, this Bolshevist battalion was obliged to retreat and he left this north way into the town. He went back, further. From the south side was an attack against us, also very difficult. In this direction was the First Battery, First Regiment, of the Soviet on the station Krivozerovka which got an order to attack the town from the south.

"But during all the day the Bolsheviki did not attack and Penza belonged to our soldiers. One night later, on the 31st of May, we received a telegram that our Third Regiment took Cheliabinsk, took more than 18,000 rifles, 80 machine-guns, and 20 guns. We have two victories!

"So our soldiers who were to be 'shoot like dogs,' have defeated the Red army in Penza, together, also, the Germans and Magyars prisoners."

Not all of the Czecho-Slovaks recalled in such details the story of their Iliad in Russia. Some of them had been in this country over four years. Yearning for home they spoke more often of their families they had left behind than about their fighting. Others, who were engaged in the supply division of the army, and who had been promised assistance by the United States and Allies, were bitter in their denunciation of the Allies' failure to send aid, and they appealed to me as an American correspondent attached to their army to "tell the United States to send something besides money."

"We have millions of dollars and hundreds of millions of roubles. We have money, money, money, but no supplies. What good does all this money do us when there is no market in Russia where we can buy food, clothing, ammunition, or guns. We can't fight with money. We need help," they complained.

And they did need help, indeed, but the possibility of aid ever reaching them had already been destroyed. They, too, were destined to be exiles in Russia, whose fate, as the fate of Russia, was soon to be placed in the hands of the statesmen in Paris and the League of Nations. But they did not know this, and in order to have one more frantic appeal appear in the United States, they were willing to assist me on my journey eastward to Vladivostok so that I might telegraph a description of their predicament to the newspapers which I represented.

Although I had travelled over 7,000 miles in Siberia and Manchuria before I reached Ekaterinburg I had never purchased a railroad ticket! Travelling is vagabonding in Russia. Few travellers purchase tickets. There are no regular collections and often one can travel as far without a ticket as with one, but these were not my reasons for travelling free of charge. On the journey I took with Major-General Graves I was a guest of the American commander, and he, as an Allied officer, could travel wherever he wished on any campaign or mission, whenever he received the approval of the inter-Allied railroad mission in Vladivostok, or by simply notifying Japanese headquarters, because he and all other Allied generals were officially under the command of the Japanese commander-in-chief. The American Red Cross had a different status. This was a recognized relief organization whose object was to assist the Russian people, and this society paid no railroad fares, although it was said the Russian railroad officials were keeping a careful account of every mile travelled by American and Allied officers so that a bill could be rendered after the war! Be that as it may, on my 7,000-mile journey I had neither the opportunity nor permission to pay railroad fare.

I was not alone in enjoying these free rides. I do not recall meeting any foreigner in Russia who ever bought a railroad ticket, just as I do not recall having seen any one travelling in Russia with a properly vizaed passport, or card of identification. There was no check on the travellers except in Harbin and Vladivostok. I met Russians, frequently, who had crossed the Bolshevist front into Siberia without being questioned. I do not doubt but that others travelled from Siberia to Moscow and Petrograd. In Omsk, on my way East, I met the Russian wife of a Czech soldier who had been back and forth into European Russia several times as a "Bolshevist Red Cross sister."

But now that I was prepared to leave the Ural district for the coast, I encountered every possible obstacle. There were no Red Cross or Y.M.C.A. cars returning. No Czech supply-trains were scheduled to leave. No Allied officers contemplated a journey in less than a fortnight or three weeks. The only possibility appeared to be a post train which left Cheliabinsk every Thursday. I was offered a corner to sleep in in one of these cars, but, because I expected to do some writing during the nineteen-day journey, I appealed to the Czech National Council for the use of one of their "office" cars. The National Council, however, was anxious to keep all the cars which had been commandeered from the railroad as near headquarters as possible so that, in case of an emergency, they could move from one city to another, because they never knew in this ambush warfare what would happen from one day to the next.

I searched the railroad yards of Ekaterinburg and Cheliabinsk for a car, and was about to ask for the use of an abandoned and dilapidated hospital-car, which was standing idle in the yards of the former city, when it was suggested that I go to the Russian station-master and make an appeal.

After repeated calls with another correspondent, and receiving no encouragement or help, I was on the verge of deciding to travel in one of the post-cars when I discovered on a siding a heavy passenger-car, in fairly good condition, with heavy iron bars over the windows and doors. This car, according to the sign on the outside, was a prison-car which the officials of the Tzar's government had used to transport political prisoners from European Russia to Siberia in the days when the will of one man was supreme over 170,000,000. This car was a sort of useless emblem of the old order, and the possibility of travelling through Siberia in a prison-car with the freedom of an ordinary citizen had its fascination, but the following morning, when I called upon the station-master again, he informed me that the night before a small office car had been brought to town by one of the Czech officials, and that if I went to the Czech National Council again I might be able to obtain the use of this coach. After appealing to various members of the Czech staff, my colleague and I were given authority to use the car. General Gaida issued an order for it to be attached to the regular train leaving that night for Omsk.

To have succeeded after some four or five days of constant effort in obtaining a "private car" was an accomplishment which can be appreciated only by those who had endeavored, in a country at war and disturbed by civil unrest, to travel under somewhat better conditions than those confronting the public. After searching for some war prisoners or baggage-men to help lug my supplies to the car, and after having them securely placed in one of the berths, I sauntered off to the station to thank the Russian railroad man for his help, because I felt greatly indebted to him. Before I had entered Siberia I learned that cigarettes and cigars were almost unobtainable, and I carried a good supply of both with me. Walking into his office with several packages of cigarettes and tobacco, I asked him, through my companion, whether he would permit me to give him something for his assistance, and he remarked as I began to take the packages out of my overcoat pocket:

"I see you know the Russian custom of bringing gifts!"

I continued to take the valuable presents out of my pockets and to place them on a desk, when he smiled and became embarrassed, finally remarking: "Thank you, but I do not smoke." There were several other Russians in the office, and I suggested that he give the tobacco to his friends. And then I beat a hasty retreat back to my car, only to find that two officers had taken possession of it in the meantime, and to find a young Russian girl in a heated argument with a Czech soldier as to who should be the porter on the train.

It is the custom in Russia even under revolutionary conditions to have a porter on all special cars. The young girl had been assigned by the Co-operative Conductors' Association to take this car to Vladivostok and bring it back. The Czech soldier had written orders from the Czecho-Slovak National Council to do the same thing.

In order to settle the dispute we paid the girl twenty roubles to leave, and then went into the other compartment to settle the matter with the officers, who declared that the car belonged to them. This dispute was of a much more serious character because these officers had been given the number of the car by the Czech soldiers who brought it to Ekaterinburg, and they were told that if they went down and took possession of it, that possession was ten points in law in Russia. We finally relied upon the order which we had received from the Czech National Council and from General Gaida, and delivered an ultimatum to the officers, informing them that unless they left the car we would appeal to the Czech staff and have them ousted.

It was late at night before these domestic problems were settled and we were comfortably lodged in our private car with the Czech soldier as a guard, when the young Russian girl again appeared with her bundle of clothes and tears in her eyes to inform us that the organization she worked for had threatened her with court-martial unless she returned to the car and went to Vladivostok and brought it back again.

The scene of our activities was then shifted from the car to the headquarters of the Conductors' Union, and the correspondent who accompanied me, and who spoke such excellent Russian that he could argue in all of the intricate ways of the Slavs, went to the headquarters to settle the dispute while I walked to the station to make sure that our car would be attached to the midnight train for Omsk.

Both of us were away for several hours. When we returned to the siding where our car had been we found another line of freight-cars and no coach answering the description or the number of the car which we had left. Then began the search for our private car, which we were about to give up as having been lost to the two officers to whom the ultimatum had been delivered earlier in the evening. Walking through the yard during one of those black nights of Russia, for all nights are not white as many imagine, we searched every track in vain and decided, finally, that our only hope lay in the possibility that a switch engine might have picked up the car and attached it to the local train at the station.

We returned to the depot, where hundreds of refugees were awaiting an opportunity to take the same train. About two hours after the train was scheduled to depart a switch engine appeared pulling our car and a freight-car across the yard to the first track from which all trains depart. "Matusick," the Czech soldier-guardsman, was on board. Our baggage was piled securely on the seats. Candles were lighted. The stove was red with heat, and, with the thermometer still forty degrees below zero on the outside, we climbed into our "private" car, wrapped up in our army blankets, and trusted to luck that the well-known "cooties" of Russia would not disturb us. But that night it was not only the jostling of the four-wheeled coach, which finally collapsed before we reached Harbin, and the red sparks from the wood-burning locomotive, which flew in the air and bathed the train with a spray of burning cinders, that kept us awake!

In this little car with its single sleeping-compartment, its small room with tables for office use, its kitchen and wash-room, I journey from the Ural Mountains to the capital of Manchuria with my colleague of the *New York Herald* and two Czecho-Slovak soldiers. One of them, "Matusick," was supposed to be the "guard," porter, valet, and cook, but none of these tasks fitted in with his trade or ability. All he could do was to master the heating-plant and steal coal from cars and bins as we travelled across the country. And as none of my companions could cook the task fell to me. For seventeen days I prepared three and often four meals, from breakfasts to midnight lunches, for four hungry vagabonds.

At the beginning of our journey we purchased some rice, honey, bread, butter, and meat at the markets of Ekaterinburg, and begged some coffee, tea, and sugar from the Red Cross canteen. The rice was almost as expensive as platinum. Honey cost about two dollars a pound. Butter was reasonably inexpensive to an American but dear for the Russians. In Ekaterinburg I paid the equivalent of thirty cents a pound, while later on the road I bought the best creamery butter for nineteen cents.

Salt could neither be purchased nor begged. Coffee, tea, and sugar were forgotten articles to the Siberians. The only sugar I saw in Siberia was at a market-stand along the railroad. A Russian soldier brought five pounds to one of the women at the stand. Where he obtained it he would not say, nor did any one seem to know, but he sold it for two dollars a pound.

With these supplies we travelled to Omsk where we obtained chickens, geese, and the finest cuts of beef at prices varying from twenty to thirty cents per pound. Food in Siberia appeared to be abundant, especially between Ekaterinburg and Irkutsk, but between that city on Lake Baikal and Manchouli Station in Manchuria people were starving to death because of a lack of food. This was but another result of the revolution. In those districts where food was produced there was plenty. In other sections where the inhabitants had been dependent upon food shipped to them from other parts of Siberia there was nothing. This was but one more evidence of the failure of the industrial revolution. Until the overthrow of the provisional government in November, 1917, food was brought into these barren communities, but after that it stopped and every one suffered, rich, poor, industrious, and lazy citizens alike, for famine makes no class distinction.

Along the route in western Siberia we had no difficulty obtaining all the provisions we needed. Often at the markets we bought roast goose, boiled pork, and fried veal and beef which the peasant women brought to the depots, as the "regular," to which our car was attached, pulled into the cities and towns. But it was pathetic to travel through those districts which were foodless, especially when enormous quantities of food were known to be stored in various parts of Siberia. An official of the Siberian Co-operatives told me that these unions had 20,000,000 roubles' worth of butter in cold storage and 40,000,000 roubles' worth of raw materials and other food-supplies in their warehouses between Irkutsk and Vladivostok. This 60,000,000 roubles' worth of supplies can neither be shipped to the famine districts of Siberia, because of the collapse of the freight traffic, nor can it be sent to foreign countries in exchange for manufactured articles, such as clothing and household goods, which the Russian people need.

It was a slow journey back to the Pacific coast. Sometimes the train would make forty miles an hour only to be delayed from one to seven hours at some station. As our car was the last one of twenty-eight we had the conductor with us frequently, and from him we learned of the uncertainties of travel, of the murders and robberies which occur in the night.

All night long the passengers would be crowded in the box-cars and coaches. In the morning, at the first stop, they would climb out into the snow and run, like prisoners fleeing from a guard, to the shanties where boiling water was kept for the travellers. After their tea was brewed from chunks of "tea cake," a preparation of tea dust and some solid matter, they rushed back to the cars, placed their kettles inside the doors, and washed their faces and hands in the snow. Until the three bells were sounded, the Russian railroad custom of announcing the departure of a train, they would remain outside and climb into their "cells" on top of each other after the train began to move.

Between my first and second journeys across Siberia the armistice was signed, and although Russia was not a party to the convention the end of the war in Europe had its decided reactions in Siberia. One of the most noticeable changes was the collapse of the German Secret Service system, which fell like a house of cards. In every Siberian city there had been a powerful and efficient organization under the chief direction of neutral business men. In Omsk the chief was a Swiss; in Ekaterinburg he was an Austrian; in Khabarovsk a Swede, and in Vladivostok a Dane. But that which was evident in the remains of the organization was that those who were intrusted with the direction of this work were experienced business men, and commerce was the basis upon which the system was built. This was not only a symptom of the past but an omen of the future. It was but another indication of the big business interests linked with the old German military machine.

While I had encountered evidences of Bolshevist propaganda in Siberia on my way West, I noticed a decided growth after the signing of the armistice with Germany, and representatives of the Czecho-Slovaks in nearly every city confirmed the growth of Bolshevism. In Irkutsk, the Czech commandant of the municipality said the Bolsheviki had the strongest propaganda organization in Irkutsk and, by using vast sums of money, were obtaining the control of most of the newspapers. While it would have surprised me to have heard this statement on my first trip, it was not astounding at this time, because I had observed the laxity of the control of travellers in Omsk and Ekaterinburg, and learned how easy it was for agitators to travel back and forth between the Bolshevist districts of European Russia and Siberia.

After seventeen days, travelling at the average rate of seven miles an hour; after passing through Tchita, where General Semenov and his 15,000 Cossacks maintained their reign of terror; after experiencing discomforts of travel the like of which I had not encountered in any war country of Europe, I reached Manchouli Station, to be welcomed at the depot by members of the United States Railway Service Corps and a young lieutenant, whom Lieutenant-Colonel Barrows, chief of the Intelligence Division, had sent there as an observer.

Manchuria seemed like a civilized nation compared with Siberia. It was busier than it had appeared two months earlier. The streets were filled with Chinese and Russians. The markets were overflowing with supplies of every description. Tobacco was abundant. Sugar, tea, rice, and other foodstuffs were plentiful, and clothing could be had at any shop. But the chief joy of the city to every traveller from Siberia was the city bath-house, and to this monopoly of cleanliness I hurried, together with scores of other travellers who for more than two weeks had been vagabonding in Russia. At the bath-house scores of other citizens had come—Chinese, Russians, Burats, Mongolians, Englishmen, Frenchmen, Japanese, and Americans. I bought my ticket, entitling me to one hour's standing-room under a spray of hot water, and stood in line with the others, waiting patiently for my turn to come; but some thirty-two others were ahead of me, and I went out to roam about the city until it was my turn.

After this recreation was over I sauntered to the home of the American officer, to be treated with the best of the United States army rations, which were a relief even to my own cooking! And from him I learned that 400 Canadians were on their way into Siberia, and that, after travelling in box-cars from Vladivostok, every man was begging and demanding a bath, and the British representative in that city had been ordered "to prepare baths for 400 men!" Those who have not travelled in a revolutionized country cannot appreciate the feelings of those soldiers from Canada, but I could. I had already experienced the same discomforts that they had.

Fortunately the "regular" was delayed an unusually long time at Manchouli Station, and in and about the city I learned of the "antics" of Semenov and his brigands. Semenov had refused to recognize Admiral Koltshak and was believed to be supported by the Japanese. My first intimation of this was during the stop at Irkutsk. Two days previous to my arrival there three Russian officers, said to be attached to Semenoff's staff, came to the city and were arrested by officers representing Koltshak. The following day when they were brought to court the Japanese military representative in the city appeared to ask their release on the ground that they were attached to the Japanese staff, and the Japanese contention was approved.

I had been away from Vladivostok several weeks and had not heard of the change in the relationship between the Japanese and the Americans, but as soon as I reached Manchuria the Japanese influence was felt. The delay in the departure of our train was due to the movement of Japanese troops which passed through the city all day and night en route to the coast from Tchita and the surrounding country, and I learned for the first time of the extensive withdrawal of Japanese forces, the details of which will be given in the following chapter.

After a day's delay in Manchouli Station our "private" car was attached to a slow freight. Before we reached Harbin the rear springs of the car broke, as a result of the freight-train "drag" and, at the peril of changing to another car of the moving train or being dashed to pieces in the "private," we abandoned our eighteen-day-old "home" for the safe compartment of a coach belonging to the British railway mission, and rode into Harbin, thankful to the Czechs and Fate that we were so near to Vladivostok and Peking and so far from Siberia proper. The exodus was not as fascinating as the entrance, although the way station of Harbin was like a visit to America, because the doors of the United States Railway Service Corps barracks were opened to two correspondents, who accepted the proffered hospitality of Colonel Emerson with the enthusiasm of wayward sons returning to the shelter and food of an abandoned home. After a bath and a night's rest I proceeded to Vladivostok, where the "Japanese question" had long since superseded the Russian "problem" in the interests of the Allies.

## Chapter XI
## JAPANESE ACTIVITIES IN SIBERIA

To travel from Omsk to Vladivostok, after the armistice, was to pass from one centre of politics to another. The former city was the capital of anti-Bolshevist Russia. The latter was the capital of the Far East, and while the days of October were decisive for Russia, the months of November, December, and January marked another critical period between the relations of the United States and Japan. Before the war no one would have thought of Vladivostok as a meeting-place for Japan and the United States to discuss Far Eastern problems and politics. No one would have considered it even after the Russian revolution, but during the winter this Siberian city was as much of a diplomatic centre as it was a military headquarters, and Asiatic Russia was more of a political battle-field than a war theatre.

Even a short residence in Vladivostok was sufficient to convince one that politics was of more importance than military strategy, and after a journey into the interior and back again this city looms above the horizon of the East, above Tokyo and Peking, as the meeting-place for statesmen and generals of two different civilizations, of the Occident and the Orient, to discuss and solve the Janus-headed Siberian problem—Siberia and its relation to Russia and the world, and Siberia in its relation to Japan and China.

That the Great Powers understood the importance of Japan's relations to Siberia was indicated by the men they selected as envoys and generals. Fully eighty-five percent of the Allied officials in western Russia had represented their governments in the Far East. The French, Italian, and American diplomatic representatives were or had been ambassadors to Tokyo, and most of the military men had been attached to foreign posts in the East both before and during the war.

In considering Japan's activities in Siberia it is not only essential, however, that the reader should know the type of men selected by the Allies to deal with these dual Japanese-Russian problems, but the attitude of the Japanese toward Siberia. To keep in touch with Japanese opinion I followed closely the editorial comment of the leading Tokyo newspapers as reproduced in *The Japan Advertiser*. One editorial, which I considered a fair statement of the attitude of the majority of Japanese, was published in the *Chugai Shogyo*. I shall give it in its entirety here because of the information it contains about Viscount Uchida's[1] attitude and because it reflects the general impression of the East regarding the "success" of Allied intervention—a belief which was to give way very soon to criticism and disappointment.

"The Allied Siberian campaign has proved a greater success than was generally expected," the editor of *Chugai Shogyo* wrote....

> The Allied troops are now occupying all important points in the regions which have formerly been the sphere of interest of the Bolsheviks and Austro-Germans. In short, it is now revealed that the world has overestimated the strength and influence of the Bolsheviks.
>
> In the past, especially in an earlier part of this year, there were many among the Allied diplomats and publicists who entertained a view that the Bolsheviks under the leadership of Lenin and Trotzky were the only political power in Russia which had a possibility to organize a strong central government in that country. Viscount Uchida, present foreign minister, who was then the Japanese Ambassador to Russia, was also one of those who overestimated the Bolshevik influence in Russia. In an interview with press representatives, which took place at Harbin when he was on the way home from Moscow, the viscount declared that Russia would be controlled by the Bolsheviks unless some new political faction would come to existence, to displace the government of Lenin and Trotzky. He further said that the Bolshevik influence was far stronger than the German influence, so that there would be little prospect for the German aggression in Siberia as was feared by many Allied politicians. By saying this, the viscount apparently, if not directly, opposed the scheme of an Allied expedition to Siberia then under consideration among the Allied Powers.
>
> The situation in the last few months, however, has shown that the view entertained by those diplomats like Viscount Uchida regarding the Bolshevik influence was entirely mistaken. The Allied campaign, in spite of its comparatively small scale, was not only quite enough to drive out the Bolsheviks in Siberia, but has even caused the fall of the Bolshevik authorities in European Russia.
>
> Now the general situation in Siberia is still in the course of settlement, and it is hard to predict as to which one of the so-called "governments" of Siberia would become the central Power to take up the administration of the region.

---

[1] Count Uchida Kōsai (1865–1936) was a Japanese statesman, diplomat, and interim prime minister. He was also known as Uchida Yasuya. He served as ambassador to China, Austria-Hungary, and to the United States. He served as Japanese foreign minister from 1911 to 1912 under the second Saionji Kinmochi administration. Appointed as ambassador to the Russian Empire just before the Bolshevik Revolution, Uchida returned to Japan to serve as foreign minister again from 1918 to 1923.

But one thing is at least certain, that is, Siberia in the future will be governed by a government which is extremely pro-British or pro-American. Vologodski, premier of the Omsk Government, for instance, is an extreme pro-British politician. Admiral Kolchak, minister of war and navy, of the same government, is also known to entertain friendly feeling toward Great Britain. Judging from these facts, it is easy to observe that the British and American influences are speedily growing among the Siberians, and that these two countries would be able to hold a supreme position in the affairs of Siberia after the war, both politically and economically.

What will be, then, Japan's position in Siberia when the war is concluded?

Undoubtedly, none can deny that the success of the Allied campaign in Siberia was chiefly due to the strength of the Japanese troops. In fact, it was Japan who really saved the Siberians from the tyranny of the Bolsheviks. But is it possible for Japan to maintain the prestige she has obtained through her successful expedition even after the conclusion of war? Lamentably enough, it is doubtful under present circumstances. In a word, Japan needs a wise and fair policy in Siberia if she is really desirous of maintaining strong influence in the region after the war, and it is our hope that the Hara[2] government will exert itself for the purpose by establishing a definite policy, in accordance with which the Japanese Government can handle the affairs concerning Siberia fairly and successfully. Especially, we are quite anxious to hear our foreign minister make public his view regarding the future of Russia. Certainly we suppose that Viscount Uchida has already realized the mistake he has made in his judgment concerning the Bolsheviks. But we hope to know as to what is the conclusion he has reached through his knowledge and experiences concerning Russia and Siberia in regard to the policy Japan should take toward Siberia after the war.

Something which was symbolical of the importance which the Japanese Government attached to the Siberian expedition was the presence of a Japanese battleship in the centre of Vladivostok bay. The ship commanded the whole situation and could be seen from every hill of the city. After I reached Vladivostok almost the first information I received from Russians was that this Japanese war-ship was one of those which Japan captured from Russia at Port Arthur in 1904, and they did not like this "flaunting" of Russia's defeat in the Russo-Japanese War at this critical hour in Russia's history. The question those Russians asked was:

"Is Japan coming to Siberia as a conqueror of Russia or as an ally?"

---

[2] Hara Takashi (1856–1921) was a Japanese politician and the tenth prime minister of Japan from September 29, 1918, until his assassination on November 4, 1921.

In that question there was the kernel of the whole Siberian situation as viewed by the Russians themselves.

"If Japan has landed troops as a conquering nation," the Russians argued, "then the United States, England, France, and Italy are here with Japan to exploit Russia under the guise of peaceful military intervention. If Japan is our ally why does she act like our owner?"

The Russians did not state their case alone to an arriving correspondent. They had already stated it in much plainer words in the Siberian newspapers, and their official representatives had called upon the envoys and generals of the Allies to question them.

After hearing so much anti-Japanese gossip, however, I became immune to it for a while until I had made my own investigation, because I learned that the Russians were inclined to be anti-Japanese to an American, and anti-American to the Japanese. They would remark to an American:

"We do not like to have the Japanese here but we hope the Americans will stay," and, a few moments later they would bow to a Japanese business man and tell him, the Americans are all "millioniares" and the future of Siberia "rests with Japan." And this was not confined to the Russian citizens but to government officials. General Ivanov-Rinov, former minister of war in the All-Russian Government, complained to General Graves in October about the activities of the Japanese soldiers and denounced the Island Nation in the most hostile terms. A few days later he gave an interview to the Siberian newspapers in which he praised Japan as the greatest of the Allied nations.

I did not go to Siberia harboring any anti-Japanese sentiments, and I did not become hostile toward these energetic people of the East during my travel in Russia or the Far East, which included both China, Manchuria, and Korea. One does not have to travel very long in the Orient to learn that there are two parties in Japan, a "war party" and a "peace party." Ever since the United States has been a belligerent there has been a herculean contest between these two parties for control of the government. Shortly before the signing of the armistice in France the "war party" was in control of the Cabinet. Since then the peaceful statesmen of Japan, backed by the business interests of the country, have been in authority. At this writing the "peace party" is still in power, although the opposition is so strong that it might be able to wreck the Hara government if an internal crisis developed.

By a "war party" and a "peace party" I mean, first, a power within the country supported by political interests which believes that it should go ahead with aggressive policies in Siberia and China contrary to the policies and opinions of the rest of the world, and, secondly, another party which has as its basic principle the peaceful solution of Far Eastern problems through diplomatic discussions and concerted action of a League of Nations.

Before I went into the interior of Russia I heard many American officers comment upon their relations with the Japanese. With the exception of individual fights between Japanese and American soldiers, which were adjusted in each instance that I know of, by the trial and punishment of the guilty offenders, there was complete harmony between the officers of the two headquarters' staffs and between the American and Japanese officers in the field. In Khabarovsk I asked an American colonel, who commanded the United States troops on the only fighting expedition in which the Americans took part, what kind of orders the Japanese gave.

"Their orders were as clear as a bell," was his immediate reply. "Any officer who cannot understand Japanese army orders, when issued in French as ours were, knows nothing about military affairs. From the time we left Vladivostok until we reached Khabarovsk there was not a hitch in operations and not a doubt in the mind of any officer. Our orders were perfect. We never had to ask a question."

In Vladivostok I had an opportunity of interviewing General Otani, through his second chief of staff, General Inagaki, but while the general expressed the belief that he was "sure the Japanese-American relations would always continue," as they were at that time he would not discuss policies beyond remarking that "military operations in eastern Siberia are ended, but the Allies cannot leave, because as soon as they would depart the Bolsheviki would return and become very disorderly. Until Russia can organize a strong army the Allies will have to remain in Siberia."

This was the chief plank in his platform for the reorganization and reconstruction of Russia. Without an army the general did not believe it possible for Russia again to be a great Power. "And in this work," the commander-in-chief of the Allies added: "I think the Allies should help the Russians. To-day Russia has not the power to form a militia, or army, and it can be accomplished only with Allied co-operation."

One of my first observations in travelling through Siberia was that there were several times as many Japanese troops in Russia as those of all the other Allies combined. East of Lake Baikal, Japanese soldiers were stationed in every village and city. Every railroad-station from Vladivostok to Tchita along both the Amur and the Chinese Eastern Railway line, flew the Japanese flag. Every railroad bridge and nearly every public building was guarded by Japanese.

The Japanese literally covered Siberia with troops and commercial agents. The latter leased every available building and bought up supplies, so that, in case of extensive Allied operations, everything would be under Japanese control. Whenever the commanders of the British, French, or American armies would order a lieutenant or captain to another village or city, away from the base at Vladivostok, on some special work, the Japanese would despatch a major to the same place. If an Allied general sent a major, the Japanese staff sent a colonel. Japan's object was to maintain the seniority of the Allied agreement which made the Japanese commanders of all Allied armies and missions in Russia.

# JAPANESE ACTIVITIES IN SIBERIA

Each time the American, French, or British commanders moved a soldier or regiment; whenever an Allied soldier or officer landed in Siberia, the Japanese General Staff had to be informed, but the Japanese, in turn, never informed any of the Allies how many soldiers they had; how many were being brought into Siberia, nor where they were being sent.

At first the Allies did not protest nor question the Japanese policy. They had agreed to work in Siberia under the supreme command of the Japanese, and they continued to give the Japanese supreme command their respectful support until the opposition within Siberia to the activities of the Japanese army became so great that, in justice to the Russians and their own countries, the Allies had to take cognizance of the antics of the Japanese soldiers and of the policies of the Imperial General Staff and its political and secret military agents.

Although under the original agreement the number of Japanese troops was limited to 7,000, Japan was the first nation to break the agreement. Instead of sending that number, the "war party," which was in power in Tokyo and had its secret agents in Russia, sent 73,400 men.

When the United States and Allied governments learned this, they had their suspicions confirmed that Japan was not "playing the game" according to written agreement, and still they made no diplomatic representations.

Meanwhile the Japanese seized all caravan routes and blockaded all ports. Japanese gunboats and monitors were sent up all navigable streams and rivers into the interior. No caravan could move into or out of Manchuria, Mongolia, or Siberia without passing Japanese guards. No railroad could be run without being under the constant scrutiny of the Japanese. No ship could arrive or depart except under the ever-present gaze of a Japanese naval officer. By October Japan had Siberia and Manchuria entirely under her power. Japan was in a position at any time to challenge Russians and Allies combined, because the military and naval strength of Japan was greater than that of all the other Powers combined.

By the middle of October this situation was causing a great deal of concern. The war was at its height, and the Allies could not understand this policy of Japan, especially in view of the constant reports that the German military party and the Japanese military party had come to a secret understanding. There were reports also that Japan and Germany had a secret agreement under the terms of which Japan was to be given control of Siberia from Lake Baikal to the Pacific. This was immediately denied by the Tokyo government, and I do not know of any responsible people in the Far East who believe that the Japanese Government ever listened seriously to the separate peace proposals which were being sent from Berlin at regular intervals.

The Allies, however, could not help but observe that, even if there were no grounds for these reports, nevertheless the Japanese army and navy in Siberia and its ports were in a position where they could defy the Allies at any time. Their hold was so firm that if the war was compromised or if the Germans were to win, nothing in the world could force Japan from Siberia, and that country would become what Korea is to-day.

Still the Allies were silent. The fighting in France was attracting all of their attention and demanding all reserves.

There were in the Far East, however, some men who went there for the purpose of helping Russia. These men, after making thorough investigations, reported to their governments that the Russian railroads were in a terrible state of disorder, and that Russia could never be helped militarily or economically unless the Trans-Siberian Railway was reorganized and placed upon an efficient business basis. At this time there was present in Harbin and Vladivostok about 200 experienced American railroad men under John F. Stevens and George Emerson. These men had been brought to Siberia under an original agreement with the Kerensky government, but they had been waiting patiently nearly a year for something to do.

The Japanese attitude, however, toward the Trans-Siberian Railway, which differed from that of the other Allies, was reflected in an editorial in the *Hochi*, one of the leading newspapers of Tokyo, which commented as follows on the "Future of Siberian Railroads."

> When America sent Mr. Root[3] and his mission to Russia, we sincerely hoped that the Japanese people would realize the importance of that mission and its effects upon the commercial and political situation in Siberia. But, strangely enough, our countrymen overlooked the activities of the American mission in Russia, paying no attention to the outcome of negotiations between the mission and the Kerensky government. Then, as the consequence of an agreement concluded by the mission, an American railway corps headed by Mr. Stevens came to Siberia. Undoubtedly, the event was of special importance, as it was necessary for Japan to watch, as carefully as she could, what the railroad men from America were going to do. But even then the public in general paid no special attention to the event. Of late, the question relating to the administration or management of railroads in Siberia has become one of the most significant current topics of the Far Eastern politics. It is reported that Mr. Morris, American Ambassador to Japan, is now in the course of an important diplomatic negotiation with the Tokyo Foreign Office, and there is reason to believe that the question now pending between Japan and America chiefly concerns railroad business in Siberia. Foreigners, especially Ameri-

---

[3] Elihu Root (1845–1937) was an American lawyer and statesman who served as the secretary of state under President Theodore Roosevelt and as secretary of war under Roosevelt and President William McKinley. In June 1917, Root headed a mission sent by President Wilson to revolutionary Russia, the Root Commission, to arrange American cooperation with the new revolutionary government. Root was the founding chairman of the Council on Foreign Relations, established in 1918 in New York.

cans, are paying much attention to the outcome of the negotiations, and what they want to hear is what the Japanese people are thinking about the problem. But, strangely enough, no definite opinion regarding Siberian railroads has yet been expressed by men in public life here, as if they were entirely indifferent to the future of their great neighbor.

Certainly, the question relating to the management of railroads in Siberia is complicated, but we can simplify it by separating the question regarding the Chinese Eastern Railway from that in regard to the trunk line of the Trans-Siberian Railway. The territory where the Chinese Eastern Railway is running is not Siberia but China. Secondly, the railway is financed not by Russia alone, but by France and China too. And lastly, the southern terminal of the railway is directly connected with the Japanese railway. Recently, a rumor was in circulation that America has concluded a loan of $5,000,000 with the officials of the Chinese Eastern Railway, but the rumor is indeed too absurd to believe, as such things cannot be realized, entirely regardless of Japan's paramount interests in China, especially in Manchuria.

As to the question relating to the management of the trunk line of the Trans-Siberian Railway, our opinion is that the urgent question is to make the railway efficacious for military purposes. We think that it is not advisable to begin negotiations as regards the future of the railway at the present moment. It is too early, and it is at the same time doubtful as to who can represent the interest of the Russian people in the negotiation with the other Powers.

We are confident that America would not ignore the prestige and interests of Japan by secretly concluding agreements with the officials of the Russian railways in Siberia. We are convinced that America knows the gravity of the problem, and, indeed, it is our earnest hope that the governments of both America and Japan carefully avoid any troubles which will endanger the friendly intercourse of the two nations.

This editorial, while evidently written to influence the negotiators, was intended, nevertheless, to strengthen the influence in Japan which was working against exclusive American control. Despite this, however, England, France, Italy, and later China, together with the new Russian Government which had been formed in Omsk, gave the United States power of attorney to take over the Trans-Siberian Railway and run it for the benefit of Russia. These six Powers realized that nothing of importance could be accomplished in Siberia until the railroad was in efficient hands. When Japan was asked whether she would give her consent she asked time to consider the proposal.

For two months, September and October, the question was debated in Tokyo. The "war party" objected to any control which was not Japanese from top to bottom, and through an "invitation" from Ataman Semenov, in Tchita, sent 150 railroad men to Siberia. This party maintained that Siberia was one of Japan's spheres of influence and that no other nation and no group of nations had a right to interfere with what the Japanese military party was doing. Another group of Japanese statesmen, backed by all of the Chambers of Commerce and big financial institutions of Japan, wanted to compromise with the Allies. But the military party won its point, and Japan made counter proposals which destroyed all possibilities of an Allied agreement regarding the Trans-Siberian Railway.

For the first time the Allies were convinced by the attitude of the Tokyo government that Japan's policy in Siberia could not be reconciled to the Allied policy.

Meanwhile, also, there were other developments to cause international apprehension. Two Cossack atamans, Generals Semenov and Kalmykoff, in Tchita and Khabarovsk respectively, were carrying on obstructive work. They were terrorizing every Russian community through which their armies passed. Under the guise of fighting the Bolsheviki they were doing the same things the Bolsheviki were doing in European Russia. They were robbing banks and murdering peaceful, respectful Russian citizens with impunity. Although Russians themselves, they were terrorizing their own country. Their activities, however, came to a head when they interfered with the rights of foreigners.

In Khabarovsk, Kalmykoff arrested three members of the Swedish Red Cross on the ground that they were German agents. When word reached Sweden the Stockholm government protested to the Allied governments. The Allied consuls in Vladivostok were instructed to appoint a committee to investigate the charges and the conditions of the imprisonment of the three Swedes. Before the committee was organized a report reached Vladivostok from Khabarovsk to the effect that the Swedes had escaped from jail and "disappeared." The last word was significant. Whenever any one "disappears" in Siberia, he never reappears. Within a few days came other reports to the effect that the Cossacks had murdered the Swedes and destroyed their bodies.

It was obvious then that the Allies had to make an investigation, and the committee was ordered to proceed to Khabarovsk at once, but it received word from the Japanese General Staff before leaving Vladivostok, that an Allied investigation was not necessary because the Japanese staff in Khabarovsk was making a thorough investigation. The result was that the Allies were never permitted to investigate, and they never received a report from the Japanese investigators.

At this time a Japanese officer, General Nakashima, was working in Siberia in a secret capacity under orders from the Japanese War Office in Tokyo. He had a large secret fund at his disposal, and he was known to have very close connections with both Kalmykoff and Semenov although he was technically not under the jurisdiction of General Otani, the Allied supreme commander in Vladivostok. The Allies soon obtained proof that General Nakashima was using money in Siberia in a way which was calculated to bring about more disorder and confusion.

By November 2, there were so many activities of the Japanese in Siberia which were causing dissension and disunion that Secretary of State Lansing, having all the data in his possession, sent for Viscount Ishii, the Japanese ambassador in Washington.[4] The envoy came to the State Department about four o'clock one afternoon, and Mr. Lansing called his attention to various facts which he had about the obstructive tactics of the Japanese military party in Siberia, pointing out the violation of the original agreement regarding the number of troops, showing how the settlement of the railroad problem was being postponed by Japan's opposition, and calling the ambassador's attention to the work of General Nakashima. The secretary of state pointed out the obvious outcome of the developments in Siberia if the Japanese military party was permitted by the Japanese Government to continue its policies and activities in Siberia. Just what words the secretary used to impress Viscount Ishii with the seriousness of the situation I do not know. One version is that he told the Japanese ambassador that he hoped the work of the military party would not cause a break in the good relations between the United States and Japan, and another version says that the secretary pointed out how the activities of the Japanese military party were very similar to those of the German war party, and that the latter had already led to a war between Germany and the United States.

Viscount Ishii returned to the embassy in Washington, and despatched a long code message to Tokyo which arrived there on Sunday night. As is customary, Secretary Lansing sent a copy of his remarks to Ambassador Roland S. Morris, in Tokyo, for the information of the ambassador.

On Monday morning Ambassador Morris called at the Tokyo Foreign Office only to be informed that the minister of foreign affairs could not see him for two or three days.

During these critical days of early November there was a political storm in Japan. Information as to the attitude of the United States quickly reached the Japanese statesmen and business men, through the Foreign Office. Word was sent, too, to the Japanese War and Navy Departments, and a series of conferences were begun which were to determine the future relations between the United States and Japan. The "war party" was in favor of defying America. The business interests and peace statesmen, who learned for the first time of the activities of the Japanese army in Siberia,

---

[4] Viscount Ishii Kikujirō (1866–1945) was a Japanese diplomat and cabinet minister. After a term as Japanese ambassador to France from 1912 to 1915, he became minister of foreign affairs from 1915 to 1916, playing a major role in the normalization of relations between Japan and Russia. As special envoy to the United States from 1917 to 1918, he negotiated the Lansing-Ishii Agreement, which was intended to defuse tension between the two nations, but was limited in its effectiveness due to the reluctance of either government to make any concessions. Ishii stayed on as United States ambassador from 1918 to 1919, attempting to reduce tensions created by the Siberian Intervention of Japanese forces into the Russian Far East. Ishii served as a member of the Privy Council from 1925 to 1945, in which he was highly outspoken in his strong opposition to the Tripartite Pact between Japan, Nazi Germany, and fascist Italy.

sided with the United States. For three days the debate continued and during this period no one knew whether war or peace was ahead.

But the sane elements of Japan triumphed. The "war party" met its first great defeat at the hands of its own people. The Japanese Government telegraphed new orders to General Otani immediately. He was instructed to send back to Japan 35,000 soldiers. A few days later another order was sent to him in Vladivostok ordering the return of 17,000 men. Another order still was despatched recalling General Nakashima to Tokyo.

After most of these troops had left Siberia General Inagaki, second chief of staff of the Japanese General Staff in Vladivostok; a gentleman and a diplomat who was with General Otani, was not in thorough sympathy with the tactics of General Nakashima, called upon Major-General William S. Graves, the American commander, to express the regrets of the Japanese staff for past practices and to state that hereafter Japan and the United States would work together in complete harmony in Siberia.

For the present it looked as if the victory in Japan over the "war party" was complete, but those who thought all difficulties were at an end underestimated the influence of General Nakashima. He was the chief politician of the Japanese military party. He was Japan's "General Ludendorff," and when he arrived in Tokyo another political storm appeared which resembled a typhoon in its suddenness and effect. All of the anti-American sentiment in Japan came to his support. The military and naval parties united, and for a time it looked as if the Cabinet might fall because of the opposition of these two groups. In the United States, perhaps, the extent of this power is not realized but it can be easily explained.

According to the Japanese custom and law no Cabinet can be formed without a secretary of war and a secretary of the navy, chosen from the highest ranking officers in the War and Navy Departments. These two departments, combined, lead the "war party." They control the secretaries of war and navy as long as they are members of the Ministry, and they decide whether a new forming Cabinet shall have their support. Thus, in practice, no Cabinet can be formed and no Cabinet can live without the support of the War and Navy Departments or the "war party."

This club was in the hands of General Nakashima, and many well-informed people believed that he was on the point of wielding it with great power when Germany collapsed and the armistice was signed. The fall of the German military party was something which the Japanese military and naval leaders never expected and their power was so great, their astonishment so complete that they would not believe the telegraph news of Germany's humiliation. For twenty-four hours they prohibited the Japanese newspapers from printing the terms of the naval armistice, and withheld the details of the land armistice. Finally when the news despatches were confirmed by official telegrams they realized that, for the time being, their fight was at an end and the "peace party" in Tokyo could not be overthrown.

By the first part of January, however, the war party again appeared on the political horizon, and had a sufficient amount of influence with the Tokyo Cabinet still to block the efforts of the United States, acting on behalf of all other Allies, to bring about an agreement as to the reorganization and operation of the Trans-Siberian Railway. The Japanese military party had been working secretly in Siberia despite the events of early November. Through financial and moral support of the Japanese, General Semenov in Tchita was interfering with the transportation of supplies to the Czecho-Slovak armies. Semenov was refusing, also, to recognize the Kolchak dictatorship. At one time the Czecho-Slovaks were on the point of attacking Semenov when the Japanese stopped their military trams. Major-General Gaida had already sent a curt note to the Japanese commander in Tchita, asking what attitude Japan would take if the Czechs were forced to move against Semenov.

In January the State Department in Washington was compelled again to bring the issue of the operation of the Trans-Siberian Railway to a decision. Again the attention of the Japanese Government was called to the fact that a policy which the Allies had agreed upon seven months previous was still undeveloped because of the opposition of Japan's "war party."

At this time every Chamber of Commerce in Japan, every large importing and exporting house, every large financial institution, and every statesman who had been working for Japanese-American friendship united in supporting that party in Japan which sought a solution for the difficult Russian railroad problem and an agreement was reached—the understanding which was announced by Acting-Secretary of State Polk in Washington. By this agreement the Trans-Siberian Railway was to be operated under the direction of an Allied board and under the protection of an Allied military staff. The Japanese "war party," for the present at least, was impotent.

Now that the League of Nations is in process of formation another important question develops with regard to the policies of the league in Russia, and one of the first questions which may face the league may be whether the Japanese military party is to be permitted to send these forces into Siberia. It will be a concrete issue which will test, almost immediately after its formation, the power and authority of the league. Japan has been sharply divided by the question of a League of Nations. The present Japanese Government supports it, but the "war party" continues its opposition and the influence of that party with the anti-American press of Japan is very great.

The great peace leaders of Japan, however, are expected to win out in any fight which develops in Japan in the future with the militarists.

It is not necessary to go into further detail about Japan's activities in Siberia, for in this volume my object is not to discuss Japanese-American politics, but to follow the trail of the Bolsheviki. The past attitude of Japan's military party was one of the reasons the Allies could not agree upon policies in Siberia and Russia. It was one of the reasons for a lack of Allied unity, and one cause for the growth of Bolshevism and the resumption of the trail of the Reds across Siberia. Happily at the Paris Conference many of the disturbing questions of Siberia and the East have been discussed, and the "war party" of Japan is expected to disappear with the jingo parties of the other Powers.

## Chapter XII
## BOLSHEVISM OUTSIDE OF RUSSIA

Before the revolution of March, 1917, most of the ties which bound the United States to Russia stretched across the Atlantic. Before the war our interests in Russia were centred in Petrograd and Moscow. Siberia was a name but not a nation in reality.

To-day, while we still have a news interest, a political interest, and, to a limited degree, financial interests in European Russia, there are shuttles busy on the Pacific stitching our western seaboard to the coast of the extreme Northwest. New ties bind us to Russia via the West. Sailing from San Francisco and Seattle, Portland and Vancouver to-day are government transports and privately owned freighters and steamers bound for the beautiful, deep-water harbor of Vladivostok and Golden Horn Bay. Within a fortnight, three weeks, or a month, depending upon the speed of the vessels, they will be tied up to the docks of Siberia. As they swim across the arc of the Pacific they pass other ships bound for the United States and Canada; ships which a short while before left the rocky cliffs of Russia for the Sea of Japan and the Pacific. These ships are weaving a net of trade routes between western America and eastern Russia, a net of trade which is the garment of progress. They span the Pacific from the Golden Gate to the Golden Horn.

Sailing from San Francisco for Siberia I was impressed, as many Americans are, by the distance between the two continents, but as I returned to Seattle, believing that I had left the trail of the Bolsheviki in Russia, I crossed it again in that seaport city of Washington, and I realized that Bolshevism had crossed the Pacific and that the distance of space and time were no longer barriers to the radicalism of the East. Russia and Bolshevism were not as far from the United States as I had imagined. Bolshevism had spread to Seattle, via Siberia, as it had crossed European Russia to Austria, Rumania, Germany, Bavaria, France, England, and Italy. Siberia, the land of "Nitchevo," which was a vision before I went there, was a reality when I returned, a real country, inhabited by real people with desperately real problems and possibilities. Bolshevism which seemed to be an Eastern menace only last year, now threatened America and the world.

With the signing of the armistice, instead of collapsing with the Central Powers, as was expected, and as might have happened, had their been action, instead of Allied indecision in Siberia, Bolshevism spread throughout the universe so that its trail glistened over the face of the globe like the tracks of the silkworm. Beginning in Minsk, Russia, at a conference in 1898, the trail extended over plains and mountains from Russia to Scandinavia and Europe; from Siberia to the United States and Canada.

Bolshevism is spreading to-day because it is a revolutionary movement similar to a world storm, which gains strength and volume as it travels; which destroys as it goes and which leaves unstable social, industrial, and political conditions in its wake.

Why does this revolution succeed?

Why are efforts made to have the League of Nations recognize the Bolshevist regime in Russia?

What is the secret of Bolshevism which makes it succeed where other policies and governments fail?

If Bolshevism follows the failure of other policies, what will follow Bolshevism?

One is disturbed by these questions in Russia. When I arrived in Vladivostok in the late summer of 1918, I found the sentiment almost unanimous against the Bolsheviki. The Allies, the Czechs, and the Russians neither sympathized with nor approved of the Bolshevist platform. Still, after they had been there a few months, after they had seen the difficulties before the reconstruction of Russia, after they had seen the limits of their own ability, they had tempered their judgment of the Bolsheviki, and by the beginning of 1919, most of the Allied soldiers wished to leave Russia. The sentiment among the Allied officials was still divided, but the feeling was growing that the Allies would ultimately have to withdraw and let Russia work out her own reconstruction problems without either the assistance or the handicap of foreign belligerent forces.

It is not difficult to understand the reasons for this change of sentiment. It may be illustrated by an incident which happened to me in Khabarovsk. I was riding in a droshky from the station through the village to the headquarters of the American regiment under command of Colonel Styer.[1] The old man who was driving the carriage was an ex-soldier. His home had been in European Russia, but after the revolution when he left the army he returned to his home, and finding a great deal of unemployment, he decided to venture into Siberia. I asked him, as I asked a number of droshky drivers, why he did not join the Russian army to fight the Bolsheviki.

"Nitchevo," he said. He did not wish to worry about fighting any more when he could earn a living with his Siberian pony and Odessa carriage.

"Well, how did you like it here when the Bolsheviki were in power?" I asked him.

"Not so bad," he answered.

"You know the Bolsheviki made a droshky driver one of the commissars!"

---

[1] Henry D. Styer (1862–1944), US military officer, brigadier general. In the rank of colonel, Styer was the commander of the 27th Infantry Regiment, first arriving in Vladivostok on August 16, 1918, and act as a temporary commander of the American Expeditionary Forces in Siberia before the arrival of General William S. Graves.

The confession of this poor workman shed an interesting and true light upon one of the chief reasons for the success of Bolshevism in Russia. The Bolsheviki made the common people government officials, gave them part of the responsibility of administration—a voice in the affairs of the government.

Russia, for centuries, has been not only an oppressed nation, but a country where none of the poor or middle-class and even thousands of educated citizens had anything to do with the government itself. The idea of the Russian state before the revolution was that the mass of humanity was made to be ruled by a small class. Following the revolution, the idea of democracy appeared, and the situation was changed. There was a feeling that the mass should rule itself and determine its own government by election. But the radical change from an autocracy to a democracy brings with it tremendous handicaps because success in government is essentially a matter of precedent, and there were no precedents to guide the new democracy of Russia. So the provisional governments failed, and the Bolsheviki came into power with their platform that society as it had existed was founded upon the wrong basis, and that the future could only be made secure if the past were forgotten and the present destroyed. The Bolsheviki carried the nation from one extreme to another, instead of arguing that the mass was created to be led by a class which it maintained by its work, the Bolsheviki said that the mass was created to work for itself and to maintain only its own leaders in power by military force. What the old Russian of Khabarovsk meant when he said that he approved of Bolshevism, was not that he approved the doctrine of Bolshevism but he approved of the democracy of government, which enables the simple, uneducated, inexperienced carriage-driver to have a part in the government.

One can understand how Bolshevism might readily succeed in autocratic countries, but why Bolshevism should develop and increase in countries where there are parliamentary and representative governments is more difficult to explain. We find Bolshevism growing in the United States, and we imagine that it is due to the propaganda of the Soviet representatives in this country. But what we have in the United States is not a party which believes in the Bolshevism of Russia, but a class of working people and factory directors, school-teachers and college professors who are dissatisfied with the present government, and disappointed because of the imperfections of the democracy, the slow methods of change, and a system of party "bosses" who control the government for business interests.

The trail of the Bolsheviki in the United States goes through our factories and our schools. It is something of a fad. Any one who says anything against the existing order is called a Bolshevik. Those who talk of great industrial changes are placed in the same class. In a drug-store in New York I heard the proprietor shout to the boy behind the soda-water counter, "You are a Bolshevik" because the boy had burned the bottom out of the hot chocolate cooking utensil, because he had failed to fill it up the night before with water, and turn out the gas.

In a professional office in New York in March, two employees who had been with the concern over ten years asked for a conference with the president. One of the men was earning a salary of $14,000 and the other had an income of $20,000, annually, out of this business. They informed the head of the concern they believed his business was run on the wrong principle, and that the 250 employees had decided that the business really belonged to them, because they had been the ones to build it up, and that they thought the business should be reorganized and run by a committee appointed by the employees. The president was informed that he would be considered one of the employees, and that he would have a voice with the others in the management of the business!

One can easily imagine the astonishment of a successful business man when he was confronted by such a statement from two of his oldest and most successful employees. He asked them whether they felt that they ought to have an increase in salary, but neither of them desired an increase. He asked them what had given them the idea that they had a right to ask for the business, and they said that they had just been discussing the matter with the other employees and they felt that in the reorganization of industry in the United States all businesses should be turned over to those who work and taken out of the hands of the old directors.

The proprietor of this business house waited several weeks to watch the developments and discuss the matter with his employees because he was anxious to know what was responsible for this radical suggestion. Finally in conference with his general manager he learned that the employees knew that he was carrying a balance of one quarter of a million dollars in the bank, without interest. They knew that this money had been earned by the corporation, and they felt that if this money was not needed by the directors and not needed to run the business, because money could always be borrowed from the banks to conduct the business, that the surplus ought to be divided among the employees!

In Cleveland, the board of directors of a large manufacturing institution held a meeting to decide about the disposition of a surplus fund which they were carrying. The directors had practically agreed upon the voting of an extra dividend, when the general manager of the business, who is also a director, arose and informed the directors that it would be impossible for them to dispose of this fund in the manner contemplated.

"I have been the general manager of this business, and you gentlemen have relied upon me to keep labor in line," he said, in substance, to his fellow directors.

"I have been able to do this only by explaining to the workers your balance-sheet—by showing them that the profits of this business have been divided equally between employees and employers. The employees know by your balance-sheet that you have this surplus on hand, and they are watching to see what disposition you will make of it.

"If this surplus is divided, gentlemen, it will have to be on a fifty-fifty basis, one-half to labor and one-half to capital."

These two incidents of what we look upon as Bolshevism in the United States, I encountered trailing the Bolsheviki upon my return from Siberia.

After I had travelled from Seattle to New York and from the Atlantic coast west again to Philadelphia, Pittsburgh, Cleveland, Indianapolis, St. Louis, Chicago, Des Moines, and Kansas City, I learned that there was a definite revolutionary organization at work in the great industrial centres striving to bring about national strikes, set at present for July fourth and November first as demonstrations for Debs and Mooney.[2] I learned that "masked balls" were being organized among the working people, and that after the dancing and celebrating an agitator spoke of the plans for a national strike. By May, I was reliably informed, four million letters had been sent to workers by this strike organization.

In Switzerland I found similar tracks. Switzerland is an industrial country. The life of Switzerland is in her industries. Business is the power which drives the nation ahead, and still there is the trail of Bolshevism in that country despite its democratic form of government and despite the fact that Switzerland is the oldest republic in the world. The employees of the big factories have been in communication with the Russian revolutionists in Switzerland, and there is a strong anticapitalistic sentiment growing in that country. Bolshevism in Switzerland is not caused by a lack of food, nor by a lack of work nor because of a scarcity of the comforts of life. Food and clothing, all kinds of household articles and supplies, are obtainable in Switzerland, but prices are extremely high, as they are all over Europe. So we cannot look for the causes of Bolshevism in this little republic as being due to chaotic conditions or an imperialistic form of government. The explanation can be found elsewhere, and it is

---

[2] Eugene Victor Debs (1855–1926) was an American union leader, one of the founding members of the Industrial Workers of the World, and five times the candidate of the Socialist Party of America for the President of the United States. Through his presidential candidacies, as well as his work with labor movements, Debs eventually became one of the best-known socialists living in the United States. Debs's speeches against the Wilson administration and the war earned the enmity of President Woodrow Wilson, who later called Debs a "traitor to his country." On June 16, 1918, Debs made a speech in Canton, Ohio, urging resistance to the military draft of World War I. He was arrested on June 30 and charged with ten counts of sedition. Debs was sentenced on November 18, 1918, to ten years in prison. He was also disenfranchised for life. Debs went to prison on April 13, 1919. In protest of his jailing, Charles Ruthenberg led a parade of unionists, socialists, anarchists, and communists to march on May 1 (May Day), 1919, in Cleveland, Ohio. The event quickly broke into the violent May Day Riots of 1919. On December 23, 1921, President Harding commuted Debs's sentence to time served, effective Christmas Day. He did not issue a pardon. Thomas Joseph "Tom" Mooney (1882–1942) was an American political activist and labor leader who was convicted, along with Warren K. Billings, of the San Francisco Preparedness Day Bombing of 1916. Believed by many to have been wrongly convicted of a crime he did not commit, Mooney served twenty-two years in prison before finally being pardoned in 1939.

in the simple belief of the working people that the factories and industries belong to them, just as the government belongs to them. Essentially it is a Socialistic movement, just as Bolshevism originally sprang from the Socialist platform of Karl Marx. But the new Socialists contend that they can only be successful in their industrial revolution by completely overturning society and business and government—by destroying the world in order to rebuild it.

In England, what is spoken of as Bolshevism, is essentially not Bolshevism at all, but a demand of the working people for a greater share in the profits of industry and for greater responsibility in the management of business.

Thus, Bolshevism as a world doctrine is assuming a different form all over the world, but the trail which it makes is everywhere the same, the trail of revolution. That there must be and will be a great change in industry and business, in government and society during the next decade is obvious: the change is inevitable. But the growth of Bolshevism outside of Russia and possibly central Europe is artificial. Those who talk Bolshevism in this country, or in England, or in Switzerland merely use the Russian word to define this extensive public demand for changed conditions. The solution of these industrial problems, as a solution of international political dispute, cannot be forecast. Only the tendency of the times may be indicated, and the one factor which appears at the bottom of nearly every political and industrial dispute is secrecy. Where there has been secret diplomacy practised by the world governments, there has been suspicion among the people and foreign Powers. In a sense, a similar secrecy has been practised in our industries, and we are only now beginning to notice the decided reaction.

Secrecy is one of the fascinating facts of life. Russia has been fed on secrecy for so many decades that the temperament of the people has been affected to a serious extent. Even before the war, there was a press censorship in Russia, and during the war this censorship was extended to such ridiculous proportions that the mass of people relied upon rumor for information about the war, conditions in the country, and the policies of the government more than upon the statements in the newspapers or the official announcements. All information travelled by rumor, and the result was that there was suspicion of government authorities everywhere and a lack of confidence in anything the government stated. This was one of the greatest factors in the revolution. The censorship which was organized for the purpose of keeping information from the enemy and of sustaining the morale of the people became a sort of cloak under which the Bolshevist agitation developed and spread. Wherever there is secrecy, in government or business, the result is the same.

In the industrial centres of such representative governments as the American, the British, and the Swiss, Bolshevism as an industrial doctrine has been spreading because of the censorship of the directors of our industries, which they have maintained by withholding information from the employees about the factory itself. The employee has been considered, too often, simply as a tool to be used so many hours a day and paid for the day's work. But employees are human and they have naturally had an interest in the business itself, even if that interest has been the interest of an employee who was wondering how much the directors were making out of his labor. This secrecy has bred suspicion and nourished radicalism.

John Galsworthy[3] declared in New York that "understanding is one of the greatest things in life," and designated the chief qualities of the Anglo-Saxon peoples as "energy and common sense." Understanding is what the world is coming to, because of the universal feeling of its need. A League of Nations is only the name for an organization to bring about an understanding between world governments. Bolshevism is only a Russian name for a revolutionary movement to bring about an understanding among the proletariat.

The world movement which is discernible in every country is basically an expression of human sentiment seeking understanding. It has been suggested that open diplomacy will solve many international disputes, but it will be decades before anything like open diplomacy may be practised because suspicion is not national but personal, and wherever there are suspicious officials there will be suspicious governments. The only way such a situation can be effected is through public opinion. The inclination of statesmen is the same as that of industrial leaders who are looking forward to the time when free diplomacy may be not only practised in foreign politics but applied to industry. The quintessence of world-wide revolutionary movement is mutual understanding.

That trail of the Bolsheviki which I have crossed and recrossed in Europe, Asia, and United States, is not only a trail of discontent but the track of expectancy. To swing from autocracy to Bolshevism is to go from one extreme to the opposite, and neither of them are related at all to the normal. The senseless demands of the radicals find no support among the great mass of people in any country where the facts can be shown. Facts are the deadliest arguments against reaction and revolution, but the Bolshevists are masters at propaganda because in Russia, for instance, their campaign has been conducted for twenty-one years entirely by propaganda. The success of Bolshevism is closely related to the propaganda appeals which they distribute throughout the country. In Russia I found a copy of an appeal addressed to Hungarian prisoners by the Magyar section of the Russian Communalistic party. This document will show something of the propaganda methods of the Bolsheviki, and in every line one can discern not the statement of facts but of opinions.

A translation of this "Appeal to Hungarian Prisoners to take Arms," reads:

Comrades! An enormous danger is approaching us. The Czech formations which were bought by the Tzar, and afterward by the government of Ker-

---

[3] John Galsworthy (1867–1933) was an English novelist and playwright. In 1919, he traveled to the US and made several speeches there.

ensky, have sold themselves to the counter-revolutionary Russian bourgeoisie. Under the pretense of being despatched to the French front, they are travelling to the heart of Siberia, to the grain-producing regions. When they saw they were many, they treacherously fell upon the Soviet authority and introduced in Cheliabinsk a regime of terror. They shot and robbed the town, and the Soviet who attacked unexpectedly, were not in a position to resist. Seizing the power, they began a bloody reckoning with the prisoners. If some Magyar or German prisoners of war fell into their hands, not one was left alive. They murdered mercilessly under the influence of national hatred. This corrupted miserable band sprang from Cheliabinsk to Omsk. The Omsk-Soviet of workmens' and soldiers' deputies took steps to prevent this dangerous company from reaching here. To meet them, was sent out a delegation for negotiation accompanied by two hundred Red Guards. According to the order of the commissary for foreign affairs, they were told to lay down their arms. The rascals did not submit to the order, and began to fire at the Red Guards. A fight ensued. Comrades Rakop and Babka were taken prisoner and slaughtered without mercy. In every place hitherto occupied by them, they have opened fire on the German-Magyar prisoners and slaughtered mercilessly whoever fell into their hands. Savage national hatred has transformed them into mad animals, and now they wish to take into their hands our fate.

Comrades! It must not be permitted that we sit idly like dolls while this band fastens itself on our necks. The Soviet has decided to defend itself. The Omsk proletariat is fighting against the Czech formations at Marianofka. But the Soviet forces are insufficient. Every moment threatens danger, and therefore we must prepare for defense in the widest measure. Before us stands open the question: To exist or not to exist. The Soviet has placed at the disposition of the central organization 1,000 rifles. These thousand rifles we must use if we wish to guard ourselves and the Russian revolution, which is our ally and the basis of our future revolution.

Comrades! The leaders of the country call to arms. Every organized workman must take arms. As soon as we shatter the formations, peaceful relations will again ensue and we will lay down our arms, but until then we must hold them in our hands.

Comrades! The innocent blood of our brothers must be avenged. Our lives and the salvation of future proletarianism demands that we honorably take our place in the fight of the Omsk proletariat.

Each foreign organized proletarian to arms!
Long live the world revolution begun by the Russian proletariat!
Away with the corrupted troops falling upon us!
Long live the victorious proletariat dictature!
Long live the armed foreign proletariat!

In Canada and the United States the Bolshevist propaganda spreads like proverbial wild fire. The head of the Canadian Department of Public Safety stated in February that there was a large Bolshevist element in that country, which if not dealt with promptly "will almost of a certainty lead to trouble which may assume most serious proportions and consequences." When I arrived in Seattle a revolutionary strike had been declared there by strikers who were only prevented from taking over the city government by the sanity of union labor and the courage of the mayor. The Department of Labor in Washington estimates that there are 6,000 Bolshevist agitators in the United States, and the American Government permits official representatives of the Bolsheviki to open offices in New York although neither Lenin nor Trotsky will permit any American officials in Petrograd or Moscow.

In April the American public was astonished by reports of the mutiny of United States troops in the Archangel district of northern Russia, and the War Department, confirming press despatches, gave out copies of propaganda documents appealing to class hatred of Allied troops.

One appeal was addressed directly to the British soldiers sent against the Russian Reds. It was officially issued by the "Russian Socialist Soviet Republic," and was signed by "Lenin, President of the Council, People's Commissary," and "Tchitcherin, People's Commissary of Foreign Affairs." This appeal said:

Fellow Worker: Do you thoroughly realize what you are doing when you advance against us?

You have not come here to fight for liberty. You have come here to crush it. You have not come here to establish the rule of the people. You have come here to overthrow it.

You know that Russia was, up till last year, ruled by the most brutal, tyrannical and corrupt autocracy known to history. You have known of the terrible struggle we have had against our tyrants; of the imprisonments, of the hangings, of the deportations, to the mines of Siberia.

You, British fellow workers, sympathized with us then, and often helped us.

Did you not rejoice when we overthrew Tzarism? You did. Yet you have come here to restore it.

It is the intention of the Tzarist officers who are attached to your General Staff. When you obey their orders you are carrying out their object. They are not democrats. They are militarists and monarchists. They have a supreme contempt for the people, and they believe that they alone have the right to rule. They hate our revolution and want to crush it.

English fellow workers, don't do it!

A second poster signed by the same officials gave these reasons which they said the Allies had advanced for having sent troops to Russia:

"That they have come to stamp out anarchy and restore order.

"That they have come to help the Russian people.

"That the Allied invasion of Russia is welcomed by the Russian people."

These declarations are printed in large type, each followed by the words "It is Not True."

The British and French Governments are said to be "responsible for what disorder there is in Russia. Your government does not want to help the Russian people. It is helping to fasten the yoke of capitalism and Tzarism on them again."

Nothing is said regarding the assassination of Tzar Nicholas and his family which the Bolsheviki officially announced.

"Do not put your trust in this reactionary gang," continues the second poster. "Do not permit yourselves to be used as tools of the enemies of liberty. Fellow workers, be loyal to your class and refuse to do the dirty work of your masters.

"Fellow workers, here is positive evidence of the real purpose for which you were brought to Russia. Be honorable men! Remain loyal to your class and refuse to be accomplices of a great crime."

And Company I, 339th Infantry U.S.A., refused to go to the Bolshevist front in Russia as the Czecho-Slovaks refused six months earlier in Siberia!

In following the trail of the Bolsheviki I have found the propagandist always in the vanguard with his appeal to class hatred. Bolshevism, he states, is the rule of the proletariat, and the proletariat he recognizes, is only one class of working people, but there is something besides this propaganda of class strife which causes Bolshevism to spread; there is something more fundamental than the failure of governments and the directing forces of industries. The basis upon which Bolshevism makes its appeal to working people in such countries as England, France, and the United States, Canada and Australia, if not in Italy and Germany since the overthrow of the Kaiser, is the Bolshevist claim to the slogan "an industrial democracy." That is the bottom rock upon which Bolshevism, as a political and industrial programme, bases its success in democratic foreign countries. And, "an industrial democracy" to the Bolshevists means the destruction by revolution of all classes excepting the labor element of society and the creation of an industrial state where everything is taken over by the Soviet.

In Article One, Chapter Two, Section 3 of the Constitution of the Russian Socialist Federated Soviet Republic, under the title "Declaration of the Rights of the Laboring and Exploited People," is the following:

> Bearing in mind as its fundamental problem the abolition of exploitation of men by men, the entire abolition of the division of the people into classes, the suppression of exploiters, the establishment of a Socialist society, and the

victory of Socialism in all lands, the third All-Russian Congress of Soviets of Workers', Soldiers' and Peasants' Deputies further resolves:

A. For the purpose of realizing the socialization of land, all private property in land is abolished, and the entire land is declared to be apportioned among husbandmen without any compensation to the former owners, in the measure of each one's ability to till it.

C. As a first step toward complete transfer of ownership to the Soviet Republic of all factories, mills, mines, railroads, and other means of production and transportation, the Soviet law for the control of workmen and the establishment of the Supreme Soviet of National Economy is hereby confirmed, so as to assure the power of the workers over the exploiters.

D. With reference to international banking and finance, the third congress of Soviets is discussing the Soviet decree regarding the annulment of loans made by the government of the Tzar, by landowners, and the bourgeoisie, and it trusts that the Soviet Government will firmly follow this course until the final victory of the international workers' revolt against the oppression of capital.

These clauses in the Bolshevist constitution confirm the indictment of Bolshevism, that it proposes to "take from those who have and give to those who have not" by revolution not by readjustment, or compromise or gradual change. There is no mistaking either the method or the object of Bolshevism. Both are stated clearly in the fundamental law of the Soviet Republic.

And, Bolshevism spreads in every country where there is discontent and dissatisfaction, social unrest and agitation.

The red flag is the red emblem of revolution and it may be seen to-day in practically every nation in the world. I saw it in Russia, in Germany, in Seattle, in Chicago, in France, in Switzerland, in Austria, in Mexico, and in Spain. The flag of Soviet internationalism has preceded the establishment of every revolutionary government in Europe, and the grave problem facing world governments and world peoples to-day is:

"Can a League of Nations, or democratic representative national governments or reorganized industrial standards stop the revolution?"

That there is a conflict between Bolshevism and a union of world governments is evident. That the trail of Bolshevism encircles the globe is equally clear, and in this crisis in the development of the world today the decision as to the final outcome does not rest alone upon those who direct governments and industries but also upon those who vote and labor.

Under these circumstances what will be the outcome?

## Chapter XIII
## THE RUSSIAN CO-OPERATIVE UNIONS

Because the trail of the Bolsheviki is world-wide does not mean that all days of the future will be sinister ones. Even in Russia there are clouds with silver linings. Despite appearances and the propaganda of the Bolshevists there is one organization in that country which is stronger numerically, financially, economically and morally than the Soviets. It is the Russian Co-operative Unions, or Consumers' Societies, with a membership of 20,000,000 heads of families, controlling 50,300 shops, stores, factories, mills, and warehouses in all parts of Russia. And this group of business units is not alone important for its material strength, but because during the past two years it has been fighting the Bolshevist decree abolishing private ownership in property—a contest which resulted in a victory for the Co-operatives whose members refused to permit the Soviets to confiscate their holdings in Russia.

At a time when the situation in Russia was about as discouraging and hopeless as it ever was, or could be, there appeared in England, France, and the United States representatives of this non-political organization with a plan of action in Russia which was considered at the Paris Conference, and which may be the means for a League of Nations to begin its reconstruction work in northern Europe and Asia.

In an earlier chapter I referred to the conflict between the Soviet and the Co-operatives over the operation of the mills of Moscow. Representatives of these unions who have arrived in New York confirm the reported outcome of the struggle over the question of the confiscation of the union property in Russia. They state that although the Soviet Federal Constitution provides for the confiscation of all property this was not executed against the Co-operatives.

This is, in fact, the biggest defeat the Soviet Government has suffered in Russia. It was a direct blow to their plans for an industrial democracy which Lenin himself acknowledged in a recent pamphlet which he wrote to explain why Bolshevism as an industrial programme had failed. The Bolsheviki, however, have been endeavoring to obtain support outside of Russia by contending that the industries which are now being operated in Russia are being operated by Soviets and workers, which is not a statement of fact. What industrial life there is in Russia to-day is due entirely to the work of the members of the Co-operatives, who have steadfastly refused to work for the Bolshevist government and who have been and are now running their factories, stores, and mills entirely on behalf of the unions without any help or interferences from the Soviets.

This utter failure of the Bolshevist industrial millennium, as planned by Lenin and Trotsky, is undoubtedly the greatest indictment of the practicability of Bolshevism as an industrial reconstruction programme about which the outside world has been able to learn. And the credit for this, if due to any one organization, belongs to the Co-operatives, whose members have remained firm and unyielding in their opposition to the confiscation of their property.

In Omsk, Irkutsk, Ekaterinburg, Vladivostok, and other Russian cities I visited the stores of the Co-operative Unions, and although the supplies which they had on hand of manufactured articles were very meagre compared to the regular stocks, these stores were the only ones having new things for sale to their members. Every other store had only second-hand and worn materials, books, shoes, samovars, cloths, and similar articles. But in one of the Omsk Co-operative stores, for instance, I found everything from cloth for dresses to soap, schoolbooks, toys, furs, rubber goods, and machinery for farmers and peasants. Everything which might be of use to a Russian family, excepting stocks which were exhausted, and there were many of these, was handled by the Co-operative stores. But in Omsk, Vladivostok, and Irkutsk, as in other Russian cities, neither the officials nor the members of the unions were taking part in politics. The Omsk representatives of the Co-operative Union were carrying on their business without any dealings with the government of Admiral Koltshak, and his officials were not disturbing the activities of the Co-operatives just as the Soviets under Lenin have long since ceased attempting to interfere with the work of the societies in European Russia. Neither Koltshak nor Lenin have been able or willing to fight the Co-operatives because they have grown to their present strength after years of struggle with the Tzar's Government and after repeated contests with the autocrats of his administration, out of which they have always emerged successfully.

Because the conflict between the Bolshevists and the Co-operatives has been centred almost entirely upon the question of the rights of private property the outcome has not only an important bearing upon the situation in Russia but upon the Bolshevist propaganda throughout the world. It being the chief defeat administered to Bolshevism in Russia, reports of it naturally have not spread outside of that country, but upon the arrival in the United States and England of representatives of the Co-operatives, who have been sent abroad by the Russian unions to purchase manufactured goods in exchange for raw materials or money, some additional details of the clash between the Bolshevists and the Co-operatives have been given.

In Russia where community enterprises have been common for decades the growth of the Co-operatives has been very marked. In 1865 where there was but one Co-operative society in Russia, there were 800 in England, and some 200 in Germany. Nine years later when the number in England was doubled and Italy had 1,013, Russia had but only 353. By 1917, however, there were 39,753 Co-operative Unions in Russia compared to 12,000 in England and 10,000 in Germany, Japan, France, and Italy. The following year, despite the revolutions of March and October, 1917, the number of Co-operative societies increased to 50,000 while 300 regional unions were formed with an individual membership of 20,000,000 heads of families. Last year these unions handled 8,000,000,000 roubles' worth of materials.

While the societies, stores, and factories of the Cooperatives are scattered throughout Russia and Siberia there are five central organizations, of which the All-Russian Central Union of Consumers' Societies, organized in 1898, is the largest. The capital of this union alone is 100,000,000 roubles and they operate flour and paper mills, candy, shoe, soap, chemical, match, syrup, and tobacco factories, refrigerator plants, and fisheries valued at some 800,000,000 roubles. The financial centre of all the Co-operatives is the Moscow People's Bank, founded in 1909 with 33 branches in Russia, capitalized at 100,000,000 roubles, with deposits amounting to 650,000,000 and loans aggregating 900,000,000 roubles, according to the last bank statement of 1918 received in the United States.

The second oldest union is that of the Siberian Creamery Associations, which has 27 branches in Siberia, and 3,000 factory plants and distributing centres. The union operates factories for making oil, rope, and soap, and for rebuilding agricultural machinery, and when I left Vladivostok it had 20,000,000 roubles' worth of butter in cold-storage and over 40,000,000 roubles' worth of grain, furs, and other raw articles in warehouses and elevators.

Organized in 1915, during the war, the All-Russian Co-operative Union of Flax Growers grew to an organization of forty-six unions with more than a million and a half members by the beginning of 1918. In 1917, during the two revolutions, it collected 40,000 tons of flax, and distributed 3,000 tons of flaxseed to its members. Last year these unions sold 18,000 tons of flax in foreign countries, and the proceeds of this sale are being used in the United States and England to purchase goods and machinery for use of the farmers of Russia. This union, despite all the handicaps of disturbed economic conditions in Russia, expects to export during the coming flax season about 55,000 tons of flax valued at $38,500,000.

In 1918, while the Czecho-Slovak troops were fighting their way across Siberia and while the United States and Allies were landing troops in Vladivostok, a union of Siberian Co-operative Unions was formed by 9,162 local societies and a capital of nearly 30,000,000 roubles for the sole purpose of marketing abroad lumber, meat, eggs, hemp, and dried vegetables. This union has also gone into the fur business, and in 1918 bought from Siberian dealers more than 2,000,000 pelts. It is also operating paper, woollen and cotton mills, potash, lanoline, and dye-oil factories, and expects to develop the salt industry which promises to be one of its biggest businesses because of the abundance of salt in the lakes of Siberia and the great scarcity of that article of food, for which the Siberian people have had to depend almost entirely upon foreign shipments.

This great 8,000,000,000 roubles business society has been the only staple organization in Russia during the past two years and two months of disorder and social unrest. These societies are the only ones which were able to defy the Soviets and refuse to permit the confiscation of their property. Their holdings, which are entirely the private property of the individual members, have not been disturbed by the Bolshevists, and as a result of two years of trial under abnormal conditions which they have successfully weathered they have sent official representatives abroad on economic missions with the dual object of buying and selling for its members in Russia and of bringing about commercial intercourse between its societies and foreign manufacturers. And, as to the attitude of the unions toward the United States and the Allies, it is significant that they have endeavored to centre all their business in Allied countries, with headquarters in New York and London.

Their plan of action is purely economic. They wish to ship to Russia clothing, household goods, and farm implements. All of their purchases will be consigned to the unions so that no possible benefit can come to the Bolsheviki either directly or indirectly. After a two-year contest with the Soviet Government the Cooperatives have emerged stronger than the Soviets themselves, and they are in a position to-day where they can be of immense assistance to a League of Nations in its reconstruction work in Russia. And from present indications it appears as if the newly organized world society of governments will seek to co-operate with the consumers' societies after the peace treaty is signed in Paris.

The development of the Co-operatives in Russia, which was due to a great extent to the lack of private commercial activity, promises to have a far-reaching effect during the coming reconstruction period. To have grown from an organization of 39,000 societies under the Tzar, to have increased 11,000 more during two revolutions and the disturbed conditions which followed, and to have been successful in defeating the application of the Bolshevist decree confiscating private property is to have made a record unequalled by any business organization in any country during a great international and civil war.

## Chapter XIV
## THE FUTURE OF PEACE

Travelling through Europe during the war I heard in every neutral and belligerent country, time and time again, that magic word: "Revolution." In Spain, Switzerland, France, England, Belgium, Germany, Austria, Poland, Hungary, Rumania, and Scandinavia revolutions were gossiped about in the streets, palaces, and lobbies of Parliaments. The supreme aim of the propaganda of each group of contesting Powers was to cause internal industrial and political dissension within the realms of their opponents. Their object was to sow the seeds of revolution abroad and crush them at home. The German propagandists I met in Switzerland, Holland, Denmark, Spain, and Mexico were but agents of the German Great Headquarters carrying out instructions in the final attempt of the Militarist of central Europe to destroy the fabric of government and industry in France, England, Italy, and the United States. Even President Wilson spoke with the ardor and genius of a revolutionist when he arbitrarily separated the "German people" from the German Government," and the Allied statesmen accepted his leadership when they approved his ultimatum of October, 1918, that the associated Powers would not make peace with the "King of Prussia."

Long before the Bolshevists were in control of European Russia revolutions were advertised in the world. Millions of dollars, francs, gulden, pounds, and marks were spent in Europe, Asia, and the Western Hemisphere to bring about revolutions. But the object of this propaganda was distinctly national. Each belligerent worked for a revolution in an enemy country. They did not advocate a class war or a class revolution.

When the Bolshevists came to power in Petrograd and Moscow they took advantage of this world revolutionary agitation and began to advertise and labor for a proletariat revolution.

As a result of the combined efforts of the statesmen of belligerent countries during the war, and the leaders of the Bolshevists preceding and following the signing of the armistice, there is to-day a world-wide revolutionary movement against all authority—governmental, industrial, and religious. In trailing the Bolsheviki in Russia, and, in tracing its track across Europe, Asia, and the United States, I have, in fact, not been following the route of Russian Bolshevism but of the world revolution.

We are in the midst of that revolution to-day, but because it has not taken the form of extreme violence in the United States we do not recognize it. A revolution of action, however, only follows a revolution of opinion, and that which we call "revolutionary propaganda" is but another name for the vanguard of a revolution of destruction.

In brief, that is the condition which exists to-day, and it is with this condition that the two reconstruction forces, Bolshevism and a League of Nations, are confronted. The one seeks to rebuild the world by razing it; the latter by adjustment and evolution.

Bolshevism has made such rapid progress during the past year that at the very beginning of the period of peace it appears to be the stronger. But I am confident that this is only temporary. The Bolsheviki have not yet succeeded in conquering any democratic country. Bolshevism has spread most effectively in autocratic countries. In Russia, Hungary, and Germany Bolshevism is the price the people are now paying for militaristic governments. The old German cannons used to have the following legend stamped on them: "The last resort of Kings." Before the Tzar was overthrown the Russian peasants sang, "The Funeral March of the Proletariat," because of the oppression of the government. Bolshevism in these countries is extreme reaction against extreme autocracy.

Bolshevism in the United States, England, and France is essentially industrial. It is a movement against "industrial militarism," and it is still in the early stages of a "revolution of opinion." There is a universal feeling among all people that the world after this war must be a different and a vastly better world than it was before, but the mind of the mass of people has not yet formulated a programme or platform for the new reconstruction, but what is gradually developing in this country and England is an "industrial democracy" without the Bolshevist method of destruction.

Lenin has stated that Russia's civil war would last fifty years and that it would be fifty years before the Soviets could control the world.

During a conversation in the late summer of 1918 with Colonel Edward M. House this quiet observer for President Wilson and American peace delegate remarked that it might be fifty years after the signing of peace before the world would know whether there was to be, or could be, such a thing as universal peace. And the point he made in this connection was that the essential question for world governments to decide was whether they desired to use this fifty-year period to prepare for peace or another war. If they were sincere in their wishes for peace then a League of Nations would be an organization to aid them in realizing their ideal. Before the armistice it was Colonel House's idea that a League of Nations was to be considered a League of Governments to prepare for peace.

If Lenin speaks for the Bolshevists and if the ideas of Colonel House are shared by the statesmen of the Peace Conference then for the next fifty years these two reconstruction forces will clash.

After trailing the Bolsheviki, after following many Allied armies and enemy forces in the field, and after watching the fluctuations in public opinion through the press of various former belligerent and neutral countries I have come to the conclusion that this generation, and perhaps the next, will see the end of wars of nations but the beginning of class conflicts. The latter will develop in every country, not excluding the United States, but in each they will assume different forms and formulate different demands. In those nations whose governments are most reactionary, in those industries whose directors are least progressive this revolution of opinion may and probably will assume the form of Bolshevist action.

Like all great problems, the solution is largely a matter of leadership. Bolshevism has always succeeded so far where governments and industrial leaders failed. In Russia, Hungary, and Bavaria Bolshevism succeeded because those who directed the old governments and businesses failed. While the experiences of the Allies in Siberia appear discouraging, while their failure to co-operate there was a direct aid to the Bolshevists, this is not an indication of the future course of a union of governments. When the people of the world and the governmental leaders themselves recognize that during the period of reconstruction there can be only two forces: (1) a union of governments, or, (2) a union of Soviets, it will be easier for governments to get together, for in unity there is not only strength but order, and the demand of the people throughout the world is not disorder and Bolshevism, but order, food, and work.

Bolshevism, while it succeeds where others fail, is a programme of industrial failure, as has been demonstrated already in Russia. Against the combined leadership of men who have made democratic representative governments a success, against the united leadership of men who have built great industries and working nations neither the Bolshevist form of government nor the Bolshevist plan for an "industrial democracy" will succeed, because there were democracies in Switzerland, England, and the United States centuries before Bolshevism appeared, and during the past decade the industrial establishments of these three countries have been gradually transformed. "Industrial democracies" are being realized in these countries without destruction of property and life, and of society and government.

Militarism was the "last resort of Kings," and Bolshevism is the "Funeral March of the Proletariat."

Over the face of the globe winds the serpentine trail of the Bolshevists. The United States and the Allied governments, which have been successful against militarism, have now united in a League of Nations to bring about world peace and to combat Bolshevism. The outcome of this reconstruction war is as certain as the finale of the contest between the two groups of belligerents in the Great War. Trailing the Bolsheviki this New World League, backed by Public Opinion, will eventually encircle the globe. Bolshevism, a goblin of reconstruction, will gradually disappear and Civilization will advance safely and cautiously toward that period of universal happiness which has been the dream of prophets and the goal of all Mankind.

# INDEX

A. E. F. (American Expeditionary Force), xiii, xiv, 12, 14, 28, 87n1, 101n1, 105, 113, 114, 150n1

Afkzentieff (Avksentiev), Nikolai D., xii, 86, 94, 96, 97

Allied Powers, Associated Powers, Allies, x, xii, xiv, xv, xxi, xxiii, 3–5, 7–9, 11, 12, 23, 24, 28, 32, 45, 48–51, 58, 67, 82–85, 87, 90, 91, 95–115, 117–21, 125, 129, 130, 135–42, 144, 147, 149, 150, 157, 158, 162–66

America, vii, viii, ix, xii, xiii, xv, xviii, xxiv, 8, 9, 10, 21, 22, 44, 50, 76, 110, 121–23, 135, 142, 143, 145, 149

American Red Cross, 34, 36, 38, 42, 43, 109, 113, 129, 130, 132

American West, 7, 9, 149

Amur, 5, 10, 11, 14, 26, 27, 29, 30, 36, 40, 74, 98, 107, 113–15, 140

Angara, 32

Antonov-Ovsejenko (Antonov-Ovseyenko), Vladimir A., 69

Archangel (Arkhangelsk), 23, 24, 46, 47, 71, 77, 95, 104, 118, 157

Armistice, 3, 4, 46, 98, 109, 110, 120, 124, 125, 134, 137, 139, 146, 149, 164, 165

Asia, 3, 13, 15, 21, 24, 34, 96, 155, 160, 164

Associated Powers. *See* Allied Powers

Astroff (Astrov), Nikolai I., 86, 87n1

Atlantic Ocean, 7, 8, 99, 149, 153

Austria-Hungary (Austria, Hapsburg Monarchy), xviii, xix, 3, 4, 15, 43, 67n3, 68, 71, 73, 76, 82, 85, 100, 120, 124, 125, 137n1, 149, 159, 164

Austrians, 28, 42, 43, 83

Babka, 156

Bachmac, 69

Baikal, lake, 30, 32, 39, 42, 45, 75, 110, 115, 118, 133, 140, 141

Baker, Newton D., 105

Balkans, xix, 15

Barrows, David Prescott, 105, 134

Bavaria, 45, 150, 166

Belgium, xxi, 3, 8, 48, 105n9, 120, 164

Berlin, vii, xvi, 8, 73, 76, 103, 114, 141

Bira, 36

Blagovestchensk (Blagoveshchensk), 113

Blok, Alexander, 30n1

Bohemia, 124, 125

Bolderoff (Boldyrev), Vasily, 86, 87n1

Bolsheviki, Bolshevist, Bolshevism, vii–ix, xii–xiv, xvi–xxiii, 3–5, 7–11, 12n4, 14–25, 27, 29–33, 35–38, 42n5, 45, 46, 48, 50, 52–54, 58n12, 60–68, 69n6, 70n7, 72, 73, 74n10, 75–77, 79, 81–84, 86–88, 90, 91, 97–102, 106, 107, 110–14, 116, 117, 120, 121, 123–26, 128–30, 134, 136–38, 140, 144, 147, 149–51, 153–55, 157–61, 163–66

Bolshevist. *See* Bolsheviki

Brest-Litovsk, 50
  peace of, 17, 69

*Brooklyn*, U.S.S., armored cruiser, 14, 105, 112

Budapest, 43

Bulgaria, 4, 79n16, 122n3

Bunakovhky, 60

California, 8

Canada, xix, xxi, 15, 42, 135, 149, 150, 157, 158

Central Empires (Central Powers), 3, 66, 69, 76, 88, 101, 104, 108, 111, 113, 120, 149

Chaikovski (Tchaikovsky), Nikolai V., 86, 87n1

Charles I, 76

Cheliabinsk, xi, 30, 31, 32, 33, 48, 51, 59, 67, 71, 72, 75, 78, 79, 82–84, 91, 122–24, 126, 129, 130, 156

Chicago, xviii, 9, 10, 44, 153, 159

Chicherin (Tchitcherin), Georgy V., 75, 82, 157
China, xi, 3, 8, 9, 31, 38n1, 47n6, 54n2, 89n4, 90n6, 92n12, 94n14, 98n20, 103, 104, 107, 108, 110, 119, 136, 137n1, 139, 143
Chinese, 8, 9, 10, 12, 27, 28, 29, 41, 113, 115, 134
Chinese Eastern Railway, 38n1, 39, 40, 97, 140, 143
Chita (Tchita), xi, 26, 33, 39, 40, 43–45, 70, 98, 134, 135, 140, 143, 144, 147
*Chugai Shogyo*, 136, 137
Cleveland, 105n7, 152, 153
Columbia University, vii, ix, x, 13
Columbus, 10
Constitutional Assembly (National Assembly, Constituent Assembly), viii, 12n4, 16–18, 47, 86n1, 88, 93, 97
Co-operative Unions, Russian, 17, 19, 20, 46, 125, 133, 160–63
Cossacks, xv, 24, 29, 33, 43, 48, 52, 54n1, 55, 56, 62, 68n4, 80, 81, 82, 90–92, 96–98, 134, 144
Council of Working Men's Deputies (Soviet of Working Men's Deputies, Soviet), 16, 56, 77, 156, 159
Czechs, xxiii, 18, 28, 42, 45, 76, 78–80, 82–84, 91, 92, 94, 96, 97, 101, 110, 120, 124, 126, 135, 147, 150
Czecho-Slovaks, 14, 18, 45, 54, 61, 62, 67–77, 79–87, 95, 98, 99, 100, 101, 108, 109, 118–20, 123, 124, 129, 134, 147
Czecho-Slovakia, 12, 33, 38n1, 66, 67n2, 73, 79n16, 85, 87n1, 90n8, 122n3, 125, 126
Czecho-Slovak National Council, 18, 47, 67–71, 75, 78, 79n16, 84, 95, 120, 123, 125, 131
*Czecho-Slovenny Dennik*, 68, 69

Debs, Eugene V., 153
Denekin (Denikin), Anton I., 24, 48, 54, 56n6, 58, 62, 87n1, 95, 96
Denmark, 22, 122n3, 164
Department of State, US, xvn27, xxi, 85, 103, 145, 147
Des Moines, 153
Dietrichs (Dieterichs, Diterikhs), Mikhail K., 92

*Dixie*, transport ship, 113
Dnieper River, 18, 68
Dogert, 54, 56–58
Dominin, Parfen A., 54, 59, 60, 65
Dutoff, Alexander I., 54, 58, 62

East Prussia, 27
East Side (New York City), 9
Eastern States (US), 8
Eichelberger, Robert Lawrence, 114
Education, 17, 22, 44, 46
Ekaterinburg, vii, xi, xii, xiv, xvi, xxi, 3, 20, 24, 26, 30–33, 46–55, 58, 59, 61–67, 75n12, 80, 92, 97, 110, 111n15, 123–25, 129–34, 161
Ekhart, 57
Eliot, Charles Norton Edgecumbe, 106, 111
Emancipation of Labor, group, 16
Emerson, George, 39, 106, 109, 135, 142
England, xix, 8, 9, 12, 14, 15, 21, 22, 30, 87n1, 94n13, 96, 97, 100, 103, 106, 108, 110, 111n16, 118, 119, 139, 143, 149, 154, 158, 160–62, 164–66
Englishmen, 11, 134
Europe, xv, xix, xxi, xxii, 3, 7, 8, 12, 15, 21–25, 34, 37, 49, 76, 96, 99, 100, 121, 125, 134, 150, 153–55, 159–61, 164
exiles, xi, xiv, xviii, 3, 8, 9, 14, 40, 44, 101, 102, 111, 112, 127, 129

Far East, viii, xxi, 7–9, 13, 40, 42, 45, 87n1, 98n21, 103–05, 107, 114, 136, 139, 141, 142, 145n4
Flanders, 7, 29
Foch, Ferdinand Jean Marie, marshal, 103
France, 3, 5, 7–9, 12, 14, 18, 20, 22, 31, 38, 40, 63n15, 66, 68, 76, 82–84, 94n13, 96, 97, 100, 102, 103, 106–08, 110, 118–20, 126, 139, 142, 143, 145, 149, 158–60, 162, 164, 165
Fredericks, baron, 60
Frenchmen, 11, 101, 134

Gaida, Radola (Geidl, Rudolf), 66, 97, 123, 124, 131, 147
Galicia, 27, 125
Galsworthy, John, 155
Gattenberger, Alexander N., 94

# INDEX

Gendrikoff (Gendrikov), Alexander S., duke 56,
Germans, 8, 28, 42, 43, 57, 69, 74, 75n12, 79, 82, 83, 102, 103, 127–29, 137, 141
Germany, 58, 68n4, 71, 74, 76, 84, 85, 99–101, 103, 104, 107, 114, 118–20, 134, 141, 145, 146, 149, 158, 159, 161, 162, 164, 165
Golden Horn Bay, 7, 13, 27, 105, 113, 149
Gratzianov (Gratsianov), Alexander A., 91
Graves, William S., major general, xiii, xxii, 10, 28, 105, 106, 109, 111, 113–15, 117–19, 123, 124, 129, 139, 146, 150n1
Gray, L. S. (US consul, Omsk), 85
Grebyonka, 69
Grimm, Robert, 21
Guinet, Alfons, 83, 84
Gukovsky, Isidor E., 35

Hapsburg Monarchy. *See* Austria-Hungary
Hara, Takashi, 138, 139
Harbin, xi, 26, 27, 31, 32, 35, 39–41, 97, 109, 111, 119, 130, 132, 135, 137, 142
Harris, Ernest L. (US consul general, Irkutsk), 85
Hawaii, 7, 8
Henrikova, countess, 60
*Hochi*, 142
Holland, 22, 164
Hong Kong (Hongkong), 8, 106n11
Hooverized land, 8
Horvath (Horvat), Dmitry L., 98
*Hozan Maru*, 14
Hrbek, J., 122

Imokentjeska (Innokentievka), 72
Inagaki, general, 140, 146
*Independent, The*, 101
India, xix, 9, 15
Indiana, vii, xvii, 29
Indianapolis, 153
Inter-Allied Railway Commission (Railroad Committee), 38, 39n2, 114, 129
Ipatieff (Ipatiev), Nikolai N., xvi, 47, 52, 53, 61, 64, 65
Ipatieff house, 47, 52, 61–65
Irkutsk, xi, 24n5, 26, 31–33, 39, 40, 42, 45, 46, 49–51, 66n1, 67n2, 70, 72, 74, 75, 82n18, 84, 107n13, 121, 133, 134, 135, 161
Ishii Kikujirō, viscount, 145
Ishim, 74
Isilkul, 82, 83
Italy, 7, 8, 38n1, 53, 108, 110, 118, 139, 143, 145n4, 149, 158, 161, 162, 164
Ivanov. *See* Ivanov-Rinov
Ivanov-Rinov, Pavel P., 90, 91, 139

Jakushev (Yakushev), Ivan A., 90
Janin, Pierre-Thiébaut-Charles-Maurice, 106, 107, 110
Japan (Nippon), viii, xxi, 3, 7–9, 12–14, 38n1, 40, 63, 87n1, 96, 99, 103–04, 106–10, 118, 119, 136, 137n1, 138–49, 162
*Japan Advertiser, The*, 136
Japanese, the, xiv, xx, 9, 11–13, 38, 50, 98, 101–04, 109, 110, 134–36, 139–43, 145, 147

Kalmykoff (Kalmykov), Ivan P., xiv, 98, 144
Kansas City, 29, 153
Karlsbad, 125
Katherine the Great (Catherine the Great), 47
Kedrinsky, 60, 61
Kennan, George, xi, xiv, xvii, xviii, xxii, 8n1
Kerensky, Alexander F., 41n5, 68n4, 95
Kerensky Government. *See* Provisional Government
Khabarovsk, xiv, 10, 29, 30, 33, 40, 44, 113, 115, 134, 140, 144, 150, 151
Kharkoff (Kharkov, Kharkiv), 50, 69
Kharkoff, University of, 14
Kieff (Kiev, Kyiv), 48, 50, 62, 68, 69, 103n3
Klinov, 77
Knight, Austin Melvin, admiral, 105, 106, 109, 112, 119
Knox, general, 96, 106, 107, 110, 118, 119
Kobe, 9
Kocubinsky (Kotsiubynsky), Yury M., 68
Koltshak (Kolchak), Alexander V., xii, xiii, 24, 45, 47, 54n2, 67, 74n10, 86n1, 87n1, 89n3, 90n6, 91n11, 92n12, 94, 95n18, 96–98, 107n13, 121, 123, 124, 135, 138, 147, 161
Kowno, 37, 50
Kozek, 92, 97
Krapotkine (Kropotkin), Pyotr A., duke, 57

Krasnov, Grigory A., 95
Krivozerovka, 129
Kroutofsky (Krutovsky), Vladimir M., 89, 90
Kurajev (Kuraev), Vasily, 126, 127

Lansing, Robert, xv, 145
Latin-American, 8
League of Nations, viii, xix, xxi–xxiii, 3, 4, 5, 23, 51, 99, 100, 107, 110, 111, 117, 129, 139, 147, 150, 159, 160, 163, 165, 166
Lenin, Nikolas (Lenine, Lenin, Vladimir Ilyich), xix, 16, 21, 22, 24, 30, 41n5, 69, 70n7, 99, 137, 157, 160, 161, 165
Liaodong Peninsula, 40n4
Libau, 50
Liebknecht, Karl, 21
Ligeti, Karoly Sandor, 74
Lincoln, Abraham, 14
Llinsky, 57
Lodz, 19
Ludendorf, x, 146
Lvoff (Lvov), Georgy Y., prince, 63, 95

Magyars, 36, 72, 74, 79, 127–29, 156
Manchouli, 31, 32, 133–35
Manchuria, xxi, 9, 13, 26, 28, 31, 32, 39–43, 97, 98, 104, 109, 129, 132–35, 139, 141, 143
Manchuria City, 40–43
Manila, 9
Marianovka (Marianofka), 72, 156
Marinsk, 51
Marne, 9
Marx, Karl, 11, 16, 154
Marxism, 16, 79n17
Masaryk, T. G., 12, 68, 79n16
Matsudaira, Tsuneo, 110
Mavor, James, 16
Max (Maxa), Prokop, 79
McCormick building, 9
Menshevist (Mensheviki), 10, 11, 16, 17, 58
Mesar, I., 81
Mexico, vii, xxi, 3, 48, 159, 164
Michailoff (Michailov, Mikhailov), Ivan A., 89
Militarism, xiii, 103, 157, 165, 166
Minikin (Minkin), Alexander, 126, 127
Minsk, xix, 16, 22, 150
Mirbach, Wilhelm von, 74
Mitsui, 13

monarchist, xiii, 8–11, 24, 29, 32, 95, 98, 157
Mongolia, 43, 141
Mooney, Thomas, 153
Morris, Roland S., xv, xxii, 106, 109, 111, 119, 123, 142, 145
Moscow, xvi, 10, 14, 17, 19, 20, 23, 24, 32, 34, 38, 39, 49, 50, 58, 63, 67, 69, 70, 72, 74, 75, 77–79, 84, 85, 87, 89n4, 124, 127, 130, 137, 149, 157, 160, 164
Moscow, University of, 46
Muravjof (Muravyov), Mikhail A., 68

Nakashima, 144–146
Napoleon, xii, 62
Navy Department, US, 120
New Jersey, 9, 10, 42
New York, vii, x, xi, xiii, xxii, 3, 5, 7, 8, 10, 13, 14, 24, 42, 44, 142n3, 151–53, 155, 157, 160, 163
*New York Herald*, 132
Newark, 10, 11
Nikolsk, 29
*Nippon Maru*, 8, 10
Norway, xix, 15
Novonikolaevsk (Novosibirsk), 66n1
Novosilov (Novoselov), Alexander E., 90

Odessa, 27, 50, 61, 62, 150
Ohio, 8, 105n7, 153n2
Oldenburg, Alexander Petrovich, prince de, 56
Olssufieff (Olsufuev), Dmitry A., count, 56
Omaha, 29
Omsk, xi–xiii, xv, 24, 26, 27, 30–35, 37, 38n1, 46–49, 51, 64, 70, 72, 74, 76, 81–84, 86, 87, 89–92, 95–98, 108, 110, 120–25, 130–34, 136, 138, 143, 156, 161
Orenburg, 37, 80
Orlov, 94
Otani, Kitsuzu (Kikuzuo), 104, 107, 118, 140, 144, 146
*Outlook, The*, xviii, 104

Pacific Ocean, 7–10, 12, 14, 26, 29, 30, 48, 99, 112, 115, 120, 133, 141, 149
Pale (of Settlement), 22
Palmer, Henry L., 111

# INDEX

Paris, viii, xxi, 9, 11, 24, 49, 62, 101, 102, 103, 106, 107, 110, 111, 129, 147, 160, 163
Paris (French general or captain), 106, 107
Patoushinsky (Patushinskii), Grigory B., 89
Pavlu, Bohdan, 122
Peking (Pekin), xi, 98n21, 108, 135, 136
Pennsylvania, 42, 43
Penza, 69, 70, 71, 72, 125–29
Perm, 37, 66n1, 84, 86, 123
Peter the Great Gulf, 7
Petrograd, xviii, 10, 11, 14, 16, 17, 23, 26, 29, 30, 32, 37, 49, 50, 52, 67, 68n4, 87, 96, 106, 124, 130, 149, 157, 164
Petrov, Nikolai I., 94
Petrova, Elena (Elena Petrovna), grand duchess, 60
Philadelphia, viii, 7, 153
Pilsen, 125
Pittsburgh, 153
Plekhanov, Georgy V., 16
Podvoisky, Nikolai I., 78
Poland, xvii, 3, 17, 37, 79n16, 103n2, 125, 164
Poltava, 69
Poole, 82, 85
Portland, 149
Prague, 125
*Primorsky Jizn*, 35
Provisional Government (Kerensky government), 12, 17, 23, 33, 35, 39n2, 41, 57n12, 63n15, 68n4, 86n1, 89n4, 95, 106, 133, 142

Rausher, 126
Reading, Pennsylvania, 43
Red Army, 7, 18, 24, 33, 35, 48, 53, 55, 56, 59, 61, 65, 66, 67, 69n6, 71, 73, 74, 75n12, 76, 78n15, 80, 85, 86, 87n1, 89n4, 99, 101, 112, 117, 118, 123, 126, 128, 129
Red Guard, 30n1, 53, 68n4, 80, 82, 114, 156
refugees, xxi, 3, 9, 10, 15, 16, 26, 34–37, 46, 49, 96, 132
Regnault, Eugene, 106, 111
Revolution of 1905, 16
Revolution, Russian, of 1917, x, xii, xiv, xxi, xxiv, 5, 10, 12n4, 16, 17, 21, 24, 25, 27, 30n1, 31n2, 33, 37, 41n5, 44, 46, 56n5, 68n4, 69n6, 70n7, 75n12, 77n14, 86n1, 87, 89, 96, 101, 107, 121, 137n1, 149–51, 156, 162–64
Richter, Fr., 122
Riga, 50
Robinson, Oliver Prescott, xxii, 105, 110, 111
Rockies (Rocky Mountains), 7, 45
Romanoff (Romanov) family, xvi, xvii, 48, 53, 54, 60, 62
Romanoff, Alexandra Feodorovna, tsarina, 52, 53, 59–65
Romanoff, Alexis, tsarevich, 53, 54, 59
Romanoff, Mary, 52
Romanoff, Nikolas (Romanov, Nicholas, Nicholas II), tsar of Russia, vii, viii, xiv, xvi, 12, 16, 26, 47, 48, 52–65
Root, Elihu, 142
Rtishevo (Rtishchevo), 128
Rumania, xix, xxi, 3, 15, 149, 164
Russo-Japanese War, 24n5, 40n4, 54, 56n8, 98, 104, 138

Samara, xvii, 30, 58, 70, 82n18, 83n20, 84, 86
San Francisco (Frisco), 7–9, 14, 29, 44, 105, 114, 149, 153n2
Sapozhnikov (Zapoznikov), Vasily V., 94
Savinkov, Boris V., 57n12
Scandinavia, 150, 164
Schwarzenstein, von, Philipp Alfons Freiherr Murom (Mumm), baron, 103
Seattle, 10, 149, 153, 157, 159
Sedkovkin, 79
Sedlutsky, 79
Semenov, Grigory M., 74, 75n12, 77, 98, 105n9, 134, 135, 143, 144, 147
Serdobsk, 126
Serebrenikov (Serebrennikov), Ivan I., 90, 94
Serfdom, abolition of, 22
Shanghai, 9
Shatiloff (Shatilov), Mikhail B., 89, 90
Shekin (Sukin), Ivan I., 94
Shthegtovioff (Shcheglovitov), Ivan G., 60
Shvetz, 127
Siberian-Manchurian border, 40
Siberian Provincial Duma, 88, 89, 90n8, 91, 93
Siberian Provisional Government (Siberian Government), 46, 47n6, 77, 86–90, 91n11, 91–94, 96, 98n21, 113

Sierra Nevada, 45
Skoropadskie (Skoropadsky, Pavel Petrovich, Skoropadskyi, Pavlo), 82
Slaughter, major, 124
Slovaks, 101, 125
Smugglers, 29, 43
Social Democratic Party (Social Democratic Working Men's party of Russia), 11, 16, 97, 123
Social Revolutionists (Socialist Revolutionary Party), 47, 50, 57n12, 58, 66n1, 68n4, 71, 74n9, 86n1, 89, 90, 91
Soviet. *See* Council of Working Men's Deputies
Spain, vii, 3, 24, 159, 164
St. Louis, 153
Stalin (Jughashvili), Joseph V., 70, 77
Starenkevitch (Starynkevich), Sergei S., 95
Stevens, John F., 38n1, 39, 41, 106, 111, 109, 142
Stockholm, 16, 144
Styer, Henry D., 150
Sumarokov Elston, count. *See* Yusupov, Felix
*Sussex*, H. M. S., 112
Svetlanskaya, 14
Sweden, xix, 15, 144
Switzerland, vii, xviii, xix, 3, 5, 15, 16, 21, 22, 24, 28, 45, 46, 102, 103, 153, 154, 159, 164, 166
Syrovy, Jan, general, 67, 91, 123, 124

Taft, William H., xxi, xxii
Taiga, 31, 32, 51
Tartars, 14
Tashkent, 46
Taube, von, Alexander A., 75
Tchita. *See* Chita
Tchitcherin. *See* Chicherin
Terauchi, Masatake, 104
Thompson (Thomson), Alfred R., 82
Tiumen, 51, 64
Tobolsk, 52, 53
Tokyo, 9, 13, 24, 101, 103, 104, 106, 107, 136, 141–47
Tolstoy, 34
Tomsk, xi, 26, 32, 33, 46, 47, 51, 77n14, 86, 89, 90, 92, 93, 94n17

Trans-Siberian Railway, 13, 14, 26, 28, 33, 39, 41–43, 49, 66, 81, 84, 86, 106, 108, 142–44, 147
Transylvania, 45
Treaty of Peace (peace treaty), 3, 5, 163
Troitsk, 75
Trotzky (Trotsky), Leon, xvii, 16, 17, 20, 24, 48, 67, 69, 73, 79, 81, 104, 126, 137, 157, 161
Tsing Tau (Qingdao), 104
Tsuruga, 7, 13
Turkestan, 36
Turkey, x, 4

U-boat, 8
Uchida Kosai, viscount, 137, 138
Ufa, 47, 70, 86, 87, 90, 91, 93, 97
Ukraine, 66, 68, 69, 81, 103n3
United States Railway Service Corps, 39, 106, 108, 113, 134, 135
Ural District Soviet, 52, 55, 56–58, 61, 63
Urals, 24, 32, 35, 47, 48, 54n2, 62, 72, 73, 121, 123, 124, 128
Ustrugov, Leonid A., 38n1, 94
Usuri Valley (Ussuri), Usuri River, 9, 29, 98, 113
*Utro Sibiri*, 59

Vancouver, 149
Verknoturie (Verkhoturie), 60
Vladivostok, xi, xii, xiii–xv, 3, 7–9, 11–14, 17, 18, 26–30, 32, 33, 35, 37–42, 44–46, 48, 49, 63, 69, 70, 72, 73, 75–78, 80, 82, 86, 87n1, 90, 95, 98, 104, 106, 107, 109–16, 118–20, 123, 124, 126, 129–31, 133–36, 138, 140, 142, 144, 146, 149, 150, 161, 162
Volkov, Vyacheslav I., 90, 91
Vologda, 85
Vologodsky (Vologodski), Pyotr V., 46, 47n6, 86, 86n1, 88–90, 94, 138

War Department, US, 105, 156
War of Nations (First World War) (Great War), vii, viii, x, xviii, 3, 7, 21n4, 24n5, 29, 56n9, 67n3, 79n16, 103n2, 105n8, 107, 153n2, 166

Washington, vii, viii, xi, xxi, 7, 8, 11–13, 24,
    49, 85, 94n13, 101, 103, 104, 107, 108,
    112, 119, 122, 123, 145, 147, 149, 157
William II, 76
Wilna (Vilnius), 46, 50
Wilson, Woodrow, vii, xv, 10n2, 85, 103, 120,
    121, 142n3, 153n2, 164

Y.M.C.A., 14, 42, 109, 130
Yakolev (Yakovlev), Nikolai, 77
Yokohama, 7, 8, 13
Yusupov, Felix, prince, Count Sumarokov
    Elston, 56

Zhitomir, 69
Zlatoust, 70, 72, 78
Zmrhal (Zmrhal-Sázavský), Karel, 122

www.ingramcontent.com/pod-product-compliance
Lightning Source LLC
Chambersburg PA
CBHW032025230426
43671CB00005B/200